# CRAZY BOSSES

*Books by Stanley Bing:*

*Biz Words*
*Crazy Bosses*

# CRAZY BOSSES

SPOTTING THEM     SERVING THEM     SURVIVING THEM

## STANLEY BING

WILLIAM MORROW AND COMPANY, INC.

New York

Library of Congress Cataloging-in-Publication Data

Bing, Stanley.
    Crazy bosses : spotting them, serving them, surviving them /
Stanley Bing.
        p.   cm.
    ISBN 0-688-07073-6
    1. Managing your boss.   2. Executives—Psychology.   I. Title.
HF5548.83.B56   1992
650.1'3—dc20                                                              91-8962
                                                                            CIP

Printed in the United States of America

First Edition

1  2  3  4  5  6  7  8  9  10

BOOK DESIGN BY MN'O PRODUCTION SERVICE

To my wife,
without whose squinty-eyed skepticism
I would never have summoned up the determination
to sit down at the computer
and get started on this thing, let alone finish it.

# AUTHOR'S NOTE

My correspondents who are quoted in this book have no desire to have their feelings known publicly—that is, to their crazy bosses. Nor do I think their legitimate names are essential to your understanding of the stories they have to tell, the lessons they have to share. For that reason, every name except those that belong to the crazy rich and famous are of my own fabrication, and, on occasion, when the peril of disclosure is truly immediate and forthcoming, I have taken the liberty of obscuring the nature and location of their work as well.

In other words, when I state at the beginning of a story, "Frank sells widgets in Wyoming," it is possible, to make sure Frank may remain secure in his misery, that his name is not Frank, that he in reality sells grommets, and does so in a place other than Wyoming. When, however, I quote Frank as stating, "My boss picked me up by my ears and threw me through the wall," you may be certain that he said just that, verbatim. No events or relationships have been constructed by me, for purposes of drama or otherwise. I had no reason to do so. The truth is horrible enough.

To avoid rickety and grotesque fabrications like "If the boss is interested solely in his or her career, he or she could drive his or her subordinate to drink," I will for the most part use the masculine gender when referring to the crazy boss. It is simply the poverty and archaic sexism of the English language, no more, that forces me to discriminate in my use of pronouns. No inadvertent slight to either gender is intended.

# ACKNOWLEDGMENTS

I'd like to take this opportunity to thank my first boss in business, whose name is not really Chuck, for making me aware that serious mental disturbance and success are not mutually exclusive. For similar reasons, I'd like to thank my former chairman, Carl, and a host of lesser executives who, in the early years of my career, bullied, preened, festered, and disintegrated before my eyes in a variety of ways both gratifying and terrifying.

I'd also like to thank Michael Milken, Ivan Boesky, Dennis Levine, Donald Trump, Frank Lorenzo, Larry Tisch, Carl Icahn, Henry Kravis, Saul Steinberg, and, of course, Ronald and Nancy Reagan, among so many others, for bringing us to where we are today.

On a more serious note, I'd like to offer thanks to my friend David Hirshey for his support, his commitment to humor, and his willingness to pick up a check; to my editor at *Esquire*, Anita Leclerc, for keeping me healthy and on my toes since 1985; and to the incomparable Jeanne Bernkopf, for helping to turn my original ravings and disorganized rantings into a book.

# CONTENTS

you can shine your shoes
and wear a suit
you can comb your hair
and look quite cute
you can hide your face
behind a smile
one thing you can't hide
is when you're crippled inside
John Lennon
*Crippled Inside*

# INTRODUCTION

Feelings and attitudes are to an amazingly high degree molded by the conditions under which we live, both cultural and individual, inseparably interwoven.

Karen Horney

e begin with the case of J. Walter Thompson, because those looking for crazy bosses need look no further. At Thompson in the 1980s, all the bad things that can happen under crazy management came together—and killed an organization.

It's an ugly tale, a saga of opportunism rewarded and institutions destroyed. So buckle up. Here we go:

The year is 1868. Commodore James Walter Thompson joins the Carlton and Smith Agency, which chiefly brokers space in the religious journals of the day. By 1878, the good commodore has bought the agency for the princely sum of five hundred dollars, and names it, as all good advertising men have done ever afterward, for himself. By 1890, the agency is billing in excess of $1 million per year. As time passes, it adds such clients as Unilever (1902, the oldest client/agency relationship in advertising), Eastman Kodak (1930), and Ford (1943).

By 1964, agency billings have reached $500 million, and five years later the company goes public.

Our story truly begins, however, in 1974, when Don Johnston takes over the company. Johnston, then forty-seven and a career J. Walter man since 1951, begins pursuing an aggressive vision, selling nonsynergistic businesses and acquiring public-relations firms. In 1980, Johnston creates the JWT Group as parent corporation of J. Walter Thompson Company and a number of smaller subsidiaries.

In 1985, massive corporate power at JWT Group is still concentrated in Johnston, but there are three individuals in charge of the $3 billion advertising agency: Walter O'Brien, Burton Manning, and Joseph O'Donnell.

In March 1986, O'Donnell is named chief executive officer of J. Walter Thompson and immediately sets about the task of naming his choices to key management positions and of reorganizing the majority of the field offices. By the end of the year, O'Brien and Manning are gone, and profits at the JWT Group turn up basically flat for the year. Emma Hill of Wertheim Schroder & Company tells *The New York Times* that "major management changes during the year had affected the company's ability to react quickly to the 'dramatic slowdown in its businesses . . .' "

American Management Disease has set in. The era of the crazy boss is at hand. The company, and its working shlubs, are already feeling the heat. And it gets better, if not worse.

By autumn of 1986, JWT stock has dropped from a high of approximately 41 to 25.

On New Year's Day 1987, O'Donnell becomes chairman as well as CEO of the J. Walter Thompson Agency. Two weeks later, he meets with John Cirigliano, head of a Wall Street investment-banking company. Enter the grease to lubricate the engine of destruction throughout much of the decade: Where investment bankers led, crazy bosses followed, drooling.

Cirigliano presents his old college buddy with a plan to accomplish the leveraged buyout—the purchase through debt, not assets—of the entire corporation, including parent JWT, and to assume the top notch himself, supplanting Don Johnston.

Sometime in the next three weeks, Johnston is informed about the incipient palace coup. We know this because, on or about January 20, he collects an in-house lawyer and meets with his subordinate. At this get-together, O'Donnell reportedly tells Johnston that he no longer has the confidence of the organization. He further complains that he has been forced to spend too much of his time cleaning up Johnston's shoddy business practices. Heated words are exchanged.

Johnston leaves the meeting and calls a gathering of the outside members of the JWT board of directors for January 23. O'Donnell, too, requests an audience at the confab. There, O'Donnell presents his plan for a leveraged buyout, then leaves before the meeting is concluded.

Before he goes, O'Donnell raises the issue of questionable accounting procedures and, according to sources, "the issue of integrity and morality overseas." This laundry list of questionable policies has been put into letter form by O'Donnell and signed by at least four other executives, including president Jack Peters.

The entire series of allegations is presented to the five outside board members and, after consultation with in-house counsel, the matter is then referred to Price Waterhouse for investigation and subsequent report.

O'Donnell "sounded so immature, so naive, that it shook the confidence of those hearing him," one outside director says later. "We were shocked that he would even raise an LBO in that manner. He was rambling on, sounding like Captain Queeg in *The Caine Mutiny.*" That same outside director, Yunich, the former vice chairman of Macy's, speaks to virtually every trade publication and also *New York* magazine, portraying O'Donnell as uninformed, childish, and sort of, well, stupid: ". . . his speech was incoherent, unprofessional, and highly emotional, to the point that it was upsetting to everyone," he tells *New York.* "We moved him up to his post so there would be three years' exposure to the board and so he'd learn. Lord knows, he had a lot to learn. His performance tried our intelligence. He rambled, showed he clearly did not grasp the subject, that he was in over his depth."

Moments later, Johnston goes to O'Donnell's office with the message that O'Donnell is to leave immediately and never return to this or any other office of the company. "Don demands absolute loyalty, and in return he gives absolute loyalty," says a former JWT executive. "His sense of betrayal is as profound as a human being can experience."

Between January 26 and 30, a lot happens, none of it good for O'Donnell, who resigns from the board of JWT Group, Inc.

Johnston takes O'Donnell's job and title as his own, and begins further consolidation of his power. He fires Jack Peters, the agency's president and COO, a thirty-year veteran of the company, who allegedly aided and abetted the O'Donnell coup.

On February 1, *The New York Times* reports: "Wall Street analysts . . . are concerned about how the return of Mr. Johnston to day-to-day control will affect employee morale, client relations and profitability. 'Under Joe O'Donnell, the pieces were in place for an upturn in profits in 1987,' said Mr. Anschel of Dean Witter. 'Now, who knows?' "

In general, Wall Street, hungry for lucrative exchanges of ownership, is disappointed by O'Donnell's failure to make the buyout stick, and by the total control exerted by the older, more bureaucratic Johnston. *Advertising Age*, the comprehensive voice of America's most nervous business, sports a headline that reads: J. WALTER TUMULT: JOHNSTON'S REIGN QUESTIONED AFTER O'DONNELL OUSTED.

But Johnston tells *Adweek*, "There is no chairman; there is no president. There is just an office of the chief executive. That's all. Everybody's back to work. There were no defections whatsoever. We've had total, unanimous, spontaneous support from our clients and our people."

Further speculation centers around the personalities of the combatants: With Johnston, words such as *icy, rigid,* and *cornered rat* seem to proliferate. O'Donnell, on the other hand, is often described as self-confident, perhaps even to the point of arrogance, but more generally good-natured, charming, and efficient. Most observers express surprise and dismay only that O'Donnell would try such a major reorganization and personal power play without being sure beforehand that he could without fail pull it off.

As the business and management environment spirals downward into madness, the clients begin to leave the sinking ship. On February 9, *Adweek* reports that IBM, which had awarded JWT a significant share of its $60 million in domestic bookings, is close to shifting its entire creative account to Lord, Geller, Federico, Einstein, a smaller sister division in the JWT Group. It is also reported that JWT's 1986 earnings will be "even more disappointing than anticipated."

February 16: "In all honesty, I am terribly disappointed to be back here," Johnston states, speaking of the position once held by his protégé, O'Donnell. "Ten months ago, I turned over my duties, thinking this would be indefinite, forever. The whole thing is sad, a personal tragedy, but it's his story, not mine."

Observers disagree. Emma Hill of Wertheim Schroder, working her side of the street, once again is sought out by the media: "Joe O'Donnell, in his short tenure, restructured and thinned out executive ranks and closed the Washington office and implied more consolidations were to come. There was talk of a new era. We felt he was moving in the right direction."

*Ad Age* publishes a long, detailed list of Johnston decisions that O'Donnell felt were sufficient reason for his boss's early retirement, matters that were taken up with the board and discarded as naive and of questionable taste.

Talk of weak financial performance and impending takeover fills media discussion of the coup, although the consensus seems to be that unfriendly takeovers in the ad business don't work, that Johnston will hang tough. Several note that the stock price is depressed, however. "I'll stay with my investment for now," states one analyst, "but if the price is right, well, yes, I would sell."

Asked by *Fortune* about the extent of the "misdoings" laid at his door by O'Donnell, Johnston says that "misdoings" is "a strong word." Board member Yunich of Macy's is once again drawn into battle in support of Johnston, saying that the charges amounted to "picayune things . . . latrine gossip." By this time, Price Waterhouse has investigated O'Donnell's charges of misconduct, and dismissed them. That doesn't prevent unattributed reports on the subject from surfacing in the coming months.

Don Johnston announces that there will be no major changes in management for the foreseeable future. "What this place needs is calm, unruffled waters," he says. A couple of weeks later, it is announced that Bert Metter, fifty-nine, chairman and CEO of J. Walter Thompson USA, has resigned and will be replaced by Don Johnston. Less than a month later, W. Lee Preschel, agency president for Latin America and the Central Pacific and a thirty-year veteran of the firm, is dismissed.

James Dougherty, an analyst with County Securities USA in New York, finally aerates what so far has gone unvoiced in more statesmanlike pronouncements. "What you're seeing is an ongoing pattern of Johnston trying to protect his position at the agency," he tells *The Wall Street Journal.* "It just seems to go from bad to worse. At some point, it seems to me Johnston has to be ousted." The *Journal* goes on to drive the knife home: "Analysts say JWT's financial problems lie largely in Mr. Johnston's persistent inability to keep costs down. . . . Moreover, the latest shake-up may alienate otherwise loyal clients and scare off new prospects." Dougherty delivers the coup de grâce. "Major companies deciding what to do about advertising have to take into account this rather evident management failing at the top," Dougherty says, one sober, dispassionate observer doing his small part to make things happen.

In May, rumors are incessant that Thompson is about to lose the Burger King account, one of the largest in its portfolio. The sharks are circling. *Business Week*, generally the last and more definitive dispenser of Islamic business judgment, writes, "Although JWT has enhanced its creative reputation in recent years, financial results haven't followed suit. Analysts have criticized the agency for poor financial management and bloated executive ranks. Company profits fell 69% last year, to $5.0 million, and analysts say that JWT may well show a loss for the first quarter of 1987."

*Business Week* concludes in its patented bleak-scenario mode: "Ad executives have long considered it axiomatic that the hostile takeover of an agency is impossible because the only assets are employees' talents. If Johnston can't soon put JWT in order, however, that theory may soon be obsolete."

The week of June 7, JWT files with the Securities and Exchange Commission a plan for golden parachutes for twenty-five members of its top management. In the plan, senior officers will get almost triple their compensation if they leave the company due to a takeover. Don Johnston will receive only twice his compensation.

On June 10 or so: Enter WPP Group, a British firm roughly 5 percent the size (in revenues) of Thompson. On the prowl for American agencies, WPP fields an unfriendly offer for JWT. The company, in return, shoots back a suit against WPP and against former JWT president Jack Peters, who has joined the invasion force. The claims in Johnston's lawsuit include alleged abuse and misappropriation of information by Peters and other top executives, and asks that WPP be prevented from achieving any profits from the inside info that made the raid possible. Peters, incidentally, will become president and chief operating officer if the British invasion is successful. He is reportedly earning more than twelve hundred dollars per diem during the takeover attempt. If the bid succeeds, he will get $1.3 million in thirty-six monthly payments, plus base compensation of $500,000 per year until 1990.

June 27: JWT falls to WPP. BRITONS' NEW BID WINS JWT, reads the headline in *The New York Times*. Three of the five largest U.S. ad agencies are now owned by British firms. Martin Sorrell, CEO of WPP, was a former financial officer of Saatchi & Saatchi, which is now the largest advertising agency in New York, London, and the world, positions once enjoyed by J. Walter Thompson.

In the final minute that attends the closing of the deal, Don Johnston inserts a vindictive clause into the deal that specifies that *neither* Joe O'Donnell *nor* Jack Peters will be empowered to run the company after the takeover, and the board votes aye. Sorrell is unwilling at press time to comment on Johnston's future with the company, but it doesn't take a rocket scientist to figure out what it may be.

JWT is sold for a tremendous and surprising sum, more than $566 million, or $55.50 a share. This immediately creates pressure on the company to perform at peak efficiency and eradicate the debt.

Goodyear Tire and Rubber Company, a longtime JWT client, immediately announces that it will review its advertising accounts in light of recent events. Other major accounts are more cautious, although Burger King says that the merger will not affect JWT's chances when the $200 million in billings comes up for review that following fall.

In September, N. W. Ayer, Inc., the nation's oldest ad agency, wins the $200 million Burger King account from JWT.

Under the new regime, Sorrell must keep profits afloat by cutting operating expenses. In April of 1988, six executives of Lord, Geller, once a boutique division of JWT and now a subsidiary of WPP Group, defect en masse to start a new agency. *Advertising Age* reports that the IBM account is now in danger, citing "the apparent lack of management skills exhibited by WPP Group Chief Executive Martin Sorrell in dealing with the acquired people and businesses." In August, Lord, Geller, stripped of its talent and management, loses 80 percent of its business when IBM flies the coop.

With Sorrell installed, Johnston takes his leave. Thompson, thanks to the diseased management of its American bosses, is now firmly in the grip of debt-berserk management imported from abroad.

All this would be strange and horrifying enough, if it were not so typical of the business landscape of the 1980s, from which we are feeling the horrible effects to this day.

Today, American management has become the craziest and least effective in the world. Within one brief generation, this nation, which for four decades managed the Free World back to economic good health, enjoyed a dramatic collapse of its ability to manage in virtually all corners of civilization, from sports to government, the arts to Wall Street.

Scandal and crazy management are now not the aberration, but the bedrock of our operating mentality. Working people suffer in every case. Bosses suffer, too, of course, but they make more money, so it's less easy to feel sorry for them. Unless you're a boss.

In corporations, gas stations, orchestra pits—indeed, in all locations where authority of the one over the many is at issue, the right to boss is misused and abused, and the abuser saluted for his strength and willingness to take action.

Examples of crazy bosses are so numerous today that to mention individual cases is almost to minimize the phenomenon. But let's name a few, just to get a feel for the terrain. Lou Holtz, beloved coach of Notre Dame, berating a player for lack of courage when the guy complained of a torn shoulder? George Steinbrenner, former managing nabob of the New York Yankees, destroying his reign through a combination of cupidity, rancor, and the belief that, even when he paid off a known gambler, nothing could touch him? Donald Trump borrowing himself into virtual bankruptcy?

Better still, think about the people who boss you. How many could you say, while in full pursuit of their duties, are . . . sane? I'll give you my answer. One. My chairman is sane. But then, he's only been chairman for a couple of years. Give him time.

Although this nation's problems with authority began in earnest after the Second World War, the most obvious decay of American management function—the excesses for which we are all paying today—began in the late 1980s.

Ah, what a festive time that was for those in search of the crazy boss in full and glorious plumage!

In New York City, every department head, including a former Miss America, was under investigation, if not indictment. In the religion business, Jim and Tammy Bakker wrung $92 million or so from the teat of the righteous, and acquired enough stuff—including an air-conditioned doghouse and a 1937 Rolls—to make Imelda Marcos pale in the collective imagination. On the Street, there were men like Ivan Boesky and Dennis Levine, who traded on the information placed with them in trust, rampaging dealmeisters so greedy that an annual take of a million dollars was insufficient to fill their bloated self-images. These guys saw money not as a thing-in-itself, but rather, as straight-arrow entrepreneur Jack Kent Cooke put it, "just a way of keeping score." Perhaps these deals, mergers, acquisitions, Pyrrhic divestitures, and takeovers were even more offensive than the Boesky/ Levine transactions, because instead of being illegal and immoral, they were immoral and *legal.*

Up at the top, setting the tone, was the United States government. An attorney general with more apparent conflicts of interest than most businessmen are fortunate enough to assemble in a lifetime. A chief of staff fired by the president's wife. An army of functionaries awarding each other urban-development contracts like Christmas fruitcakes.

How could something like this happen? Bad management? No, worse: admiration of bad management.

If the crazy boss did not exist, the current environment would have to invent him, hold him up as a model, and discard him when he is finished. Sure he's nuts, but he gets things done in the big, dangerous marketplace. He's needed, to make the machine run. In the media, in boardrooms, at backwoods retreats, the crazy boss is respected as a truly American institution and quality after-dinner speaker. As an obstreperous people, we like anyone who makes a lot of money, enjoys a lot of power, and can still be completely and wholly himself, no matter how unsatisfactory that self may be. Until he stumbles, it will be his employees who get inhaled, chewed dry, and hawked out when their time is done.

So the crazy boss goes on, fueling his regime with the lives of those who serve, impervious to the whips and scourges that would pierce the skins of more rational men. And insanity, it turns out, is often the best defense. The crazy boss is generally the one in his management structure who suffers least for his crimes, even though he's the ring-leader and instigator of the carnage.

American business was not always thus. Back in 1946, Peter Drucker, the grandfather of all management criticism, was able to write, in his seminal analysis of General Motors, *Concept of the Corporation:*

It is characteristic of the American tradition that its political philoso-phy sees social institutions as a means to an end which is beyond society. . . . It has, at one and the same time, refused to accept that deification of society which endows the state, the nation, or the race

> with absolute value, omnipotence, and omniscience, and that degra-
> dation of society which makes the law a mere traffic rule without any
> ethical significance or reason. . . . To this social philosophy the United
> States owes that character of being at the same time both the most
> materialistic and the most idealistic society, which has baffled so many
> observers.

It is precisely this sense of moral proportion that has been drained
from the pursuit of capital in the latter part of this century, and that
shows few signs of resuscitation. As Drucker noted, American business used to enjoy the softening agent, the humanism, the shared
perception that a social agenda—both inside and outside the
company—is necessary for an enterprise to be *American* in the way
we have always understood it. Perhaps the unspoken social agenda
was something as simple as: "We'll create a product and sell it for a
fair price," or "We won't fire three hundred flight attendants who
have worked for the company for an average of ten years and replace
them with exchange students from Burkina Faso."

Today, we stand at a critical juncture. For a people to thrive and
not descend into anarchy, dictatorship, or communal living, there
must be a shared consensus that a select bunch of individuals have
the right to tell other people what to do. Without that common
assumption, there can be no hierarchy in society, and without hierarchy, no institutions.

Without rational, ethical, spiritual, religious, human underpin-
ning, the workplace—no matter what the size, shape, or form of its
enterprise—has no behavioral rudder to exercise control over the raw
pursuit of gain. Under the intense competitive pressure of the current
business environment, the Boss must struggle to find any means at all
to grow his power, his profits, his name. And a sadist who makes his
sales projections is more valuable to senior management and its stockholders than is a solid human being who misses his numbers by 2
percent. In a world where profits are the only thing that count, and the
future extends only as far as the next quarter, the crazy man may seem
the only one equipped to manage with confidence.

But authority, if it is to work *over the long run*, must have in its
tiny little heart a kernel of sanity. It cannot be wholly unreasonable,
irrational, capricious, and self-serving. Authority must be a product
of a common agreement to give up a little freedom for a little order,
and it must ultimately benefit not only the rulers, but those who are

ruled. That's always been the unspoken deal here. Any suspension of that basic agreement for too long leads to revolution, which has a tendency to create its own problems.

Since World War II, however, and at an increasing rate, authority has mutated into a beast that exists for its own sake, to feed nothing but itself, and its abuse is widely accepted as the ultimate, in fact, the only, proof of its potency. Power is now more important than law. The exercise of power is the ultimate good. That's the consensus. The spore of management insanity is carried from the general economic and political environment into the business community, where it is contracted by the big boss. From there, it radiates downward to smaller bosses, and out throughout the organization—and then back into the business community again. Something like the chart that follows:

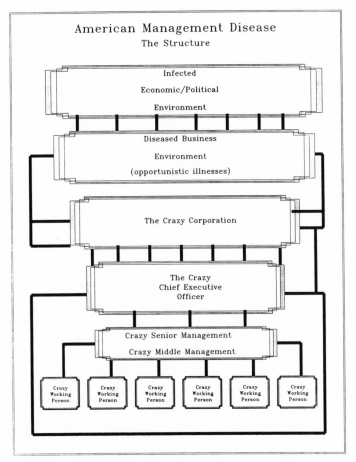

And the crazy boss himself? Each is different, and the same, a mixture of different guises, mercurial, tempestuous, and a tremendous pain in the keester.

Even if you are one, surely you recognize that.

On Monday, he may be a bully, flattening everyone in his path, spreading fear and self-loathing throughout the ranks.

On Tuesday, his aggression in temporary remission, he becomes convinced that all his subordinates are plotting against him, that all are, have always been, disloyal, ripe for extermination.

On Wednesday, he metamorphoses into the narcissistic empire-builder, castles blossoming in his fevered brain.

By 3:00 P.M. on Thursday, he's been struck inert by a spasm of bureaucratic willies, so he shuts himself in his office and won't come out except to bleat for coffee and distribute a blizzard of inane paper.

Friday morning early, his dreams are dust. He is so paralyzed, he allows several opportunities to pass, opportunities that might, if managed in a timely fashion, have brought glory to him and profit to the company.

Over the weekend, after sixteen hours of slow drinking, he subjects himself to a cover-to-cover reading of the latest Tom Peters megatome and determines to set his entire staff on the search for the next Huge Fad Management Philosophy first thing Monday morning.

And so on. And on. Until the ultimate disaster hunter puts an end to himself or, more likely, you.

In each crazy boss, the total syndrome is marked by a debilitating range of character deficiencies that, while not at all useful in private life, *are uniquely suited to a successful business career:*

- A certain *rigidity of character.* This is necessary to the functioning of the average crazy corporation. Organizational people are expected to act in coherent, predictable ways. That, in a functioning social group, is an accepted definition of sanity. In some cases, the ability to see all sides of an issue must be considered a real debility. The rigid personality may have a sense that he has failed to live up to some monolithic, mythical potential, that no matter how much he has earned or achieved, it is never enough. This quality is perhaps best expressed in today's society by a

Dennis Levine, who earned millions but needed to steal millions more.

- Next, *pervasive feelings of inadequacy* may be covered up by the need for aggrandizement from all corners. This may evidence itself in the need to show off, to impress others and one's self with all sorts of possessions valued in our culture—money, toys, women, column inches in the press.
- He also has *problems asserting himself*—either being overly aggressive or, in some cases, finding it impossibly difficult to express his wishes or to ask for something, do something in his own interest, express an opinion or criticism, order someone. He may find it hard to say no; suffer from an inability to plan, a tendency to drift. He's a bureaucrat!
- Underlying all these attributes is a *need for perfection and control* in an imperfect world. He mistrusts other people's ability to make the world what he needs it to be, and is frustrated when that world—and all the people in it—don't deliver up to his grandiose expectations. He needs to criticize, to tinker with the situation, to manipulate other people until he doesn't feel so goddamned out of control.
- Then comes the *rage*—when things don't work out, and sometimes even when they do.

That's the thumbnail profile. We'll look at more. But the bottom line on the crazy boss is this: he is sick in a lot of ways, not just one. And yes, *he will seek to destroy himself,* in time.

If you are crafty, and patient, and lucky, and determined—*you can help!* First we'll need to understand a little more about how a crazy boss works on an organization, how he is worked on by it, and, finally, how a thoughtful employee can use a crazy boss's fears, needs, and pain to manage him or, if he will not be managed, to *bring him down.*

Want to try? Sure you do.

Let's get started.

# PART I

# THE CRAZY
# CORPORATION

# CHAPTER ONE

# JOINING THE RANKS

The multitude is always ready to listen to the strong-willed man, who knows how to impose himself on it. Men gathered in a crowd lose all force of will, and turn instinctively to the person who possesses the quality they lack.

Gustave LeBon
*The Crowd,* 1879

C
ome with me to a healthy organization.
Wow. It's great here! Leaders with circumscribed powers preside over a body of workers, each of whom identifies with the group, performs a set of predictable functions, gets paid, derives some satisfaction from that process.

In this sane organization, there are certain ways an individual is incorporated into the group and fostered and rewarded:

1. People join the system and stay in it long enough to become part of the culture.
2. Dependable behavior is expected and produced in all members by a combination of incentive and reward.
3. Innovative thought and work is valued, too, since there is an understanding that spontaneous behavior is the only way successfully to respond to ever-changing business conditions.
4. People compete, sure, but they also cooperate.
5. Excellence is defined and rewarded.

Okay, that's enough of that. Let's move on to the real world.

## FIRST, YOU GET IN

Why do people give up their identity? Because the identity they gain from the corporation is greater than what they give up. The Bank

feeds off the underlying insecurities of its people. That is the quintessential parasitic act of the corporation.

Former executive<br/>Citibank

All organizations—not just fraternities—make you hurt before you
are truly accepted to the fold. The good news is that, in today's crazy
company, Getting In is perhaps the best clear view you're likely to
have at what kind of craziness is acceptable in that particular workplace. Why? Because while they are choosing you, *you are also
choosing them.* Don't forget that, in your lust to be accepted. This
may be one club you don't want to belong to, even if they do want
you as a member.

The desire to belong *somewhere,* however, is understandably
strong. Before you join a group, especially one that is willing to pay
you for being a member, your worldview may look something like
this:

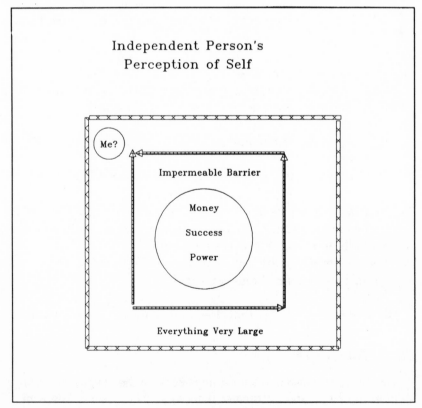

How much more comfortable is the view from within!

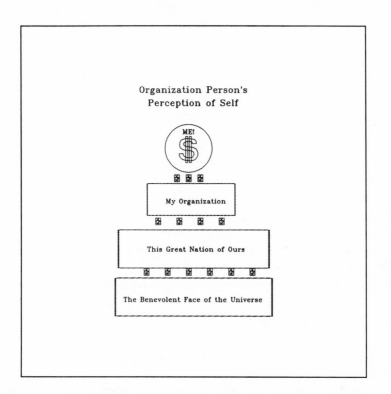

The desire to achieve satisfaction with oneself, the availability of formal solutions, and the money all combine to place the applicant in a uniquely vulnerable position, *open to psychic acquisition, hungering for it.* To get inside, however, you have to present yourself to the authority structure. And be accepted. Ah, the exquisite terror.

The world inside is effectively barred by the interview process, which is designed, like a hazing, to separate the wheat from the chaff.

The process is confusing both for the person who *wants in* and for the inside man, who can't yet afford to see the unknown quantity on the other side of the desk as a human being worthy of five minutes of time, let alone a job that will lead to human relationships laden with trust, respect, dependency, and a rudimentary form of regard approaching love. A vast cloud of unknowing, inherent in the interview process, surrounds them both. "After you've interviewed a number of people, you find out how difficult it is for anyone to get

a job, because they blend together," says Gary, a general counsel at
a growing young concern that markets cellular-communications services to pompous executives on the run. "A month after it happened,
you forget which asshole spilled coffee on your blotter, and you have
a general feeling that one of them did, so you don't hire any of them.
You start over again."

How, then, can one avoid being lost in the murk of anonymity? By
making a strong personal impression of exactly the right kind. But
applicants who display too much personality are denied entry as
often as those who display too little.

How much of you is acceptable? And incidentally, is that a threatening enough question for you?

Brad, a software designer who consults with large companies, is
sort of an inside/outside guy, seeing a lot but belonging to no one.
"There's the tension between the fact that you want to lick their
boots with your own personal tongue—and being the boy who sticks
out, which is what gets you hired," he says. "You have to judge the
interviewer's character at the same time you present your persona.
You have to figure out what kind of risks he can handle. It's like
riding a circus pony in one of those short little skirts. They want to
try to present you with hoops and obstacles you have to jump
through, in the hopes you'll bend over and they can see your un-
derwear."

The dance can extend over days or weeks, and it is not infrequent
for a serious job to take months to materialize.

Ted is a financial wizard, chief financial officer of a big rust-belt
manufacturing concern. He's been looking for a solid post in a flash-
ier Los Angeles accounting and financial-planning firm, but relates
the following sorry tale:

> In the last six months I've had about fifteen interviews. And eight have
> been with the two principals, O'Reilly and Fleiss themselves, and their
> equivalent of a little shnaps. [He snorts an imaginary spoonful.] And
> this song and dance seems to go on forever. It's been sort of like
> *Platoon.* I'm humping my pack up the mountain. Can you imagine
> having to prostrate yourself for six months and getting nowhere in
> the negotiations? We're still basically at the same starting point we
> were in January, but think of all the parties I've been invited to, all
> the good bourbon I've drunk. But we're still twenty-five grand apart,
> and I think it's now either fish or cut bait and I'm through. Do you

think I should write him a letter? If he'd only come up with five grand more, I would take the job.

After such a long siege, the *wanting* for membership is a gelatinous lump at the back of your throat that remains with you constantly. You ache to be acquired.

But you can't fool all of the people longer than about two interviews. As easy as it may be to act a phony, toothsome yahoo for three or four hours, the smart applicant offers his true self, since *that's the self he'll have to present consistently—and live with—if he gets the job.*

The eventual offering of that true self is perhaps the most frightening aspect of the entry process. Now you're playing with real ammunition. And rejection moves up from a short sting to a deep knife in the center of one's gut.

"When I was an actor," says my friend Greg, now a successful insurance executive, "the auditions that really hurt were the ones where you got close."

> I remember one where I was called back six times for a commercial. They kept telling me they loved me. And then they would call me back in, and I'd have to do it all over again. After a while, I asked them, "You guys have seen what I do. What more can I do to convince you?" And they smiled and said, "We love you, Greg, but you know how these things go. The client, you know, blah blah and so forth." It got so I really liked the fellows who were interviewing me. Finally, after all that, I got a call telling me that I didn't get it. They gave it to a well known athlete, in fact. Not long after that, I got a job here at the corporation. On the whole, it's better here. At least you know where you stand some of the time.

What is less completely understood by the supplicant is that on the other side of the desk is another employee who needs you just as much. He or she has been given the job of finding the right person. Are you the right person? Or, worse, the *wrong* one? He doesn't know!

The woods are full of people who do a great interview and bomb out completely once they are on the job. "Mary was a great interview," says Freddy, a senior counsel responsible for a lot of hiring. "Clearly intelligent. Speaks well. She also has a résumé that's very good. And she's been a number of places, great academics, which all goes to show you that résumés and interviews don't mean shit."

> How are you supposed to tell how somebody's going to be in the space of a thirty-minute conversation? The only way you're going to get to know that is making sure they have the level of competency, and then you hire or not based on personal characteristics. Does she work hard? Is she friendly? Arrogant? Well-rounded? Does she like rock and roll? Sports? *Books?* Mary talked a lot during her interview, and in that situation it was great. Now that we've hired her, I find she's the ultimate babbler. She'll make a personal call before she'll do anything, and talk about her mythical diseases until you want to throw up.

The guy known for making bad hires is widely disrespected, and I've seen more than one senior executive who failed to rise higher because his protégés flunked out.

So the stakes are high for him, too. And he's looking for some very specific things to ease his mind.

First of all, he's looking for *attitude.* "I can respond to someone who doesn't have all the answers, because it implies they're willing to learn, but I'm offput by young people whose arrogance is galling," says one CEO. "If they're too cocksure, you start to feel like their willingness to learn in situations is lousy. The idea is that you really want to be a part of this team. Most managers feel more secure with a team player. So come off as a little humble. Confident but not arrogant. Confidence tempered by humility, that's what I'm looking for."

Next comes *desire.* Better show it!

Ted, VP of Mergers and Acquisitions at a firm whose purpose seems to be the creation of debt from perfectly reasonable assets, is particularly clear on this subject:

> This guy really pissed me off. Someone who decided he really wasn't there to interview for a *job* per se, you know, he was just wanting me to know what a terrific guy he was if I was lucky enough to get him. He was very arrogant, like, "I'm not here to work for you, I'm here to help you." Ten minutes into the thing he says, "You know I'm not here for a *job* per se. I'm here gathering information." So I said, "Fine! Then get the fuck out of here, because I'm looking for some-body who wants a *job*!"

In the best of worlds, the dance of fantasy and need would be no more uncomfortable than, say, a visit to a proctologist. In the crazy corporation, Getting In is just the first stress point of many. So watch and learn. It may be the last chance you have to get out of a screwy thing. "At my job interview with K., he met me at the Century Club and we were walking up this enormous eighteenth-century staircase, and I was so nervous that I slipped a couple of steps down and fell flat on my face . . . and . . . he didn't notice," says my buddy Diedrich, a writer of direct-sales material for Fortune 500 companies that sell personal-hygiene products to a broad demographic.

> Then we went upstairs, and there was this little room where you're supposed to drink. A little salon. He has three vodkas in quick succession, pointing out Arthur Schlesinger, Jr., and I can't remember who else. We're sitting at a banquette, which I strongly advise against, and my hand is brushing against his, too much opportunity for awkward physical contact. You shouldn't touch your interviewer. Unless you're in show business.

> So he's getting sloshed, and I'm drinking club soda because I don't think it wise to lose your wits. After all, I'd already fallen down the stairs. So we finally make it to lunch. He kept trying to get me to take this other job, a job I'd told him like sixteen hundred times I didn't want, and I kept saying no no no, and he said finally, "What would it take to get you here?" And I told him some outrageous thing, and he said okay! He was already so drunk that if I had asked to be president, he would have probably agreed.

No matter how hard he tries, see, *no interviewer can completely mask his personality.* Some don't even try.

Mark, a copywriter with a Chicago advertising agency, remembers his first chat with a huge industry nabob, a famous fellow I should probably just call Leonard. The meeting took place in New York. "Leonard made me face the desk while he went behind me," Mark remembers. "I swiveled in my chair, and he said, 'No, no, you can just keep talking while you face my desk.' And then I heard a wide variety of snorting and snuffling and general snorkling from behind me. Then he came back in front of me, handed me an open bottle of Stoly, and said, 'Here. Want some?' I didn't."

The second meeting didn't go any better:

> At my second interview, Leonard had a chicken-salad sandwich, with mayonnaise dripping off his chin for the whole thing. All he wanted

to do was gossip about my current boss and whether or not he was gay. And my boss was a friend of his! So we talk for a while, then lunchtime comes and Leonard says, "Gee, I'm starved," and he gets another sandwich, stuffs his face, and doesn't offer me a single thing. He spends the entire time asking me questions about who's in, who's out, that sort of stuff. Then he says, "Nice to see you again," and walks out. I was stunned, in a daze.

By the third meeting, Mark was in awe of this sizable monster, never once thinking what such a person would be like *as a boss.* When the job offer came, he fell.

For my final interview, I had to fly to San Francisco, where they were having a company meeting. They put me up at the Francis Drake. Two days later, I finally saw him again. What a fireplug, an explosive guy. It turns out it was his birthday. In the middle of the interview, the most important moment of my life, my jump into the big time, all of a sudden the secretary comes in and says, "Leonard, could you come out here?" For the next two hours, there was nothing but champagne and stuff I won't mention. At that point, I'm sitting alone, in the corner. Leonard has had a couple of bottles of champagne, and he walks by and looks at me. I can see he doesn't really remember who I am. He says, "What am I—interviewing you?" I said yes. He says, "Come in." I said, "You sure? Maybe we should do this tomorrow." And he says, "I don't care. I like you. I'm gonna hire you. How much do you want?" And he ended up giving me about five grand more than I asked for. He wanted me to think he was a generous guy, and I guess, at that time, he was.

Mark's miserable relationship with Leonard the boss is another story. But you can't say he wasn't warned.

So beware: an economy-sized crazy boss is incapable of *not* showing himself for what he is. A word to the wise is usually sufficient. But will you take it? Probably not!

And why? Because you want to be had!

Michael, a CPA, is another sad example:

My interview was with this guy, a horrible human being I ended up having to work for for two years. He had these thick Coke-bottle eyeglasses. He asked me impertinent questions like, "How did you pay for your college education?" "How many magazines do you subscribe to and why did you renew?" I guess he wanted to know what kind of person I was. I read his notes later on my interview, rummaged through his file, you know. It was horrible. He'd asked me about myself, my philosophy, but the only thing he noted down was, "His tie wasn't knotted properly but he seems bright enough." This interview went on for two hours, *and he wouldn't let me go.* If I'd only known he was staring at my tie the whole time, I would have relaxed.

And yet—you guessed it—the boy took the job! And why? Simply because they offered to pay him money.

Yes, after all the issues of compatibility are resolved, there remains the question of money, money that lies so close to the heart of self-image. Beyond a certain minimum sum, you're looking for an amount that allows you to feel that you have just received good value for the sale of you.

You had better have a pretty good notion of that actual value, and arrive at that opinion independent of outside influence other than your spouse's. A business manager I'll call Billy works for a regional not-for-profit theater company, one that has been around for a long enough time to pay salaries in the mid–five figures. "I was interviewed for this job, and on a break I was talking to this really senior guy in the men's room," Billy relates, continuing:

And he says, "Look, this place is getting so many grants that you should definitely ask for fifty grand—don't tell them I told you this." So the managing director offers me the job and asks me how much I want. And I said fifty grand. And she said, "Actually, we were thinking of offering you twenty." I felt like an idiot. She said, "Actually, I guess we could get you twenty-five, but that's really it." I guess the guy in the men's room thought these guys in his company were assholes and would fall for a heavy pitch. From now on, I'd say beware of friendly advice from people who are making a lot more money than you are. And have some idea of what you're really worth.

And what are you worth?

You are worth *exactly the amount that would make you happy to take the job and not one penny less.*

And you can take that to the bank.

When it all comes together—a job, an interviewer, and you—it's beautiful, and really a lot like, well, falling in love. You've offered yourself and been accepted. Isn't that wonderful?

My friend Neil is a computer programmer in the management-information department of a large corporation in Cleveland. He's been a happy camper for more than a decade. He fondly recalls his introduction into the fold, which happened without the least bit of spindling or mutilation:

> Ralph said I had the best résumé he'd ever seen. I made him feel comfortable. A few people were blackballed because they weren't what he was looking for. What you wear, how long was your hair; these were issues to him. Then I had to meet about 20 million other people, including his boss, B.

> Even though B. was the top executive in the company, overlooking the river from his office, he treated me very informally, as you might treat somebody at a bar stool, and his whole tack was that the underlings had already proved the guy had the competence, he wanted to know if the guy was an asshole or not. So in the space of fifteen minutes, we talk about sports, family, other general topics of daily life. Then he had two questions that he wanted answers to: "The Company's in trouble. What do you think about coming to a company that has problems?" I said, "We all got problems." "Two," he says, "there are a lot of young people around here. Are you afraid there won't be room for promotion?" I said, "I'm not afraid, because I see Ralph has been promoted, and I think I can do the job and do the same." He said to Ralph as I walked out, "Do anything you want. The guy's okay."

Once you get in, you receive the congratulations of your friends and spouse, perhaps a company-wide or industry announcement if you're big enough, and a session, if you're lucky, explaining policies, procedures, benefits, working uniform (belts or suspenders?), place names and locations, and other orientational hoopla. You are now a member of a crazy corporation, and ready to get involved with your new workplace—and its leaders—on human levels you never dreamed possible.

## ASSUME THE POSITION!

> Each individual enters a group with the following necessary equipment: 1) biological needs, 2) psychological needs, 3) drives, 4) patterns of striving, 5) past experience, and 6) adjustive capacities. It is just this equipment which makes it possible for leaders to exploit their

members for good or evil, and which hampers the independent flow-
ering of individual personalities.

Eric Berne

You've bought the costume and think you look good in it. You start
to say things like "synergistic use of out-term operations in the
appropriate regions" without blushing. You are comfortable enough
to employ moderate profanity in certain business meetings. Most of
all, you find yourself saying "we" instead of "I," "ours" instead of
"mine." You are assimilated, not only by desire, but by the act
of performing, day in, day out, your assigned function.

Thus we come to evaluate our own worth based upon how well we
fulfill other people's expectations. "Within an organization members
behave in ways which they would not do outside the organization,"
wrote sociologists Daniel Katz and Robert Kahn in *The Social Psychology of Organizations*.[1] "They may wear uniforms or costumes
which they would not otherwise wear. They are likely to adopt certain styles and formalities in interpersonal relations which are not
elsewhere in evidence. Above all, their behavior in organizations
shows a selectivity, a restrictiveness and persistence which is not to
be observed in the same persons when outside the organization."

The first lever in this assumption of role is the acquisition of two
things:

- A function
- A title

Together, these twin attributes provide that all-important organizational asset: a sense of place.

In the crazy company, however, the title becomes more important
than the function, and juicy designations are jealously guarded by a
tree full of present and future crazy bosses. Take it from a fellow I'll
call Verne, who commands the post of "associate director" in the
public-relations department of a mid-sized national magazine.
"Since I became a full-time shitball on parade, they had to give me
a title with the word *director* in it," he says. "For a long time, they
used me as a consultant, but I got sick of not being on the health
plan."

[1] John Wiley & Sons, 1966.

I'm happy now, even if they did put an "associate" in front of my "director." Full directors around this place make only five grand more than I do and have a lot more responsibility. Even then, there are people who think a full director title is a terrific thing. This woman, Arlene Glass, was running the staff function here, and it was her job to make all the promotions and hirings. And naturally, she guarded the director title really jealously. And she sandbagged my hiring for two months so there would be one less pinhole in her importance. One less person sharing space with her and the other associates on the chart. There's more of an elite if there are fewer people there. That was a real eye-opener to me. She had always behaved well with me, and we even did the dirty hula six months later, but people get funny when you screw with their titles.

The title itself confers power. Hugh, vice president of Human Resources at a huge insurance firm somewhere in the great Northeast, synopsizes the meaning of rank:

What is a vice president? Around here, it means you've been elevated where they can't willy-nilly fire you or fuck with you, because then *the next person has nothing to aspire to*. If the security doesn't arrive at some stage, how do you keep them down on the farm?

But with rank also come certain liabilities. "The top guys where I used to work were called the Wallendas, after the Flying Wallendas," says a guy I knew who used to work at a national newsweekly. He continues:

They were called that because these guys juggle so many things at once that it's like a high-wire act. It wasn't meant as a pejorative term at all, although I will point out that the original Wallendas, most of them, did fall to their deaths.

When your title is *clear,* and your duties *defined,* the world is comprehensible and good. When your title is not—the universe is a river of anxiety, and you a very small and confused fish.

Barry, Not Yet Vice President of Publicity at a big New York–based record company, explains:

For those of us who never fought in the war, and were never Boy Scouts, a title is as close as we can get to a merit badge, or sergeant's stripes. And for those who did, it's the continuation of a hierarchical way of life. Like for example the title "deputy." What does it mean? Our deputy vice president here wants to change his title because nobody knows what he does. It's a title to joke about. Deputy dog, deputy vice president. It's a fake title, which you want to stay away from. He's never even been introduced that way. He's still introduced using his old title, associate something.

In certain afflicted bureaucracies, titles become more important than substantial things, even money, and everyone eventually gets one. Then we have something that's dangerously close to democracy, a condition that makes serious business types very nervous. Rob, an editor of internal publications at a very large midwestern manufacturer of small rotating objects, complains:

Executive editor. Editorial director. Senior editorial director. It's a semantic thing. It's when titles no longer have any meaning. Like when you go to Oakland, California, and there are no oaks there, let alone any land. What we're witnessing here is a tragedy: title depreciation. It's like the decay of the aristocracy in Europe, when titles were handed out like bonbons. What does it mean to be a duke in that environment? We've democratized titles, and it's the worst. When you democratize something, you tend to devalue it. It's a no-class action. It only has meaning if it's a small club, and when you open it up and make everybody happy, you obscure the lines of power and of communication, and pretty soon people give people underneath them titles, and there becomes a title frenzy, and the lowest person has a nice title and no one under him to do the work.

That is an insane organization, because its members know neither what is expected nor where they stand on the corporate ladder. Looking at it obversely, organizational *sanity* becomes quite simple to define: *the sane person is the one who fulfills his title, consistently doing what people expect him to do.*

Indeed, doing what people expect defines more than sanity; it defines something even more important, in the long run: *success.* In truth, aside from acceptable work, willing conformity may be the strongest bond that ties an individual to an organization, conveying the message that he's happy to be a part. "Through quite minor acts of deference and demeanor, through little behavioral warning lights, the individual exudes assumptions about himself," wrote sociologist

Erving Goffman in his work *Relationships in Public*.[2] "In fact, all behavior of the individual, insofar as it is perceived by others [is] made up of tacit promises and threats confirming or disconfirming that he knows and keeps his place."

In such a world, authority *is* sanity, and can never be crazy as long as it remains within its prescribed role. As Goffman noted: "When an act that will later be perceived as a mental symptom is first performed by the individual who will later be seen as a mental patient, the act is not taken as a symptom of illness but rather as a deviation from social norms, that is, an infraction of social rules and social expectations." Translation: the guy who's considered mentally ill is the one who fails to conform to the system. The sane man is the one who follows the rules, unless a trained psychiatrist happens to wander by.

Where predictability is all, it is the total human being who must be transformed—from unpredictable to predictable. Predictability dignifies function, cements the notion of Role over Personality, and makes people amenable to being managed by individuals whom they would not otherwise respect. In the following organizational architecture, view each unshaded space as some factor of humanity allowed to remain intact, not yet molded by the group demand:

[2] Basic Books, 1971; Chapter 7, "The Insanity of Place."

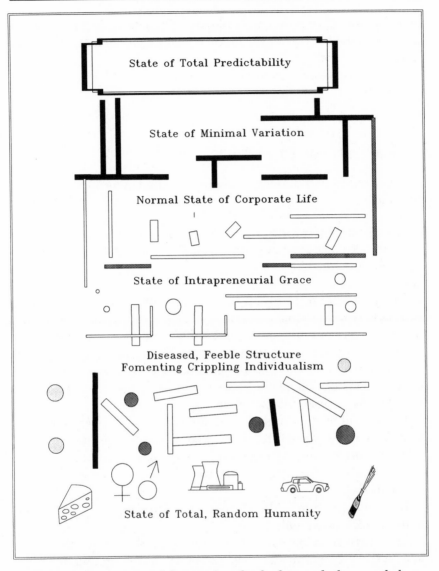

State of Total Predictability

State of Minimal Variation

Normal State of Corporate Life

State of Intrapreneurial Grace

Diseased, Feeble Structure
Fomenting Crippling Individualism

State of Total, Random Humanity

Too much structure dehumanizes both the workplace and those who labor in it. Too little structure, or too much random humanity, makes serious business relations impossible, since predictable behavior is nonexistent. Lack of organizational coherence also creates a general disregard of *authority for its own sake*, always a dangerous threat to Management.

Management's goal, therefore, is the *elimination of too much egregious humanity from its members*, since it makes them unpredictable. To manage a group of employees completely, the organization must demand and achieve, in each willing individual, deep and abiding Conformity.

And employees, seeking love and acceptance, are only too happy to comply.

## CONFORM, PLEASE. THANK YOU!

A senior officer at a national brokerage firm sets down his version of the rules:

> Investment bankers can be coke-sniffing crazies, and that's fine if they get the job done. But if they don't live in Greenwich and belong to the tennis club—then they're nonconformists.

Everyone within the group shares a certain spectrum of common needs. This unifying characteristic is based on common economic interests, common daily tasks and living conditions, and the seemingly inherent need of human beings to create meaning from what would appear to be the meaningless actions of business life. The cohesion between members grows, and like owners and their dogs, each begins to resemble the other.

In the hold of the common unifying group spirit, every man and woman is more powerful than he could possibly be alone. Alone, they are just people, a status that clearly has its limitations. Together, however, they are, indeed, the Walrus, something large and fat, with tusks.

In a sane group, it is the sense of common needs that unites and homogenizes individuals.

In a crazy corporation, it is the pathology that unites the group and, eventually, permeates each and every person up and down the organization.

Since a good many employees are also bosses of somebody, the patient is constantly reexposed, getting sicker faster.

Yet no matter how hurt or wheezing a group is, the loss of personal separateness and individual responsibility, along with the intense group emotion, and the resulting suppression of conscience, *feels good.* The price the needy conformist pays is the necessity to take his or her self, shape it, tamp it down, or pump it up, so it fits within the norm. In some places, that's a boxcar of considerable size, with plenty of room to move one's self around in. In others, *glasnost* has not yet been served.

From organization to organization, conformity is an inconstant god. Some get the ice pick because they refuse to eliminate their doggie photos from their desktops, while others wipe the halls with their drooling psyches and get away with it.

In my corporation, there are the dead, guys like my former boss Jim, who appeared at our corporate headquarters—a very buttoned-up place—fresh from Syracuse with a beard like a muskmelon and boots that squelched with the moisture of hundreds of camping trips. Or our former marketing communications guy, Herb, who liked to wear a baseball cap at his desk and do magic tricks.

Or even our former chairman, who was ousted because he insisted on drinking yam juice at board meetings while the rest of senior management had their scotch/rocks.

Nevertheless, there is also my current financial officer, who stuffs his office with miniature clocks. Or our new VP of Management Information, who is the ultimate sartorial pariah in his pocket protector and short-sleeve shirt—even in winter. Yet for some reason these guys live on, in part because they are very successful in their area and not replaceable without tremendous difficulty, and in part because the way they are odd is *not recognizable as bizarre within our culture.*

These fellows have earned the license to be strange.

In each company, in fact, there is a *sliding scale of permissible oddity.* "If you're not eccentric enough, you become a corporate drone, like most of the lemmings I work with," says a mergers-and-acquisitions strategist who insists on having an unauthorized geranium on his window ledge. "You won't find me marching into the sea. Me, I'd rather take the sharp detour at the beach and get killed on the rocks."

Those who intend to remain in the organization for the long haul must work out comfortable ways of conforming and not conforming. Some solutions can be consciously crafted to make a statement, others come from deep down.

My good friend Gray is a consultant to ailing managements from California to Manhattan. "You earn the right to your eccentricities," he says, going on to point out:

I don't know where style—which is good—ends, and eccentricity—which is not always good—begins. Maybe when you start swimming against the stream.

For example, if I'm going to an office to see some gray corporate types, I want to wear something that subtly fights their notion of what a consultant should be. I want something like I'm walking down the hall in a Paul Stuart suit and they say, "What the fuck!"

Whether it's organic or nonorganic, you've got to make it work. The worst thing is a failed eccentricity, one that falls on its face. That means you're not a nonconformist. You're just a dork.

The key is to make all nonconformance a means of communicating with, not alienating yourself from, the group. Sid, editor of a national magazine that itself sets a national standard for people between the ages of fourteen and twenty-eight, sets the rules for his shop: "You need something that sets you apart," he says, "something that makes you look different. But you have to be careful."

If your eccentricity is that you collect beer coasters from around the world, that's fine. If it's picking your nose in public, maybe it's not. And if you like miniature glass ballerinas, that's not something you bring up with the guys over beers after work. Someone comes and tells you something, you're not going to take what they say as seriously if they're . . . out of touch.

The type of eccentricities that are the most scary are the kind where a person is not aware of it and has cut himself off from human interaction. Like the old guy at work who still wears an ascot. You immediately have a picture of that guy's life—going back to his apartment and dusting. We don't want to be lonely when we're old, and we are scared. Of course, if you've got money, you can wear ascots up the wazoo and it doesn't scare anyone, because you'll always be able to *buy* a life.

Now, all this is very well and good, but somewhat useless unless you can fairly calculate your permissible level of personal eccentricity.

Here are some of the factors. Ignore these and you're likely to be gone, leaving behind but a few souls to muse, "I wonder whatever happened to that weird guy in Purchasing who used to suck his teeth?"

*Money:* "You take an eccentric homeless person and everyone wants to cart them off, but give that person a cool million, and everyone wants to have them over for dinner," says my friend Wes, general manager of a branch firm of a national accounting company. Wes believes that "money is the determining factor in conformity," and it's hard to disagree with him. "In middle ranges, conformity is a must," he observes. "You don't have to conform if you're rich, and you don't have to conform if you're poor, but being middle class prescribes the range of your behavior more than any other group. We're the downtrodden, because we can't have a lot of fun unless it's channeled into very rigid paths. Like cocktail parties."

*Power:* The farther you are from the bump and grind, the more bizarre you can be, unless you're at the center. The guy who runs things can do just about anything he likes, particularly if it's mean and tough and would be considered antisocial in any other milieu. At the other end as well, there is largess. "The lower level can have their eccentricities," says a guy I'll call Barrett, who is loan officer in a bank in Alabama. "The guy in the stockroom who's into rap music. The boss likes him a lot more, but he doesn't like that kind of behavior from his senior management people. He's entrusted his money to them. You wouldn't want to go into a bank and see the loan officer walking on stilts. It's middle management that has no fun at all."

*Age:* The greater a person's age, the more certain personal quirks are likely to be permitted.

*Uniqueness:* All men are replaceable, sure, but a guy who can tango is worth a roomful of lumpfish. "A lot of leeway is created by the inherent assumption that 'I am creative,' " states Lenny, an artist at a design firm. "There's an implicit assumption that we're out of control and kind of *have* to be in order to do a good job." He continues:

> It seems that you can get away with a whole lot of stuff if you can back it up. And the question is, Are you given the chance before they make a snap judgment about you? What my boss says to me is, "Whatever you do is fine with me, but those assholes upstairs might be different." The scoop in advertising is account-management people have a dress code, the three-piece suit day in and day out. It's

especially bizarre because one of the guys I work with, a three-piece
during the day, in the evenings is a rock musician in a sarong wham-
ming a bass. He manages it by compartmentalizing. In terms of the
creative side, you're allowed much more flexibility.

Still, creativity only goes so far. Nonconformity is seldom tolerated when the business of the company turns to business.

Burkholtz, a senior programming executive at a big-city TV station, runs his own department with impunity, but he still feels con-
strained at morning staff meetings with his tight-sphinctered general
manager. "Earl doesn't tolerate eccentricity in AM meetings," he
says. "You can't be loosy goosy, and it's gotten me into some tight
corners. He doesn't like you to bring food in. I once brought a bagel
with cream cheese into a late-morning meeting. He told me to get it
out. I said, 'How come it's okay to sit here and put a schmeer on at
nine in the morning, but not at eleven-thirty?' And he said, 'It looks
like you just got in and are having breakfast,' So I said, 'Well, why
don't we look on it as a working lunch?' He didn't like it. On the
other hand, profanity is a tolerated form of antisocial activity at any
hour. Particularly Yiddish profanity, for some reason, which is encouraged. Schmutz. Schmooze. Schmuck. Putz. 'Get the schmutz off
the desk.' That's what he told me when I had the bagel with the
schmeer. I did, too."

Lack of conformity can be tolerated in any venue, however, if the
behavior is part of one's defined role, or, better still, if you can make
people laugh. Just be careful not to let the aggression that fuels that
humor peep through.

So are you creative? Funny? Irreplaceable in any other functional
or cultural way? Congratulations, *you're nonfungible.*

Are you a desk droid with fourteen more like you waiting down
the hall? Then watch the patterns on your socks for subversive
tendencies. They could be adequate grounds for your replacement
by someone just as fungible as you.

**Bad Executive Karma:** Woe betide the guy who is too much in the
way when executive displeasure is looking for a target.

**Cultural Rigidity & Anxiety:** The fabric of all workplaces has a little
give in it, but while tartan ties may not be a felony in most locales,
even the tastiest kilt is sure to raise an eyebrow anywhere but in

Aberdeen. Conversely, an overly conservative approach in a young shop may target you as a dull wonk who just plays things safe. One senior manager says: "Polyester is definitely a drawback, especially with saddle stitching on the lapels. Still, nothing is more embarrassing than being overdressed. A three-piece suit when everybody else is in khakis and rolled-up shirtsleeves. You have to assume that everybody has read these how-to-get-a-job books, and dressed by what that guy says rather than by common sense. Those people have lost people more jobs than they've gotten."

The key is to employ the same stylistic tongue as your fellows, but with your own faint accent, one that bespeaks your background, breeding, and the remainders of your humanity. My pal Dworkin, editor at a national men's magazine, admits his differences but not his eccentricities. "I'm the only one who wears Bass Weejuns to work every day. Most people wear tie shoes," he states. "I wear knit ties, khakis, and sport coats of the stars. People are always commenting on my socks. They're argyles. It's deviant, not eccentric. My boss has asked me why is it I don't ever wear silk ties, and I said simply, I can't afford them. I also wear plaid shirts. The managing editor wears red high-topped sneakers with tight jeans."

This natural bonhomie can wear thin, however, when the culture in question comes face to face with a higher form of life. Dworkin continues:

> Everything is much more regimented around here since we were acquired, from the sort of Day-glo carpets to the rules about decor. It's okay to have a tree as long as it's not ostentatiously dead. Beyond that, it's clean desks. This is a big change for us. On Fridays the dress code still is, shall we say, lax. In the old days, you could wear a tutu to work and no one would look askance. The boss is dressed in a lime-green sport shirt, khakis, and white bucks. Last Friday the phone rang, and it was the president of the Magazine Group, and he said to my boss, "Jack, I need to see you for a couple of minutes—could you run up here?" There was a frisson of panic on Jack's face, and he hung up and turned to me and said, "Do you think I'm underdressed?" And I said, "I don't know. Where are you going—Wingfoot?" From here on in, I assume Jack will keep a tie and jacket in his office. Just in case.

The greater the rigidity of your shop in manners of dress, neatness, and profanity, the greater its resistance to any form of personal

expression and eccentricity. Employees of traveling rock musicians
have more options than employees of Leona Helmsley or Imelda
Marcos, even if those two ladies are temporarily out of commission.


## NEXT WE OBEY

> A group is an obedient herd, which could never live without a master.
> It has such a thirst for obedience that it submits instinctively to anyone
> who appoints himself its master.
>
> Freud

When we say the word *obedience,* what do we mean? In the workplace, ongoing, solid achievement should be the primary, even the
sole, requirement. Today, however, the demand upon workers is
often more global, fueled by boss anxiety and needs that are not
strictly business-related.

The crazy boss demands that his employees *make him sane.*

It becomes the job of workers, then, to restore the balance lacking
in the disturbed environment. For the average worker, disempow-
ered more than ever before, this is a patently impossible task. All one
can do is try to evaluate the demands placed on his emotional equipment, and see how much of the load he can deliver.

Yet still, we must ask: why should anyone do what another person
tells him to? Fear, of course, is a good reason, perhaps the most
effective motivator yet discovered for the short term, but it generates
a kind of obedience that is difficult to maintain over time.

Far more powerful is the force of common self-interest, mutual
identification, and the yearning for structure. The demand sent down
from the boss to those who serve him is made up of four parts:

- *Silence,* or confidentiality in the face of outside attack. The
  worker must never reveal the quirks, foibles, and operational
  eccentricities that his boss displays, the behavior that might ren-
  der him excessively human to *his managers.*
- *Loyalty:* Each manager defines this property differently, depending on his level of paranoia, but the essence of the need may be
  stated as: "Identify with my interests and take them as your own.
  Do nothing that would compromise those interests."

- *Poverty:* Bosses with plump stock-option plans that hike their salaries into the seven-figure range take a dim view of workers who yearn for a 6 percent merit increase, and immediately wax prolix about tight belts and lean machines.
- *Task Obedience:* The employee who does not deliver this essential property unconditionally is viewed with mistrust and soon ejected from the body of the group.

Employee support in the mind of the crazy boss is a complicated affair, a mixture of your assets and the money of the organization. It's an edifice that looks like this:

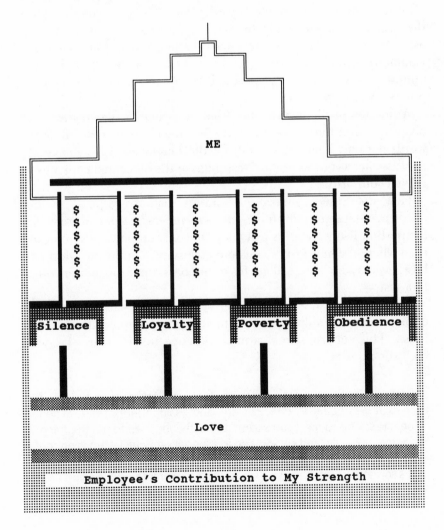

On the part of all managements, there is the endemic sense that employees are less than adult, creatures that need to be led, loved, and controlled. A supremely benevolent boss I know says:

> It's like with your children. You like to give them what they want. But if a thirteen-year-old asks for a motorcycle, the answer is no. I'd like nothing more than to see his face light up, zipping along the highway, if that's what he wants. Assuming I had an insurance policy from God to say he would not be hurt.

And the CEO of a leading telecommunications conglomerate says: "Business is not government. Government is based on consensus, on the ability of its leadership to foster compromise. Business doesn't work that way. Business can only function if it is a dictatorship. Hopefully, if it's done right, it can be a benign dictatorship, but the minute you have too many people involved in the decision-making process, you're screwed."

At the top of the dictatorship, the leader enjoys the obedience of his people and the greatest number of financial rewards. These rewards not only compensate him for the weight upon his shoulders, they also act as power totems, trappings of the office that confer even greater authority.

How does the organization, and its leaders, respond to disobedience—statutory insanity—in its members? Each culture is different. But disobedience is just about the only crime that is punished even where the hair grows long and creativity is in the air. Most any boss, even a sane one, will get his or her back up if the matter comes to a test.

Lisa, an editor at a general-interest publication with a readership of more than 17 million, recalls one former employee without fondness. "This subordinate was uncooperative to the point of saying no," she reports:

> I asked him to consider something, that's all, and he said he didn't think it was going to be necessary, and I said, Tough. Do it. When people say no to me, I can accept it; if someone tried to get the thing for me, honestly, and couldn't do it, especially if what I want is on the edge anyway, if it's a gift, or a zero percent shot, no is acceptable. If it's something you think you're due, or if it's something they didn't try

to get, or worse, both, then no is never an acceptable answer. You stew, and spend the rest of your time thinking how you're going to get back at the stupid nit without the organization knowing about it.

The smart employee of the crazy boss, therefore, *does not say no*, does not disobey per se. He becomes devious. The first tactic is simply to stay out of the line of fire. "I say never volunteer for anything, even if it's something for which you're clearly the most qualified person in the room," says Bud, a vice president of programming for a television station in the Northeast.

> I've mastered the art of enduring excruciating silences as everyone looks to me to respond. I never scratch my ear in a meeting, because it may look like I'm raising my hand. I've never flat-out said, "No, I won't do it, it's against my religion," but I have gotten out of most tasks I find odious. The trick is always appear so busy that to ask you to take on additional heavy lifting would activate that prostate condition and cause you to be out three to six weeks. Frankly, I feel nothing but awe for the people who can flout authority and never break a sweat. To be able to say no and not look like a trembling membrane means you've either slept with the person or you're otherwise confident of your résumé.

Sometimes simple delaying tactics are enough to forestall action on an insane or simply inconvenient demand. A fellow I'll call Alan is an advertising executive in an agency that serves the film industry. "Anything but constant yessing is very difficult in show business," he states. "Given the nature of this business, people are extraordinarily reluctant to give their honest opinion or assert themselves in any way. But most projects are questionable. That is, in effect, *you can question it out of existence.*"

Alan continues with some choice questions that can bollux up the works for weeks:

> What's our marketing strategy? What are we trying to do? Why? Why should we choose this format over that format? How is this responding to competitive pieces? That means we have to look at those before we do this. Is this really the audience we want to be hitting? Wouldn't this other one be a better audience? Wouldn't this package also include x, y, and z? Wouldn't this be an ideal time to tie in another

product with this one? Is the timing really right? Shouldn't we wait until budget time? If you raise enough of these, using philosophy, you've exterminated something without ever having to say no.

Which goes to show how honest discourse is the last possible choice in the crazy corporation, while, as a crazy employee, you're addressing your crazy bosses.

The senior editor at a huge national weekly news publication speaks for all bosses, I think, when she barks:

> I really hate it when people say no to me. You don't challenge authority. That's when people get my back up. When they imply that I'm being mean or unreasonable. Because I don't think of myself that way, and don't like to be perceived as being either of those things. And I don't at all like it when the implication is that this is some kind of whim I've got. This happens a lot when I have a good idea for some special project or something. They'll look at me and I can hear them thinking, Uh-oh, here she goes again. They feel I'm making them work harder to satisfy some impulse. I get resentful, and I never let them back off then. Then I really start pushing for it. I figure, fuck 'em—that's what they're paid for. And you know, when push comes to shove, they've got to do it. So they do. But it's not really a pleasant situation all around.

The granting of obedience is not solely an operational issue. It underlies the most potent demand of boss to employee (and back again)—the cry for emotional satisfaction that supplies perhaps the only true satisfaction in the workplace outside of money.

## LOOKING FOR LOVE IN ALL
## THE WRONG PLACES

Congratulations. You have endured the first four steps and are now a member of the only kind of family that must pay you to be a member and that may terminate you without cause.

Love between peers—and sometimes even between bosses and their employees—is the commodity that makes life, if not worth living, at least worth enduring. And the fact that the camaraderie, the love, is only temporary, makes it all the more precious, and doomed.

In the pathological world of the modern workplace, it is the person-to-person relationship that fritzes out, creating the leaden, miserable environment that characterizes the unsuccessful group. Worst of all, the need of each employee for an organizational "parent," a force to oversee, to care for and protect them, is frustrated.

A brilliant graphics designer I'll call Patty worked as a department head in a large audiovisual house in the Midwest. "Pam, my best friend, worked here for six years," she reports, "and for four of those years, she was afflicted with the desire for kind words from Ruth, our boss." Patty ties this desire for corporate affection to a very deep source:

> Pam never got approval from her own mother, so I guess it was kind of a natural thing to expect it from Ruth, a wise, wonderful, classy, successful woman. So I think that's how it happened. I think Pam felt she got recognition maybe for the things she didn't feel were her most valuable contributions. Not the real her. She was never validated in terms of her real center and personhood. She finally realized that and just stopped wanting it. And eventually left. It's a growth process that many people go through. Looking for approval from a father or mother, and not getting it, you start looking for it in other places. All of that gets projected onto a boss.

The leader should be presiding head of the family table. When he or she is not, all relationships within the organization are skewed. Where employees seek love and approval, confusion is returned, and when bosses seek wholehearted loyalty and obedience, no such satisfaction is offered.

Corporations continually invoke their status as a family in their internal communications and in their dealings with each other. But as in genuine families, this one has myths and traditions that lend meaning to the work, and the imaginative life, of each family member. And the leader is at the center of this, too, lending the workplace emotional continuity and rational sense.

Lack of coherent, ongoing ownership, or of continuing senior or even middle management–level people who are the bearers of the oral tradition, destroys the sense of mutual purpose that creates the family. Stories of the sizable masters/monsters who ran the business previously take up a significant portion of mid-level and even senior-level chat in a company. These myths form a crucial tie between the individual and the group.

This mutual history helps to bind people to their group. When it is absent, the demand for a common "interior landscape" does not go away, it merely remains frustrated.

The comfort the group looks to their leader to provide—a continuing sense of purpose based on a common mythology—is cold. The deprived group is not amused, and the boss knows it.

And yet he needs it, now more than ever, precisely because he has become crazy.

## LOVE IS GONE—WHO CARES?

Right! So what? What if the modern business organism is anathema to love? Does it matter? Not to shareholders. Not to security analysts. Not to the guys way up high in the management structure— who love their benefits (and each other) very much indeed.

The only people who care are the people who work and are slowly being driven crazy, bosses and their reportees alike. They're unhappy, mightily; the only unhappiness worse than unhappiness with one's job is unhappiness with one's other imperfect family, the one at home, where you spend a whole lot fewer of your waking hours.

My pal Ford, a newspaperman now happily at work in the vineyards of personality profiles, began his career in the dungeons of a daily in Newark. "The place had no humor," he remembers. "Watercooler discussions were conducted in the bathroom. It led to drinking sessions, where the laughs were really strong because they'd been bottled up for a week. They were more hostile laughs, too, full of recrimination and resentment for the boss."

What generated this resentment?

> Our boss Carl set the tone. He worked in a glassed-in office, and the first thing you'd see is him reading the morning paper, like a Buddha, and not a smiling one, absolutely grim, stoic, a deflating presence, and he was visible to everyone in the place. You tended to sit up at your desk and not laugh, too. You couldn't even talk to him. That glass might as well have been Klaus Barbie's glassed-in shield. Did anyone kid with Eva Braun?

In the numbing atmosphere of love withheld, people laugh in the bathrooms, drink at lunch, and are sad.

Today, in the absence of reliable friendship and camaraderie, with the strength and security of numbers gone in hurtful cutbacks, who is available to answer our fearful questions, guide our pressured actions, reward us when we succeed, forgive us when we fail?

Our crazy boss, that's who. And the fact that he can't meet those voracious needs doesn't help things, for him, for us, or for the crazy business organization we all serve.

The leader needs to function as a thread of meaning, of a continuing rationale. When that thread of meaning is threatened from outside, or worse, from within, the panic is severe. The danger of parental love lost is deeply threatening to the entire person, not just the part that works for the company but also the human being who gets up at 3:00 A.M. for a long leak, a short drink of water, and a lot of worrying.

Once the group stops loving its leaders, or has no leaders to love, it begins to stop loving itself. The glue that held it together, and made it feel safe, is gone, and each person is free to be as self-serving and aggrandizing as he or she sees fit. This is the end of the life throb that makes every successful company work.

The resulting "every man for himself" mentality is both the effect and the cause of the destruction of organizations, the dissolution of authority, and the deterioration of the American business mind. Yet that neuroticizing of business leadership moves on apace. And the dutiful employee is expected to accept an ambivalent sort of truth: he must fit into the criteria of rational performance, while his boss may be as crazy as suits him.

Which, perhaps, is only fair. In the contemporary business universe, the boss's craziness may be his best and only strategic defense.

# CHAPTER TWO

# CRAZY BUSINESS

## TOO MANY DEALS

T he trading of properties and assembling of portfolios is as old as the idea of the conglomerate. What has made this epoch different from any other is the fact that, at least until recently, such activity has been fueled not by market demand, or by conceivable business strategy between principals, but by the availability of money and the aggressiveness of the hangers-on who conceived the deals and made them happen. Today, we are suffering from all the excesses that preceded our sad, retrenching decade.

At its height, how bad was it? Nineteen major mergers—savings and loans, real estate firms, soft drink companies, food stores, you name it—showed up on my newswire on *one day* in 1987, at the height of deal mania.

Think of the number of people involved. Consider the paranoia. The despair. The betrayals both large and small. Was it, perhaps, an unusual day? No. The next day, when I once again entered the command "Search: Mergers" in the database to which I subscribe, I came up with no fewer than thirty more pending mergers, acquisitions, friendly and unfriendly takeovers, and other changes of management. Two small chemical labs were bought by a manufacturer supplying "specialty niche products" for a wide variety of industries. Vicorp Specialty Restaurants, operators of the Hungry Hunter, Mt. Jack's, and other dinner establishments, merged with Rusty

Pelican Restaurants, Inc. Physicians' Reimbursement Services, offering health-care services mostly in third-party insurance claims, bought Professional Management Associates, a health-care consulting service in Louisiana. And so on, and on.

Deals, deals, and more deals. Huge sums of money rocketing across hardwood tables. Enormous wealth. Devastation of existing corporate governments. Exultation among those who manage money. Confusion and terror among those who simply must earn it or give up the notion of Reeboks for their kids.

Was there nothing to protect the working man or woman?

No, honestly, there wasn't.

Virtually all of the above deals were accomplished not because they made any business sense. They were done because they made huge amounts of money for a few very lucky people: the management, a couple of lawyers, perhaps an investment banker or two. Such observations are now quite commonplace. But at the time, nobody questioned the basic ground rules.

The only ones who knew what was going on all along were the droids who saw their working environment dissolved, over and over again. One advertising sales man I know was terminated from one corporation, spent an entire year getting a job worthy of his talents, then, on the day he arrived at his new job in Dayton, was informed that his new firm had been sold *to the same people who bought his prior firm*! The guy spent a full eighteen months basically sitting on the beach after that. Of course, he had the severance to do it. That was part of deal mania, too. Nobody got hurt. Nobody big enough to care about, at any rate.

Smaller employees, however, fell hard. And our entire business universe is still paying, in the form of layoffs, bankruptcies, management reorganizations, cutbacks, and general transitional insecurities. Today, in a wide variety of companies, heads are rolling, debt is crushing investment in research and development, promised numbers are not being delivered upon. And entire industries are reeling.

This is the legacy of the 1980s.

It's difficult to say which came first, the chicken of deal mania or the egg of greed. But one thing is clear: the resulting orgy of merger, acquisition, and desperate wholesale restructuring, has produced a dramatic rise in anxiety, corruption, and pathological behavior. Underemployed workers, farmers and small-business men understand that the massive fraud and greed that accompany the proliferation of major mergers—and the mergers themselves—are destructive of America's heartland even as they 'create wealth' for the financial and investment community." Throughout the 1980s, it was pathetically easy to put a company into play.

All it took was one well-placed rumor to get the deal rolling:

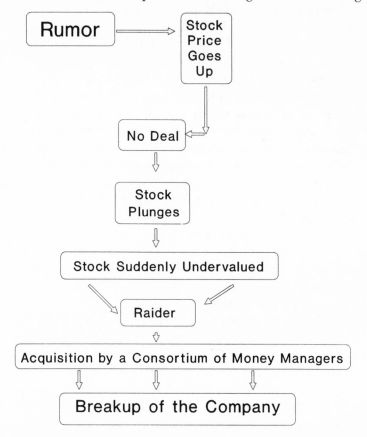

In the 1990s, the picture has already changed, but the result to employees will be very much the same. Hundreds of companies, burdened by debt, are now in the process of, Trump-like, putting up their assets for sale to meet their interest payments. These properties will be available at bargain-basement prices, so in the very near future we can expect trading to escalate anew, once again roiling a working environment that bosses had just been getting used to.

Clearly, in this whacko business universe, the crazy boss is the one best dressed for the business weather, ready to labor in an overheated business environment that fosters paranoia, insane expectations of profit and growth, the need for dramatic behavior where none is really handy, and the willingness to do just about anything that's necessary, including firing radical numbers of people, many of them in middle and senior management. "The whole climate has changed for a CEO," Andrew C. Sigler, CEO of Champion International Corporation, told *Business Week.* "There is intense pressure for current earnings, so the message is: 'Don't get caught with major [long term] investments. . . . Do all the things we used to consider bad management."

How could such a thing have been allowed to happen?

Once again, we need to focus on our national preoccupation with *results at any cost.* The majority of business pundits never questioned anything—as long as it was making somebody money. In fact, quite a few of the running dogs in the business media applauded the entire bloody phenomenon—as long as it didn't happen to them. They called it "creative destruction." *Forbes,* for instance, loved to wax prolix on the benefits of all forms of business upheaval. "Restructuring is a periodic occurrence in a capitalist economy and serves the purpose of adaptation to economic and technological change," the magazine wrote in its July 13, 1987, issue, under the headline HERE WE GO AGAIN.

It's nothing we haven't seen before. As mergers increased in number, crusades against them were waged under Teddy Roosevelt, in the Depression, and during the Nixon years. The takeover barons were hated, but the turbulence they caused wasn't entirely in vain. Along with their predatory tactics, shady bookkeeping and callous treatment of workers, acquirers brought efficiencies and necessary changes.

Take a look around you right now at the current business world. Those are the *efficiencies and necessary changes* that you see.

The *Forbes* piece cuts to the heart of the matter, however, when it quotes Milton Freeman, senior partner at Arnold and Porter, who worked at the Securities and Exchange Commission from 1934 to 1946. "Whether it's a leveraged buyout, a hostile takeover or a proxy fight," the good economist says, "it remains a war between the fellow who wants to take over a company and the fellow who wants to keep his job."

What's wrong with wanting to keep your job, anyhow! Selfishness isn't limited to the rich, you know. It's one of the last things the middle class can afford.

Let's have a little dose of realism here, in the person of a guy I'll call Larry, former director of employee relations at a now-defunct television company. He wants to tell you about the human cost of these creatively destructive deals.

"I came to my corporation in 1980," he says, "fresh off the street and totally not corporate in any way."

The president was a guy who built the company from the ground up, literally. Guy drove a bucket truck before he was able to hire somebody to do it. A great manager, always clear in what he wanted and the negative consequences if he was disappointed. Terrible temper, but always forgot about a fight five minutes afterwards. Six months after I get there, the company is "merged" with a huge multinational conglomerate with headquarters in Cleveland. All of a sudden there are tons of new people around, and they're wearing square-cut pinstripe blue suits, with little buttons in the lapels with "Excellence" written on them. A memo comes out. "We want you to know that we've acquired you because we like you. You're the kind of people we want to work with. We look forward to building our common future together in the days and years to come." Something like that.

I try to get friendly with as many of them as possible, very fast. After a while, they don't seem so bad. The old president "retires." It's only about six months later, and there's a new chairman, and a lot of new vice presidents running around who our old vice presidents have to report to. A whole bunch of memos come out, about one a week, announcing all the staff changes, all saying things like, "Charley will continue on here as vice president, reporting to me. He's made a tremendous contribution around here for a long time, and I'm looking forward to having him on my team."

In November, in the first full year of the new team, the word comes down that the new chairman has decided to "take a look" at our headcount. After a few weeks, the rumor circulates that he has found the entire company "fat," which indeed we are, since we've just added about a hundred guys from Cleveland. Headcount here is cut from 450 to less than 100 in about three months. All the guys who leave are from the old team. Because I'm a small manager, and quietly busy, I'm spared and permitted to remain and do the job formerly covered by six people.

About a year goes by, and things are better, actually. After I get over losing all those people who were once my friends and corporate clients. And I kind of get to like the new guys, and sort of get into the whole goofy Excellence thing they believe in so much, with pins and little toys for superachievers and all-company retreats with a lot of beer and talk about the customer. One day the big guy from Cleveland shows up and makes a speech in our executive lunchroom. Big, beefy guy, very gray suit. He tells us: "We're really proud of the job you guys have done and will do. To us, you're the future. You're where this company has room to grow. Our commitment to you is strong, and I commend you."

Three months later, they announce that our division is being sold to help in the "realignment of the company's portfolio," but the real reason is to drive up the stock price so the parent will be less attractive to take over.

At Christmas, the company announces that our division has been sold, and that our assets and field people will be "incorporated into the new owner." Two thirds of our people are fired, because they are "not synergistic." Around HQ, of course, we're dead meat. Everyone is given very generous severance packages and the thanks of a grateful parent. The company we were sold to, by the way, fired just about every person responsible for customer service. How could they afford them with that debt service to pay? I thought there would be a shitstorm of controversy, but it turned out the new guys were commended in the business press for running the new operation really lean.

That's right. No matter what the new boss tells you, a change of management means dead people hanging from the yardarm. As Harvard sociologist and management philosopher Rosabeth Kanter has pointed out, nearly half the senior executives of an acquired firm leave within one year of the acquisition, and three out of four are likely to leave within three years.[1]

So much for the workplace as a constant in everyday life.

A takeover is the ultimate career disaster for the dedicated employee. The more loyal and emotionally tied to the existing company you have been, the bleaker the future looms. That's not to say that with luck and a powerful craving for survival at virtually any cost, a player of sufficient moxie cannot survive a change of ownership.

[1] *Management Review*, October, 1986.

Sure, it's possible. Which brings to mind the early days of the Cuban Missile Crisis, when we were hiding under our desks, and we heard our teacher say, "In the event of a nuclear attack, children, please make sure to remove any eyewear and refrain from looking directly into the blast."

In merged corporations, as in wars, hard work and political savvy may count for little if you get in the way of the inevitable.

Considering the human cost, the craziest thing, after all this pressure from financial and market forces, the shaving of bodies, the manipulation of stock value, the jiggering with product line, and the destruction of beloved, sloppy, human organizations galore, is that most mergers—the source and font of so much radical, crazy activity—*don't make it.* In fact, of all mergers and acquisitions, perhaps as many as one half to two thirds ultimately fail, according to experts in the field.

Not that they were meant to make it, really. Their job was done when they "created wealth," or just "made money" for those who engineered them. The real people—boss and employee alike—are then left to pick up the sodden mess and heave it into some kind of shape.

But how is that to be done? Is that task—picking up from the eighties and remaking a rational and sane business environment—possible?

I don't want to be a bummer. But it just might be that the answer is no. We simply owe too much. The tab is too humongous. The time has come to pay for the feast somebody else just ordered and ate. And we don't have the dough.

## GET INTO THE KITCHEN AND
## WASH THOSE DISHES!

How does a company handle debt? Real badly, if it can handle it at all. The weird thing is, *we knew that.* As a nation, we just sort of . . . forgot it. We were too busy lathering over the notion of a "free market," as if that were some kind of good thing, a priori. In virtually every purchase financed by debt—and that means just about all of them until 1990 came and a few people woke up and began asking about assets—firms are forced to carry their own crosses to Golgotha.

The song, as Bill Murray used to say before he belted out the Star Wars theme, goes a little something like this:

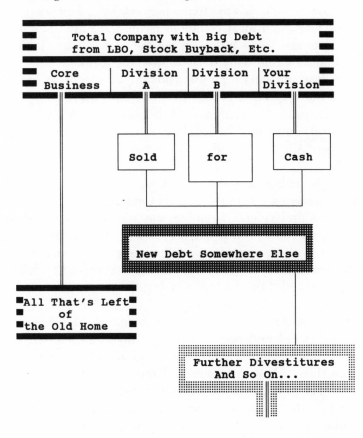

As *The New York Times* noted in July 1988, "In most cases, management of the company and the buyout investors are able to take over the company by putting up only 10 percent or so of the purchase price as permanent equity capital. . . ."

*I had to come up with more equity than that to buy my house, for chrissake!*

Well. Never mind.

And now for the kicker: doing business well doesn't matter now! The bankruptcy of Revco, for instance, came about in spite of the fact that the retail stores themselves were doing respectable numbers. As the *Times* pointed out: "Most of Revco's 2,000 stores are profitable . . . but the company as a whole was not generating enough cash to operate the business and make $150 million a year in interest payments . . ."

There are, of course, ways to manage crushing debt short of going belly-up. First, and most common, is the technique of cutting off one's nose to save one's face, or when the nose is unavailable, chopping off nonessential body parts to save the torso.

When the Campeau Corporation bought Allied Stores Corporation, owner of Bonwit Teller, Brooks Brothers, and AnnTaylor, in 1986, Robert Campeau, the chairman of the new, merged firm, gave the prototypical comment: "We will have to sell some of the less productive assets of Allied," he said, "to reduce the debt load created by the merger."

By 1989, the business went bust and brought virtually the entire retail business down with it. "Robert Campeau's history of nervous breakdowns and volatile behavior was well known to the lenders who financed his ill-conceived takeover binge," wrote *Fortune* in June 1990, "one resulting in a financial mega-bomb that was barely built before it was detonated by a business that *had* to deliver and didn't. So why did the lenders give him all that money?"

Why? *Because they liked him!*

In the wake of the insider-trading scandals of the 1980s, the junk bond market did undergo a twinge, as investors realized that the source of their strength—illegal information—might soon be drying up. Even Michael Milken, that great democratizer, found himself convicted of using his power to extort, not just leverage companies. In spite of his offer to go on a speaking tour—lecturing, I believe, on topics like "giving something back"—he was jailed and stripped of all but his last $500 million.

The whole idea of doing business without the availability of a criminal edge rose like a specter before Wall Street. And junk bonds fell. But what were we all to do—now that debt was no longer an asset? After all, the whole world, save for the few former Axis nations, has become an order based on the IOU.

Underlying each American's individual debt is an increasingly global indebtedness that, most likely, can never be paid.

Somewhere in that ocean of international debt is the total tab owed by the United States to the rest of the world. Most of the nations we owe a nice balance of trade won't even let us into their markets without the kinds of restrictions that cost jobs and price tags.

We buy TVs and VCRs and computers and cars and cheese and wine and tea and coffee and cocaine and oil. We owe the world.

The urge to live on a debt to be paid later doesn't limit itself to the mercantile or international arena, of course.

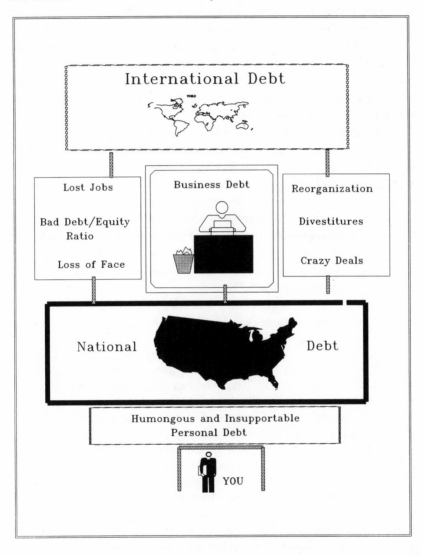

It begins at home.

As a nation, we're toting heavy plastic. Each of us has our own portfolio of stuff we owe. The more we owe, the richer we are. We have created a society based on free-floating debt.

What will be used to pay the tab? Will world creditors simply be willing to wash the slate clean? What if Mexico defaults? How can I meet my $2,500 monthly nut? Why did I buy that summer home?

And so debt is another contributing factor to the climate of anxiety that forges the crazy boss, particularly one who works in a newly minted, debt-burdened company in which the cost of his labor is one of the liabilities. Nervous management must cut costs across the board. This customarily involves everything from counting paper clips to firing people. As short-term solutions, selling assets and cutting people and services are considerably easier than the more serious alternative of *raising revenues.*

Cutting people is cheap; it only costs lives.

Of course, many aggressive nineties types of hyperthyroid mega-dudes want both to cut expenses *and* to raise revenues, which means axing people and expecting those who are left to do a whole lot more. In a variety of industries, American companies are reaming out themselves. "Mid-level managers don't exist anymore," Corinne Kuypers-Denlinger, vice president of the Naisbitt Group told me. "The economy took a downturn, and many companies thinned out their middle levels. They don't want to pass information through so many layers of bureaucracy."

But as companies work to thin out, less professional workers rush in to fill the gap. *Fortune* noted in February 1987:

> Fast growth is also ahead in temporary employment services. "It used to be that companies turned to us on a panic basis, when someone got ill or went on vacation," says Thomas Anton, executive vice president of Kelly Services, Inc. "But now companies staff up to meet their normal requirements at a lower end of their business cycle and then hire temporary employees when things pick up." There's even likely to be a market for management temps. Companies with pared-down staffs will tackle many new problems or programs by hiring hands-on management consultants—people who not only study problems and write recommendations, but also take on strategic tasks. . . .

Management temps? Spare me! Stupid, brain-dead notions from jerks who think about nothing but the short term! . . .

Excuse me. I was raving.

As we move into the 1990s, fewer and fewer white-collar types will be able to daydream about the great days when they worked their way up to the top of the tree. Management and support teams get smaller. The responsibilities grow larger and virtually unachievable. This is known in polite company as "flattening the pyramid." Presumably those affected may in the future be known as "the flattened."

The remaining mid-level boss is left with an acute awareness of his own tenuous state, and a fierce determination to do more with less—fewer people, fewer resources. This eventually finds its way to the customer, who begins to perceive a waning in quality and reliability. With so many products to choose from, products from all over the globe, the American customer can be unforgiving. "What the customer is saying is, 'We love you for your excellence as long as your product is priced competitively. And if you stumble, the hell with you,' " Professor Joseph Bower of Harvard Business School told me. But martyred companies can't keep their prices down, because they have to make lots and lots of cash—in a hurry. Reduced quality and value to today's customer means almost immediate business death. Customers now know the difference. The issue of quality screams out at them from virtually every ad in every country.

So the deal-hawking leads inexorably not just to short-term financial failure but to God's honest failure where it counts: in the marketplace; and the spiral moves ever downward into further chaos and despair.

Who brought us to this point?

Your crazy bosses, that's who!

## CRAZY BOSSES IN THE NEWS

### *Raider*

"On January 3, 1986, Carl C. Icahn changed his spots," *Barron's* noted in September 1988. "That was the day he took over as chairman of Trans World Airlines, and, suddenly, the corporate raider became a manager." The periodical continued:

> On the surface, as intimated, he has pulled the airline out of its nosedive and, in a relatively short span, turned a financially ailing company into a healthy and growing enterprise. However, careful inspection reveals that what Icahn has really done is to restructure the airline into a hollow shell filled with debt, and assure that much of the cash and stocks bought with the proceeds of the debt will wind up in his hands.

Moral? Raiders do not "change their spots." Their operational mentality is based on a perception of the *business as asset to be manipulated*, rather than as an organization filled with living people there to provide a product or service.

Then there was Ronald Perelman, a busy little raider who in the space of a few short years:

- Seized Pantry Pride in a significantly leveraged deal and sold most of its stores;
- Bought Revlon for $1.7 billion and sold off all but $300 million worth of its operations, making, as *Forbes* later wrote, "much more money breaking up the company than [founder Charles] Revson made by building it";
- Bought 15 percent of Transworld Corporation, which operated Hilton's hotel and food-service businesses. Transworld liquidated, and was bought by an associate of Perelman;
- Bought up more than 5 percent of CPC Corporation, the company that makes Skippy peanut butter and Hellmann's mayonnaise, and sold out at a $40 million profit;
- Raided Gillette, the razor people.

In 1987, Perelman made a serious but ultimately unsuccessful run at Salomon Brothers, which was highly not amused, although Perelman certainly made a number of soothing noises in regards to the company's senior management. "Despite his promises, Mr. Perelman is widely viewed as an extremely wealthy, hands-on executive who made a tremendous profit in taking over Revlon and might not be willing to watch Salomon from afar for very long," *The New York Times* speculated.

Throughout the 1980s, everybody loved a raider, especially one with a lot of endearing quirks. "Two years ago, Natalie I. Koether brought a surprise guest to a meeting with the chairman of a company she wanted to take over—Jennifer, her 10-year-old daughter," *Business Week* burbled on February 13, 1987. "After some tough negotiating, Koether netted $900,000 when she agreed to sell her shares back to the company. 'Jennifer comes with me all the time,' says Koether. 'I even had special business cards made for her.' "

"If someone wants to schedule a meeting and Natalie's taking Jennifer to a Mets game, she goes to the Mets game," says one of Koether's investors, with admiration. One can only speculate on the experience. Knowing the lady is planning to play with your stock, you fawn and suckle at a Mets game while the raider and her little daughter eat hot dogs.

So eccentric. So cute. Very good press.

In fact, until the early years of the nineties, when the passion for thoroughly irresponsible raidership somewhat abated, there wasn't one of the breed who didn't enjoy a tushie-tap from the chroniclers of capital.

"History cannot provide many episodes as exciting as the last decade in the capital markets of America," wrote George J. Stigler, 1982 Nobel Prize–winner in economics, in *Forbes.* Stigler is also director of the Center for the Study of the Economy and the State at that yeasty home of neoconservative wisdom the University of Chicago. The man could barely contain his enthusiasm:

> Corporations as rich as many nations have been conquered. Ancient protected cartels have not been able to stave off powerful new invaders. The New York Stock Exchange, the commercial or savings banks; the old-line investment bankers all face new competition. No feat of financial legerdemain has seemed impossible for a bold entrepreneur such as T. Boone Pickens or a gifted swindler such as Ivan Boesky. . . .

Nowhere has the bloodying of a once-stable business been more evident than at CBS, where the Ted Turner takeover attempt was repelled—at a terrible cost: the operation was a success while the patient died.

"This is no takeover," said Larry Tisch as he humbly accepted the reins as acting chairman of CBS. "I will hold office only during the brief transition period until the selection of a new CEO. I intend to maintain the traditions and spirit of this company as established and nurtured by William S. Paley." By the following year, Tisch was permanent, CBS was making its famous cuts, firing newswriters, and indulging in what one CBS staffer, in an anonymous letter to all his fellow employees, called "a tidal wave of budget cuts, wholesale firings and journalistic retrenchment."

Upon acceding to his throne at CBS, Larry asked one manager to describe his duties. The guy did so. Tisch then inquired how many people reported to this executive. "Twelve," the manager said. "Pick your best person," Tisch reportedly stated in reply, "and get rid of the rest." The anecdote was presented in *Business Week* as a demonstration of the kind of tough, no-nonsense management that was going to bring American business back from the grave.

A year later, rumors were rife that CBS itself was on the block, offering the ultimate specter of corporate weight loss—acquisition, reorganization, evisceration, and employee defenestration.

No one, however, could say that Tisch wasn't fair. Even as he ordered the mid-level layoffs, he also ordered the executive dining rooms closed, and cut back radically on limousine service for top managers.

The presence of the raider in the wings elicits the night terror felt by all key executives at this moment in history. And the fear has nothing to do with economics. It is personal. What's at stake, simply, are the elaborately constructed lives of people who make too much money, own and owe too much. People who have bought into the big dream with debt and are still waiting for their equity to catch up.

Today, although acquisition by leverage has abated dramatically, the danger of unfriendly onslaughts is far from over. Institutional mergers are still the method of choice to grow revenues in a tough economic environment, and stockholders are applauding companies who spurn the protection of recent antitakeover legislation.

The only protection from the predatory environment is itself another excess. Fortunately, there's a crazy boss here to get the job done as well. You know him. He probably just joined your organization, after a couple of years in management consultancy.

### Reorganizer

*Advertising Age* of July 11, 1988, reported: "The reorganization of McGraw-Hill is rocking the foundations of the company, and that could lead to the sale of more magazines, the shelving of new-magazine plans and the elimination of jobs, including more top executive posts. One top McGraw-Hill executive said, 'There is going to be a lot of blood on the floor . . .' "

Fear of takeover, merger, sale, divestiture, raid, and leveraged buyout infuses in all employees from chairman to stock clerk a powerful intimation of job mortality. The wicked mix of short-term greed and long-term insecurity is often enough to whip an otherwise-normal organization into a hypertense state well suited to the radical temperament of the crazy boss, and dependent on his decisive behavior.

And when business is bad, as it has been in the wake of the 1980s, it's even worse, particularly since most businesses were depending on things to be *great*—simply to keep up with their interest payments.

In a reorganization, the officers do unto their own company what they wouldn't have others do first. They become the enemy they have feared, ripping their houses from stem to stern in what is politely called "reorganization," or "realignment," but what is, in truth, a surgical raid from within.

Just as the Perelmans, Icahns, and Pickenses have their flatulent rationale, the reorganizer is not without his, which goes something like this: "The generally horrible business environment has done us a favor, exposing our weakness, which is based on the laziness and general unworthiness of our underperforming businesses. Okay, fine. Now we're going to get so lean you won't be able to find a place to bite!"

Let's assume, for argument's sake, that some reorganization wouldn't hurt. Nothing's perfect. Still, much of the aggressive transformation is done not because it makes the business run any better, but because it plays well with the investment analysts and other pundits who decide which stock is hot and which is not in terms of immediate gratification. Today, the ultimate terror of management is that they will be considered "soft" by those arbiters of asset value. So they prove they're hard. Hey—if you fire enough people, it may take years before folks get wise to the fact that you have a pretty weak strategy beyond that, and by then, who knows? The market might have changed! Until then, you're buying time. And time is most certainly money in this case, especially if you're making less of it than you want to.

There are few rewards for conservative, humane stewardship that stumbles.

For instance, did you know that, on the basis of raw returns, the ten *most admired Fortune* companies in 1983 would not have been as good an investment as the ten *least admired*? So while quality management sometimes pays off, inhuman management works just as well, if not better. This fact is widely recognized by the financial community. IBM, for instance, dropped in the 1986 rankings for "most admired corporations" because it didn't lay off enough employees, having, instead, a "full employment policy." This didn't stop IBM from earning more than any other company in the world. "Instead of dropping in your rankings, it should receive a special award," wrote one irate reader to *Fortune*. "The lower marks for IBM indicate to me that Wall Street's understanding of good managing is about as sound as Ivan Boesky's ethics."

Naturally, in the face of the onslaught of deal-mongering and opportunistic feeding, the ultra-senior manager must give the appearance of reacting *proactively*.[2]

While senior reorganizers and their Wall Street technicians manipulate their "assets," as a class they have achieved excellent gains. In the 1980s, bonuses at most large financial institutions went completely haywire, and even to this day management-compensation packages are inspirational to those who look up the ladder in wonder and greed.

For example: not long ago, a friend of mine reports, a guy was brought into his corporation for the express purpose of cutting 20–35 percent of the people then employed. Why? Because margins were down, and the industry growth rate was in the tank. His compensation package came to approximately $500,000 per year in cash and medium-term incentives. In his package was also not one, but two cars.

Somebody explain the thinking to me, will ya?

Without laughing, I mean.

Perhaps most irritating to employees pressed into the 3 percent annual-increase machine is the knowledge that their richer bosses are protected by juicy termination agreements.

In 1986, for instance, CBS News, in the process of being Tisched, underwent a painful series of pyrrhic cutbacks that left the division reeling and Congress questioning whether good financial performance and good newsgathering were a compatible proposition.

The gore had barely settled from these well-publicized cutbacks when the Writers Guild went on strike against the network's news operation. This strike, caused by senior management's determination to reassert control over union gains during the preceding years, amounted on the troop level to a civil war within the ranks, pitting mid-level officers against the foot soldiers with whom they usually had coffee.

[2] Buzzword unavailable in current dictionaries but still in wide use within the business universe. Implies creative thinking *before the fact*, action that anticipates its own need.

As the lifetime serfs of the organization circled in front of the CBS News operation on West Fifty-seventh Street (and continued to circle years after this particular flare-up), management shut off negotiations, and the tenor of the discourse took an even more bitter turn. Even to those who saw financial responsibility as an explanation for just about anything, the news from corporate headquarters was bewildering: Upon his ouster at the height of the company's "restructuring," it seems that former CBS President Tom Wyman was fitted with perhaps the most extraordinary parachute in the annals of corporate greed: a flat grant of *$4.3 million and a stipend of $400,000 per year for life!*

This kind of self-serving behavior is built upon a mad assumption: that parachutes of this size are necessary, as business educator Dean West puts it, "to encourage executives to behave in ways that serve the interests of the corporate shareholders."

Let's see if we've got that straight: a boss will only behave responsibly if he knows that, succeed or fail, his future well-being is provided for? Does labor enjoy that privilege? Isn't that what they were on the picket line about? This fascinating double standard must create at the very least some healthy consternation in those who labor in anxiety and uncertainty for crazy bosses whose selfishness is almost comically obvious. "We have yet to be given a definitive legal judgment why a change of control gives an executive grounds for substantial additional benefits not otherwise his on normal retirement or any other severance of employment," noted Martin Riger, emeritus professor of law at Georgetown University in the March 13, 1987, issue of *The New York Times.*

The answer is that no legal judgment is required. Executives fit their fellows with parachutes so that they may themselves be similarly equipped when the time comes. It is a dramatic example of the reorganizer's perception of himself, his perks, his divine rights.

### The Bold Deregulator and Fearful Re-Regulator

In the 1980s, religious free-market fervor was forged into a competition-free marketplace filled with quasimonopolistic unlicensed private utilities free to do as they pleased.

Working people were the losers, no matter what color their collars.

After the meltdown of the S&L industry, it's difficult to find proud, noisy deregulators these days. But their policies live on, and attempts of Congress to re-regulate certain industries have to date been unavailing.

Since the radical deregulation of the broadcasting business, for instance, all things have been possible for those with the guts to play in the big leagues.

The old names in the business, those committed to a public-service model that was established in the middle 1930s—Taft and Metromedia, for instance—were bought out, replaced by investment-banking concerns like Kohlberg Kravis Roberts and programming distributors like Lorimar-Telepictures, looking for a place to dump their programming fare.

Deregulation spurred sales in TV and radio stations, and even more dramatically in the seething cable-television business, where subscribers were for a time selling for as high as $2,500 each, and systems changed hands like baseball cards. As *Channels*, the now-defunct entertainment-business magazine, noted in May 1987, "FCC rules changes have created a new era in TV ownership, with stations being sold like so many fast-food franchises."

Not long before that, the chairman of the FCC, the body that governs the broadcast media, called television "a toaster with pictures."

In the high days of the public-service model, with regulations sprouting from every aspect of television-station operation, the business enjoyed double-digit advertising growth on a yearly basis, and customarily performed at margins that well exceeded 30 percent. After deregulation, the line industries—TV and radio stations—contracted, and sales growth slowed dramatically for the first time in living memory.

By the beginning of the nineties, station sales, too, had ground to a halt as properties reeled under the cost of the leverage that made their acquisitions possible. And throughout the industry, the first widescale cutbacks in history devastated work forces in those very departments that helped local TV differentiate its product: news, public affairs, and local programming.

But what matters to the deregulated capitalist is not operating profit. What matters is asset value, i.e., the ability to make windfall profits when the company is once again sold.

This is why a media company like TeleCommunications, Inc., which now controls some 35 percent of all cable-television subscribers in the United States—and a significant chunk of most of the programming on those systems as well—can continue to grow while it generates insignificant earnings and immense debt. The asset value of its holdings is astronomical—who cares how the business is faring?

Just the people who work in it.

Broadcasting is not the only American institution that has been assaulted by the hammer of deregulation. "The demise of the Trailways Corporation's bus lines provides the latest evidence that the widespread rush into transportation deregulation of a few years ago was ill considered," Melvin A. Brenner, former vice president of TWA and American Airlines, wrote to the *Times*. "There will soon be only one company, Greyhound Lines Inc., with a nationwide network of intercity bus routes—an unregulated monopoly of such service."

Not long after Greyhound succeeded in becoming the only national bus company, it made a healthy stab at busting its unions, generating a truly ugly strike, complaining all the while about the difficulty of operating in its business environment.

Yeah. It's tough to be a monopoly. Or certainly to work for one.

And how are airline workers faring? Between 1985 and 1987, in the first jolt of deregulation, the industry saw twenty-six mergers. "Pilots everywhere are feeling increased and conflicting pressures," reported *The Wall Street Journal.* This is bad news for the frequent flyer, considering that 60 to 70 percent of airline accidents are attributed to pilot error. Due to stress, Eastern pilots in 1988 were quitting the company at the rate of about thirty a month, twice the rate before deregulation, according to the pilots' association. A Virginia Polytechnic Institute survey of 420 randomly selected pilots at Eastern, USAir, Inc., and Piedmont Aviation, Inc., discovered that nearly one quarter of those at Eastern reported sleeplessness, anxiety, and other symptoms of depression—nearly twice the rate of pilots at other carriers.

An Eastern spokesman commented that pilots complained of stress because they had had it "easy" for so long, picking up perfectly the humane tone often adopted by his boss, Texas Air's Frank Lorenzo, nabob of the parent that then ran both Continental and Eastern. Lorenzo at that time was a prime example of a manager who learned to manage debt in a deregulatory environment.

*Fortune*'s early 1987 profile of "flinty, harddriving Frank Lorenzo" noted that the entrepreneur "first made his mark on the airline industry in 1983 when he placed Continental Airlines in bankruptcy, canceled its union contracts, and began flying again almost immediately as a cut-rate carrier with some of the lowest labor costs in the industry."

They had to be low. The guy's debt was astronomical.

"The acquisitions have stretched Lorenzo's balance sheet extremely thin," *Fortune* conceded. "Long term debt now accounts for well over 80% of total capital, vs. an average of about 50% at other major airlines." Yet the magazine was able to conclude on an upbeat note, as all business journals like to do unless their subject is actually under indictment, observing that Lorenzo "took up jogging several years ago and dropped 45 pounds. He has kept up his running, even participating in an occasional marathon, and has pared his weight to a fashionably lean 170 pounds. He also likes to ski and leases a mountain lodge in Utah."

In between skiing, running, and dieting, flinty Frank was busy:

- He bought Eastern at a bargain-basement price, essentially for nothing but debt; in fact, the $615-million purchase price for the airline was paid to the stockholders of Eastern, not to the airline itself, which immediately became cash-poor.
- He immediately called for huge concessions from employees, with Eastern pilots, who are by no means the best paid in the business, being hardest hit.
- He then used Eastern operating revenues and finances to enrich the parent corporation, the end goal being, eventually, to strip Eastern clean for the benefit of the shell company that owns it.

Texas Air, it seems, has "upstreamed" cash. Simply put, this means that all available cash is sucked out of the subsidiaries in order to finance the parent. This information comes from the Eastern pilots, a clearly partisan group, yes, but I choose to believe them.

An FBI investigation of Frank Lorenzo took place in 1988, looking into union charges of mismanagement and malfeasance. The government found that he was indeed fit, willing, and able to operate his airlines. *The New York Times* gave him a stunning endorsement the following day, one that positioned its subject as a determined, far-seeing warrior in the battle against corporate bloat. Forgotten were the tiny incidents of just the year past, such as those noted in the newspaper itself on September 18, 1987:

U.S. ORDERS EASTERN AIRLINES TO STOP FLYING DAMAGED JET

An Eastern Airlines jetliner was removed from service by Government order Wednesday because of severe damage apparently caused by a hard landing two flights earlier. The damage was not discovered after the hard landing, at Tulsa, OK, on Tuesday, or before the plane took off on two segments of a regular passenger flight on Wednesday. A spokesman for the Federal Aviation Administration said yesterday that the agency was notified of the damage by a call from an Eastern employee . . . Safety experts were concerned about why the damage had not been discovered earlier.

The article went on to recall a similar occurrence when a Boeing 727 flew five passenger flights with "wrinkles and other damage to the fusilage." The carrier in question? Lorenzo's Continental.

In 1989, Lorenzo lost control of Eastern, and a team of managers was hired to operate the property, which he continued to own and profit from until he was finally bought out in 1990—possibly the only individual to realize a profit from the holocaust he visited on the once-proud airline. And the once-successful Eastern shuttle from Boston to New York to Washington? Purchased by, of course, Donald Trump. Until, that is, the Donald was forced to take a look at his highly leveraged portfolio.

Finally, in 1991, the entire airline went out of business. On the day it did, Frank Lorenzo published an opinion piece in his great friend, *The New York Times,* mourning the demise of Eastern. He blamed everything on the unions.

The drive by American business and its henchmen in government continues to keep pushing deregulation forward on all fronts, even though it is quite clear that only one group benefits from the abnegation of the government to represent the people: our crazy bosses in both the public and the private sector. Is there a distinction between the two?

Check the board members of your major military contractors. How many guys used to work for the Reagan administration? Just asking . . .

### Post Yuppies

There's one last character who has made this all possible. He pops up in a tremendous range of roles, but his function is clear: to provide a sense of moral relativism. Sometimes he's a whiz kid in mergers and acquisitions. Sometimes he's a consultant, brought in to heal an inefficient organization and then hang around and exploit it. He is most useful in those companies that enjoy an excessively human face, tolerating a number of harebrained projects, departments boasting one or perhaps more not overly useful people, companies with a growth rate that could be goosed into a short spurt upward without too much trouble.

Security analysts, investment bankers, attorneys, and assorted hangers-on—these are the servants of big capital and, like Hegelian slaves, they came, until recently, to control their masters.

Many of them are former Yuppies gone to seed.

The classic Yupster was distinguished by a common system of no values, a sheer ethical neutrality that, after a while, accumulated the power of dogma. The worldview, if one may call it that, was a weird mixture of sixties pop psychology (I'm okay, you're okay), seventies situational ethics (If it feels good and don't hurt anybody, hey), and eighties rebuffed idealism (Bobby Seale is selling what?). What emerged from this stew was a group of people, as old as sixty-five and as young as twenty-two, who simply didn't give a honk what they did as long as it made money.

But the word is useless now, dredged as it is in goat cheese, compact discs, and other insubstantial effluvia that never really characterized these business craftspeople at all. We're going to have to find a name we can use without conjuring up BMWs and feisty little Montrachets. Say, I know. Let's call them MBAs.

"Call these corporate climbers the fast track kids," wrote *Business Week* back in 1986, when it was true. "They are impatient for raw management authority, they develop little loyalty to the institutions they work for, and they're often charged with lacking the sensitivity and people skills that typify today's most successful executives. These traits could also result in dramatic cultural changes in big corporations as the fast track kids become the chief executives of the 21st century." That's my future boss you're talking about. Let's take a look at the corporate tree that grows inside his mind:

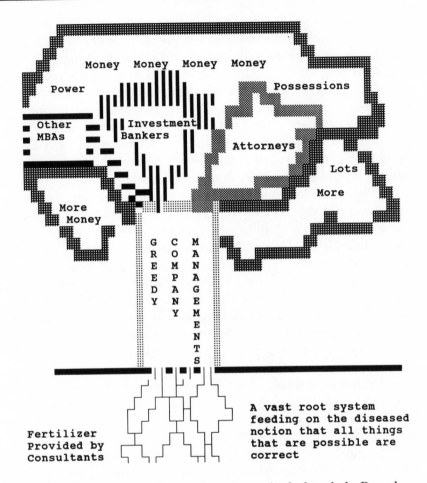

Money   Money   Money   Money

Power                                    Possessions

Other
MBAs                Investment
                    Bankers
                                    Attorneys

                                         Lots

                                    More

More
Money

G   C   M
R   O   A
E   M   N
E   P   A
D   A   G
Y   N   E
    Y   M
        E
        N
        T
        S

Fertilizer                          A vast root system
Provided by                         feeding on the diseased
Consultants                         notion that all things
                                    that are possible are
                                    correct

MBAs didn't create the environment single-handed. But they thrive in the bushiest branches of the Tree of Greed. And at the heart of that growth is the empirical Professional, analyzing, thinking, generating business, much of which need not be done.

The origin of this model of businessperson—the manager as egocentric wizard—can be traced back to the business schools that feed the Wall Street machine. The locus is the Wharton School of Finance and Commerce at the University of Pennsylvania. Graduates of Wharton represent a virtual Who's Who of Bad Guys. They include such notable figures as Donald Trump, Saul Steinberg, Michael Milken, Ronald Perelman, and Laurence Tisch, plus a whole lot of other types that might not be household names, unless your household was raided, acquired, merged, bought out, or reorganized.

As Robert Kennedy once said of the Academy: "The Wharton alumni don't look at the world as it is and ask, 'Why?' They see the world as it could be and ask, 'Can I make a buck at that?' "

Staffed with a faculty of entrepreneurial geniuses and corporate outsiders, Wharton imparts a scientific detachment to its students that is excellent. The discipline encourages them to see business as the play of numbers on an asset sheet. Quite naturally, after a time, they come to see business as essentially nothing more than assets, that's all, not as beautiful, mysterious shrines to the creativity, toughness, and enterprise of the human spirit.

To the career boss, such unambivalent corporate climbers represent a considerable danger from below, a basically alien life form uncaring of any preexisting culture, determined to *achieve* on an Iacoccatonic level. These days that's one tough order. They have minimal loyalty to their host organizations, since they look forward to what *Forbes* referred to as "a longer resume than their parents'." They're filled with a healthy urge to supplant their elders, the guys who are making all the deals, immediately if not sooner. And they have no problem in accommodating short-term fixes that hurt large numbers of people. A survey by executive-search firm Korn/Ferry International shows that only 14 percent of corporate executives under thirty-nine think "concern for people" is important to success. And when Duke University's Fuqua School of Business surveyed its students in 1987, they split 50–50 over whether price-fixing between competitors was wrong.

Most old-line operators acquire their cold blood at a more advanced age, after many hard-won campaigns. To be so young and so detached is a very powerful business asset indeed.

The only protection from their relentless, coldhearted professionalism is constant, public, daily *success*, and excellent office politics to boot.

In fact, truth be told, I lied. There is no protection from them. They aren't meek, and they *shall* inherit. The international business community is their nation. The world, quite literally, is their oyster, and they mean to eat the whole thing.

## MOVING RIGHT ALONG . . .

One argument made for the great American acquirer/restructurer is that if *he* didn't squeeze out the fat from the too-comfy organization, then Japanese, British, Saudis, whoever, would move in on our markets and put us out of business. "Global competitive pressures and gluts are the roots of the restructuring," Ed Yardeni of Pru Bache told *Business Week*. "If the Icahns and Pickenses don't do it, the Japanese will do it for us by putting our companies out of business and taking what's left of their markets."

But it's not an either/or proposition. The Icahns and Pickenses and Lorenzos and countless internal budget slashers terrorize the crazy corporation, and when they've created sufficient mergeritis, the foreign firms move in and pick up just about any piece of business they want.

In short, the restructured, paranoid, crazy boss creates an organization ripe for the kind of aggressive colonization that afflicted JWT. Even at those few American advertising agencies that have yet to be acquired, the terror of the marketplace reigns.

Listen to a guy I'll call Henry, who hunts heads for an executive-search firm that serves the advertising business. "The climate has an incredible effect on people," he says.

The relationship you've built up over the years is very transient, because everybody is looking out for their own lives. So people have their résumés very active, and they're very concerned about their future and their present. A lot of people in agencies do not tack things on walls, they put them up with Scotch tape. There's no permanency.

Though you're sitting with a contract that guarantees one or two years, there's no promise it will be renewed or that there'll be a job waiting for you elsewhere when the job is over. With mergers, there is a consolidation and a consolidation translates into fewer jobs, with more people vying for them. Overqualified people are vying for jobs that should rightfully be going to somebody on the way up. People who are on their way up feel like they're locked in to the general situation.

People who remain are working more and longer hours, and my estimation is that there are fewer people who are reporting to them, and those fewer people are working longer hours, too. So that's what a consolidation brings. It brings a bottom line. And in the long run, the burnout rate takes its toll. You truly cannot work seventy hours a week for fifty-two weeks without that having a major effect. I think you're in maximum overload right now.

And therein hangs the ultimate tragedy, for employees and bosses alike. Crazy-management costs. And it exacts the highest price from the very people who are least equipped to pay.

The result is anxiety, rampaging, electrifying anxiety.

The expression of that anxiety can be shaped by individual pathology or it can be shaped by the organization. And while he is on top, the crazy boss may look—to everyone but his employees—like someone performing on all fronts quite admirably. A madman in a lunatic organization fits right in. It's the odd-man-out of the asylum who appears insane.

To employees, however, there is no question how the anxiety-plagued boss looks: he looks *crazy*.

# PART II

# THE CRAZY BOSS

The men of higher circles are not representative men; their high position is not a result of moral virtue; their fabulous success is not firmly connected with meritorious ability. Those who sit in the seats of the high and the mighty are selected and formed by the means of power, the sources of wealth, the mechanics of celebrity, which prevail in their society. They are not men selected and formed by a civil service that is linked with the world of knowledge and sensibility. They are not men shaped by nationally responsible parties that debate openly and clearly the issues this nation now so unintelligently confronts. They are not men held in responsible check by a plurality of voluntary associations which connect debating publics with the pinnacles of decision. Commanders of power unequaled in human history, they have succeeded within the American system of organized irresponsibility.

C. Wright Mills
*The Power Elite*

# CHAPTER ONE

# THE BOSS WITH FIVE BRAINS

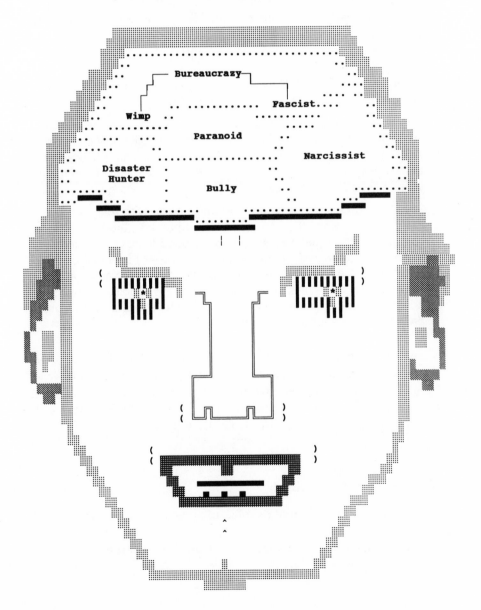

A s a carrier of unhappiness, the crazy boss suffers a lot, but his subordinates suffer far worse. They go for months without a kind word, in constant fear of arbitrary punishment, humiliation, or execution, enraged by the injustice, brutality, ineptitude, paranoia, neurotic pride, and downright stupidity that crackle in the air around them. They are not, shall we say, *empowered*.

Here are a few voices of those who suffer:

"Working for my boss is like being seduced by an Arab prince, only to find out the next day that you've been sold into white slavery."

"My boss is a raving lunatic alcoholic who is fairly reasonable at nine in the morning, but after lunch he becomes totally incoherent, or rages, or closes his door and won't come out. So you have to see him the first half hour of the day or you're wasting your time. If you miss your early train, you've blown it."

"He's an extremely forceful and dynamic person with tons of social graces, who creates the impression that when he's around he has control over the situation and all kinds of good things are bound to happen. Unfortunately, no good things have ever happened on his watch, but no one in ultra-senior management seems to have caught on. As a result of his most recent disaster, millions of dollars were lost, hundreds of innocent people were fired, and he ended up with a big promotion and a lot more responsibility."

Sound familiar? Is your management crazy? And if so, just *how* crazy is it? In milder forms, the crazy boss could bring a low-level fungus into the workplace, debilitating people far in excess of what they are paid for. The truly virulent boss can spread a fever that kills a lot of innocent people before it finally kills him.

## WHAT DOES IT LOOK LIKE?

It looks different in different people, since each mixes his own strange brew of odd behavior.

For our purposes, we're going to define five separate portions of the mind of the crazy boss.

First, there's the broad yellow backstripe of the confirmed *bully*. Maybe, as one architect reports of his supervisor, the guy likes to thunder into his space and, in front of a group of Japanese dignitaries, scream his head off just for fun—while they smile ingratiatingly and take snapshots. No kidding.

Or, perhaps, as another, very short bully is wont to do, he "periodically assigns the same project to three people, retiring in glee to watch the flesh fly." Or maybe he's just an insensitive toad who flies in the face of even the most minimal Company standards of humanity. A bully at one Fortune 500 company was keeping an eye on one of his charges who was scheduled to leave at 3:00 P.M. to have four wisdom teeth removed. "Take the rest of the day off if you have to," this boss muttered as the employee sidled out the door.

Or how about the bully at a consumer-goods company who hired a young woman specifically for her ability to "follow orders," then told the Department of Human Resources that the new employee had exactly "three months" to "become a different person, less dependent. I can't stand dependent people. Make her over."

Next comes the trembling *paranoid* who shuts his door, refers all calls and visitors to you, and won't come out—for three months. "His door was always locked," says a former project manager for a cable-television company, "and if you needed a henchman to get a message through to Charley, and a henchman wasn't around, you just slipped a note under his door. And he'd slip one back. He never wrote complete sentences or words: 'Pls Hndl,' his message would read, or 'Do Immd,' because he couldn't stand human contact, or the thought of human contact, for more than one or two seconds running."

This fear of human contact, in extreme cases, can lead the paranoid to exhibit symptoms of compulsive perfectionism in both work and personal habits. This is simply another way of exerting control over a universe that makes the crazy paranoid incredibly nervous. I mean, there are so many germs in it! And messy spreadsheets, too! The only solution is to take control of every teeny, itsy-bitsy aspect of just about everything! An old vice president of mine, who had been highly successful as an entrepreneurial type earlier in his career, was promoted to a department-head post in my company. He immediately began to fail egregiously. Why? Because he was doing just about everything himself—down to making the coffee. He had a staff, but didn't use them, because, heh-heh, they weren't to be *trusted.* By the end of the year, the entire department was under the knife of a management consultant. Before the bad boss was excised (with a hefty platinum parachute) most of his department had been sacrificed.

Third, the diseased manager is often such a self-obsessed *narcissist* that he sees all those around him as tiny flecks in the majestic spectacle that is his life story. Deadlines are blown, opportunities decay, while the executive senior VP is behind locked doors contemplating whether he'd like his portrait done in pen-and-ink or pastels. A friend recalls waiting one fine winter evening for his chairman to clear something that was needed immediately. "In retrospect, I guess I was lucky I dropped by his suite at eight-thirty P.M. to see what was going on," he says. "If I hadn't, I might never have found out that he had gone home at six, just after calling to tell me to stick around and wait for his approval."

Fourth, we'll need to understand the twofold mind of the *bureaucrazy*. On the one hand, he might be a pure wimp. A former boss of mine used to criticize employees who did not fill in the "bullets" that were used to itemize notes on memos. The "bullet" came hollow, like this:

○

and many is the memo I had to color in, like this:

●

before it was allowed to proceed its way upstairs to senior management. This is evidence of a mind paralyzed by appearances and form. When he was finally asked to leave, this boss received more in severance and extended benefits than your average steelworker makes in a decade. That's because there was nothing substantive that could be offered as reason for his termination. Except for the fact that he was, by any rational standard, operationally insane.

Recently, since the ascendancy of fad Excellence credos, a new subspecies of *bureaucrazy*—the *organizational fascist*—has gained a tremendous foothold in the world of crazy business. He's always been there, but now his pitch is falling on fertile ground. A variety of formal productivity tools are being fomented at this time. All demand not only obedience, but also the kind of selfless devotion that was previously reserved for one's nation, if not one's wife.

One engineering vice president, put in charge of the Company's Search for Excellence, decided that, in a bow to the Japanese model, people would be more productive if they had a greater stake in the decision-making process. To his thinking, participative management encourages worker loyalty and creative action, as well as more rigorous "conformance to requirements," and engenders virtual Oriental worker loyalty. The vice president immediately ordered all employees to sign a public Oath of Commitment to Excellence and mandated a series of all-employee public signings to make sure the development of participating management got off on the right foot.

Finally, when all the crazy vapors come together, we have the *disaster hunter*, working to push himself to the brink of catastrophe and, eventually, over. Disaster hunters could be addictive personalities with shades of workaholism, who hang around until midnight, return at daybreak, and expect you to do the same. "The boss here wakes up every morning at five-thirty A.M.," says a senior manager at a midwestern manufacturing company. "He jogs four miles before six, takes a shower, eats a hearty breakfast, and is at his desk by seven. He sits there, in the quiet, reading. What kind of work could he be doing? Nobody has that much work, no matter who he is, especially around a place like this that moves like a giant snail. And he's the last to leave at night, too. I try to outstay him. And no matter how late I leave, when I creep by his office, could be nine or nine-thirty, even ten o'clock, I hear this voice, 'Goodnight, Ted.' It's weird. It gives me the creeps."

Or the disaster hunter could be an alcoholic. One magazine editor, two drinks after lunch, blasted into a subordinate's office, raging with despair, and sent the work of months *flying out the window.* "Start over," he said, and walked out.

Or his could be a case of drug dependency, or chronic manic-depressive mood swings, or just notorious stupidity, exercised with regularity and éclat. The behavior really doesn't matter. The essence of the crazy boss is that he is, in everything he does, seeking his quietus with the nearest bare bodkin around, and he doesn't mind taking his nearest and dearest along with him.

"I think of my first boss, a very depressed woman who was manager of Information Services," says a current vice president of Corporate Communications at a midtown Manhattan conglomerate. "She was called into the chairman's office one day to begin preparations for an important speech the boss was making the following Monday. It was short notice, sure, but that's why people like us are making serious money—the ability to absorb that kind of short-term pressure and still make things happen. But Marla couldn't handle it.

Immediately, she started growling. Saying, 'You expect us to put this together over the weekend? With the kind of materials you have here? We'll have to be on it night and day!' and that kind of stuff, and on and on. If her looks could kill, the chairman would have been dead on the spot. When she left the room, the chairman turned to the president and said, 'Who is that woman? I want her out of here.' And six months later, she was."

## SO THESE ARE FIVE "TYPES" OF BOSSES, RIGHT?

Wrong. There is no such thing, in my opinion, as a "type" of boss. There is only the crazy boss himself, with plumes of behavior rocketing into the environment, all of it fueled by the same illness, the same etiology. It is my conviction that American Management Disease is suffered by a majority of all bosses in the United States between the ages of twenty-six and eighty-two, and by 98 percent of those who make more than $134,000 per year. I could be off by a couple of dollars, but I don't think so.

## NATURE OR NURTURE? BOTH!

The crazy boss started out as a relatively sane individual, a normal, common person. How else could God have made so many of him?

The fact is, unless a boss is born to the position, or owns a controlling block of stock—both of which represent a lifetime license to kill—there are some minimal standards of normalcy that even the most successful executive must project in his early years. And that's hard to do with hallucinations marching through your head, or delusional tics and eccentricities visible to the naked eye. So the majority of bosses decompose on the job as, under pressure, one inbred weakness or another seizes hold and brings them down. What starts as a state of simple, innate nervousness evolves into generalized disability. The severity of their problem is bred in the hothouse of the workplace.

In today's business organization, more often than not, the crazy boss is also a highly motivated and successful player, fueled by craziness, not stunted by it. His bullying, paranoia, selfishness, ruthlessness, penchant for perfectionism, addiction to drugs, booze, or work, is the only way he knows how to achieve all the good things expected of him. And as long as he does so, and makes his own boss look good, he's in no danger from the men in the white shirts. In fact, he just might be the one guy the place can't do without. This can make him kind of hard to unseat.

In a healthy company, with halfway decent values and communication between people and departments, a crazy boss will be cut off from the herd, wither away, and, eventually, find himself a job in an organization crazy enough to appreciate his strengths. In a sick company, or one under intense pressure, where people live in fear for their lives and no general standards of proper management exist, the crazy boss can find a home where he is allowed to ferment in his own bad juice. You can pretty much bet that the existence of one near you is evidence that something is wrong up above. He is the creation of, and thrives in, organizations that depend upon his pathology to get the job done, and reward it when bonus time rolls around. Except for the very few cases who end up with a lifetime supply of Thorazine, the problem is institutional, not personal.

The more extreme the needs of the organization, the more outsized the financial and human needs of the group, the more radical the demands the group will make on the leader.

In a healthy organization, the demand for the appearance of omnipotence is difficult enough to sustain. In a sick organization, the constant entreaty for decisions, affection, acumen, and brutality may amount to a burden not even a completely sane man, if any exist, could support.

The fearful leader must find an organization hospitable to his particular bent. Maybe as a young man he polished his spoon with his napkin before stirring his coffee, and the vice president who hired him liked that in a man. Twenty years later, under the pressures of his office, he demands that his executive flatware be boiled three times daily and refuses to meet with more than one or two very clean people. The gentle but relentless weight of both his function and his extraordinary importance to himself has simply finished the job he began from birth on his own personality. Along the way, he's been rewarded for *the extremity of himself,* and as he pauses for a moment in his busy day to regard the general state of the world, he's got to be convinced that it's the rest of the world that's crazy. After all, he's doing a lot better than most of it.

He has no incentive to change, because his sick crowd relies on him. Madness confers tremendous power, yes, but only when it is surrounded by a weakness that calls for that kind of leadership to keep it in shape.

A leader accrues loyalty and power by appealing to something basic in a disassociated group of people, speaks to an emotional gap in the collective mind that he can fill with his ego, his will, his myth.

In times of peace, he is its heart, in times of war, its spleen and muscle.

Today, most American workers exist in the most primitive form of group, one that is tradition-free and free of loyalty. Such an environment generates tremendous fear in people, fear of loss, of death, of dissolution and shame. Fear that drives people together. Fear that keeps people apart. It is a fear produced by the incessant demand for short-term results and the feeling of danger supplied by a variety of villains. And it is not irrational. It is real. It is sane.

As employees in virtually every American industry from advertising to manufacturing, broadcasting to finance, now know, the price of even moderate failure in the business world is often appalling. Success is no bargain either; the boss—and his people—are twisted into a variety of tortured shapes under the pressure of achieving huge short-term financial gains.

No organization can take on the task of managing people when immediate, quantifiable success is the sole criterion for continued personal health and well-being. While it's quite natural for a business to define managerial prowess by financial performance, employees yearn for more humane standards. And any organization that refuses to hold itself to that larger criterion just might be the comfy womb in which the crazy boss is welcome.

For the driven manager, the fear of failing is only part of the nightmare driving his crippling anxiety. The loss of face, the loss of place, is just as intimidating.

"If I made one big mistake, it was getting wedded to the company," a fifteen-year veteran of one large multinational told *The Wall Street Journal* when his division was sold. Another told the daily chronicle of the American Dream: "That company to me was a father, a mother, a confidante. Then in a matter of an hour, all that's severed. The camaraderie, the cohesiveness, it's all gone."

Very businesslike, eh? Anything but.

The loss of security, and the workplace hearth, is catastrophic for organization people, who come to define themselves in terms of their place in the organization. It's enough to make the strongest business, and the strongest boss, sick with something very specific and very hard to cure.

## DIAGNOSIS

In its glossary of afflictions, the American Psychiatric Association describes the comprehensive neurotic syndrome known as *Character Disorder.*

> A heterogenous group of pathological character disturbances which exhibit in common an habitual inflexibility of behavior patterns without marked subjective discomfort.

In other words, this is going to hurt you a lot more than it hurts him.

> Instead of discrete areas of symptomatic involvement, *the entire personality is usually affected,* especially those ego functions determining frustration tolerance . . .

He gets mad easily.

> . . . drive regulation . . .

He's either too impulsive or totally constipated.

> . . . affective responses . . .

He can't *feel* things quite right.

> . . . and object relationships.

And he hasn't a clue where he ends and the rest of the world begins.

Psychiatrists O. Spurgeon English and Gerald H. J. Pearson, in *Common Neuroses of Children and Adults,* consider the "illness of the total personality":

> One can probably safely say that it is these neurotic characters, living unnoticed and unlabeled within the average group, who do so much to produce frank neuroses and psychoses in much the same way that a typhoid carrier or an undiagnosed tuberculous infection can contaminate a whole family or even a whole community.

Psychoanalyst Otto Kernberg has written:

> There is the general "invasive" nature of administrative concerns—the invasion of the privacy of his thinking, around the clock, by pressing organizational issues for which no immediate solution can be found; the invasion of his life space as his public image infiltrates areas of privacy and reduces his time and space for careless leisure and freedom; the threat to the freedom of his fantasy life as his internal relations to people and nature, to art and leisure, all become contaminated by stress related to responsibilities that always remain with him.

Under such pressure, the natural reaction for many people is *regression*—childish solutions to adult problems—a return to a time when life's questions were more basic and the answers were simpler.

Pearson and English describe the result:

> There are those who demand excessive attention and petting, who cannot bear deprivation, who cannot be disappointed without being sulky or depressed, who cannot restrain impulses, aggressive or sexual, and who cannot wait for reward for effort. There are those who pursue futile plans or activities, sometimes with some realization of their futility, but seemingly with a compulsion to carry on; there are others who are not aware of the futility of their activity at the time.

That's a crazy boss, suffering from something he caught in the air around him.

Most every Tuesday in *The New York Times,* a new article appears declaring such instructive news as "Dreams Have No Meaning," or "Nervous People Tend to Be More Insecure Than Others, Studies Show." At this point, all sensible people basically sneeze on the notion that the child is father to the man. Perhaps behavioral scientists conditioned us when young to reject the whole idea of motivation per se. Yet I've got to believe that when I look at a guy sucking on a cigar and howling with rage and frustration when the third quarter numbers didn't work out, I'm looking at an infant.

The feeling of impotence, and the resulting emotions of fear, belligerence, confusion, and thwarted love, run wild in the American workplace today. Even sane people like you feel it.

And if character is substantially determined by the daily environment that works on the basic, imperfect human being within each of us—I draw my conclusion that what we have here is *a mass case of situational insanity.*

## ARBEIT UND LIEBE

Love is the main thing people demand of the organization in which they work. It may take the form of money, or praise, or title, but the demand on the family is the same. Justification. Acceptance.

Freud said it first when he defined mental health as *arbeit und liebe*—work and love. Today, while both may be available, neither can be relied on.

Maybe that's the real tragedy of the crazy boss.

The manager in today's business organization is forever shut off from the ultimate source of comfort: the sense of belonging, of being loved in a secure group; he is a being apart, separated from the Company hearth, the delicate, essentially bogus family that keeps his psyche intact. As Erich Fromm wrote in *The Art of Loving,* "The awareness of human separation, without reunion by love—is the source of shame. It is at the same time the source of guilt and anxiety. The deepest need of man, then, is the need to overcome his separateness, to leave the prison of his aloneness. The *absolute* failure to achieve this aim means insanity."

Each crazy boss displays a different amalgam of symptoms, depending on the time of day, week, month, or career, moving through pathologies as the moon does its phases. But there are some ways of handling the beast no matter how his craziness is manifesting itself at that moment in time.

I believe any successful approach to your crazy boss must incorporate the following fivefold path:

**Break the Cord:** The single most powerful weapon of the crazy boss is *your emotional dependence upon his authority.* When that need is eliminated, the crazy boss becomes simply one more tough obstacle to be negotiated—not a debilitating psychological opponent with untold power over your personality.

***Do the Job:*** Competence is always the best defense, especially in these tough economic times, when more is being demanded of each individual than used to be asked of entire departments. If your client base is substantial, you've got a source of power that transcends the vagaries of most any crazy boss, particularly the one who answers to a number of crazy bosses himself.

***Stay Frosty:*** No matter how anally retentive he might be, how firmly in lockjaw control over his exterior, the crazy boss has almost no real control over the irrational emotions that rage within. So you've got to do everything within your power to keep your shirt on while those around you are losing theirs. The ability to analyze a situation just might separate you from the rest of the loony crew. In the grip of a crazy menace from within, chill out, determine a day-to-day strategy, and live within it. The saner you are, the crazier your boss will appear by comparison. And when the fruits of that craziness come to pass, you'll be less guilty by association.

***Work His Head:*** It's his most vulnerable spot! Every bully has fears. Find them out and give them meat and bone, so they can stand and walk on his nerves when the tiny hours of the morning are upon him. When he's in a preening, narcissistic phase, be sure to pump the little part of his rusty engine that tells him nobody appreciates him as much as he deserves. If he likes to drink a bit too much—and talk likewise— over and after lunch, do what you can to make sure that his big interfaces with senior management take place at, oh, 2:00 P.M. Get the picture? His craziness makes him *more* vulnerable, not less. It's your greatest weapon against him—if you don't let it destroy you first.

***Be Prepared:*** He will fall, make no mistake. When he does, you have to have the kind of relations with his superiors that decree your continued existence after he is gone. Sure, this involves some duplicity on your part during the painful years of his tenure. Duplicity isn't the province of senior management, you know. You can do it, too!

Pursuing this five-point program will position you to outlive your crazy boss and profit from his demise.

As a long-term strategy, it's pretty good. But it doesn't take the place of daily micromanaging of the problem.

To get that job done, you'll need solid understanding of every aspect of his crazy personality—its nuances, shifts, and not-so-fine points; as well as a number of suggestions on how to manage each facet of his craziness while he's in its grip. And while I may speak at times as if your boss is exclusively one "type" or another, this is done merely for convenience. Remember that the true crazy boss is a stewpot of bad behavior. Recognizing which part of his anarchic soul you are confronting is half the battle.

The other half is up to you.

# CHAPTER TWO

# BULLY

The first thing is never to become friends, but sweetly and decisively to assert your powers. Take them out for a drink on their birthday, get to know their life, but come at them from very far above, keep them scurrying and keep them in hand. It's like handling a horse, you have to keep the reins in your hands—if they suspect you're going to give them their head, they'll bolt. You have to leave no doubt as to who would be the victor if things went to the mat. Ambition comes into it, of course. They have to have some, in order for them to be good, but they can't have too much, or everything is beneath them. They're there to do menial stuff that you don't have time to do; it's unprofitable for a company to have an executive sit down and type a letter that takes him twenty minutes, or to get coffee for that fucking matter. They have to get pleasure out of doing it well. Balance is it, I guess. Be sure and thank people if they do something good for you. Go out of your way. Keep the ball of considerateness and teamwork rolling. And, at the appropriate moment, slam dunk the mothers and let them know who's boss.

A Bully

**M**anagement by terror is a time-honored technique, because it works. The most mediocre man or woman can suddenly seem dynamic, forceful, fearful—passing anxiety and hatred down the managerial pipe until it infects all who work under him. Direct whipping is the first, worst, and most common employee complaint, for obvious reasons: while working for a guy who is predominantly a wimp may be painful in the long run, you don't lose as much skin from your back.

I begin with the bully here not because he is special—but because he is common, and all-too admired by those who seek to mirror and create the national consciousness.

## HE MAY BE UGLY: BUT HE SURE CAN COOK

American management is replete with admiration of classic bullies who, as long as they flourish, are left to operate pretty much as they will. It is no coincidence, I think, that George Steinbrenner's campaign of terror against his employee Dave Winfield was not revealed—and punished—until Steinbrenner was well into his historic fall from grace. Until then, he was just, well, the Boss.

Businessmen love sports metaphors. Which is why it is, perhaps, not beside the point to invoke the career of another dramatic and successful bully whose "two-fisted" style still provides a model for more than one crazy bully boss: Woody Hayes, legendary coach of Ohio State. Hayes was long regarded as the quintessential "tough" manager, and only when his team began to fail was his style interpreted as anything but an excess of zeal.

On March 13, 1987, *The New York Times* obit offered this assessment of Hayes's career:

> Throughout his career, Mr. Hayes, a squat, square-jawed man with a fierce visage and an even fiercer temper, was known as much for his tantrums as for his victories. During practice he would beat his fists on the helmets and shoulder pads of players who displeased him and would occasionally become so frustrated that he would fling his own watch and eyeglasses to the ground . . .
>
> Then, on Dec. 29, 1978, he erupted one time too many. In the final minutes of a frustrating 17–15 Ohio State loss in the Gator Bowl, Charlie Bauman of Clemson intercepted an Ohio State pass. As he was chased out of bounds, a frustrated Hayes stepped up and punched him. The next day, using a military term that seemed especially appropriate, High Hindman, the Ohio State athletic director and a former player and assistant coach under Hayes, announced that the coach had been "relieved of his duties."
>
> The morning after his dismissal, Mr. Hayes, describing the punch as "a matter of an instant," said, "I got what was coming to me." Then, in a rare moment of public self-analysis, he offered what amounted to

an epitaph for his coaching career. "Nobody despises to lose more than I do. That's got me into trouble over the years, but it also made a man of mediocre ability into a pretty good coach."

The bully—reaching for the stars over the wall of his own mediocrity—rears his head only in decaying organizations, organizations under extreme stress in which the orderly sense of rightful authority has fallen apart.

A corporate type describes her boss, a highly successful woman now number two in her organization:

Phyllis would dismember you. She's interesting in that her horrendous manner and temper make her an effective manager. She does it through intimidation, lying, manipulation. She exhibits many more of the traditionally male characteristics. She is egomaniacal and paranoic and wants to get somewhere. The point is, for the people above, the work *is* getting done. Sure it is. But at what cost?

## HE'S MEAN, HE'S GREEN, HE'S ALWAYS BEEN ON THE SCENE

When Suetonius wrote his disquisition on the lives and careers of the Caesars back in the first century, it was quite clear to him that as Rome decayed, so did the quality of its leadership. When Rome was strong and vital, Julius was the revered Caesar.

Suetonius brings us through the reign of Augustus (in which power was bureaucratized and reached the height of accomplishment and rationality), to Tiberius (less rational, more brutal and arbitrary as the bounds of Roman power began to stretch thin), and tells of hitting bottom with Caligula. "They set aside Tiberius's will—which made his other grandson, then still a child, joint-heir with Caligula—and so splendid were the celebrations that 160,000 victims were publicly sacrificed during the next three months, or perhaps even a shorter period," the historian observes in his dry style.

By then, all that was left of the tradition of leadership established by Julius Caesar was the degradation of the republic, the ascension of personal power to a level that could only lead to failure. No individual could really rule the Roman Empire—far-flung, corrupt, infinitely political, endangered by a host of enemies. No man but a madman. About Caligula, Suetonius writes:

> One day he sent a colonel to kill young Tiberius without warning; on the pretext that Tiberius had insulted him by taking an antidote against poison—his breath smelled of it. Then he forced his father-in-law, Marcus Silanus, to cut his own throat with a razor, the charge being that he had not followed the Imperial ship when she put to sea in a storm, but had stayed on shore. . . .

> It was his habit to commit incest with each of his three sisters in turn and, at large banquets, when his wife reclined above him, placed them all in turn below him. . . .

> Having collected wild animals for one of his shows, he found butcher's meat too expensive and decided to feed them with criminals instead. He paid no attention to the charge-sheets, but simply stood in the middle of a colonnade, glanced at the prisoners lined up before him, and gave the order: "Kill every man between that bald head and the other one over there!"

Kind of sounds like the reorganization of TWA.

The last of the Caesars descended from the original board was Nero—paranoid, lecher, narcissist, bully. "Nero died at the age of 32," the historian writes. "In the widespread general rejoicing, citizens ran through the streets wearing caps of liberty, as though they were freed slaves."

The cult of power, the respect for the divine right of management, has, throughout history, produced the destruction of the system led in that manner.

So it is today, where bully behavior is encouraged and rewarded in a wide range of business enterprises. The style itself is applauded in boardrooms and in house organs like *Business Week* as "tough," "no nonsense," "hard as nails." When you see these code words, you know you're dealing with a bully boss, and an organization on the verge of decline and eventual dissolution.

## LOYALTY *ÜBER ALLES!*

Perhaps one of the most forceful and successful bullies in the history of American business was Harold Geneen, former head of ITT. The

organization benefited dramatically—for a long time—from his philosophy and style, then suffered in predictable ways.

The following history was offered by a guy I'll call Williams,
former chief of one of ITT's operating divisions, who knew Geneen
well, and has some complicated feelings on the subject. " 'Do it
because I tell you to' was often the only issue for him," Williams
recalls, "even when it was totally counterproductive. Yes, he was
effective, because he was brilliant, incisive, devastatingly accurate
about facts and figures. He took ITT from being a large company to
being a huge one.

"But success may have been larger failure in the long run," the
former ITT executive continues. "His acquisitions were a paper triumph, and his style of management led to a terrible succession crisis.
It was never clear that ITT was more than the sum of its inefficient
parts, parts perhaps made more inefficient at a time when they
should have grown wildly. The point is that he could have been *more*
successful. And many people were made miserable along the way.
Geneen did have a larger vision of bringing American management
technique to old-fashioned clubby companies that were performing
poorly. Eventually, he had to give that up, and turn to acquisitions.
And it's not clear that he succeeded in the long run."

Williams joined ITT in the late 1950s, about the same time as his
boss, and was an integral part of Geneen's push to diversify and
expand into international markets. The boss's style, however, and
not his accomplishments, are at issue here:

"Geneen would arrive in my city, and immediately call me to his
hotel—he wouldn't wait until the office meeting," Williams says. "He
would say things like, 'Don't talk to those crazy bastards of mine in
New York,' put down his closest NYC advisers, ask me not to report
back to them, to keep our business private. I would point out that that
put me in a difficult reporting situation, since I reported directly back
to those very guys. Geneen would then go through this thing, totally
ridiculing the guys that were supposed to be my bosses."

Dividing to conquer is a well-worn bully technique. As one manager of a small textbook publishing company reports of his boss,
"He goes to two of us editors individually and says, 'Come up with
an idea.' Pits one of us against the other without our knowing it. So
I go to Lynn down the hall and say, 'You know, I'm really stuck on
what to do with this book.' And she looks shocked and says, 'But
Arnold assigned this project to me!' 'No!' I say, 'he assigned it to

*me*!' And we both look at each other. He does it as a way of seeing who will come up with the best. When I was first hired, he told me, 'I like to engender some friendly competition.' I said, 'But that competition can hurt,' and he responded, 'A little brain matter on the walls never hurt anybody.' I think he manages through division because he doesn't care who he hurts. He sees all people as replaceable. I mean, he never even says good morning. Never says good job. You never hear from him unless you fuck up."

Although such behavior would be scorned in any other venue, the business bully is blissfully unconcerned with self-examination or self-critique. Williams continues about his boss:

There was a review session of some operating subsidiaries. Geneen came in the night before and took in a huge load of material. He arrived at the meeting at ten A.M. The meeting was called for nine. He had his senior staff with him. The first to be reviewed was one of the largest subsidiaries. The head was an elegant British businessman. Geneen started off the meeting by saying, "Good morning, Bob"— believe me, this guy was never addressed as "Bob" before—and, with no notes in front of him, Geneen says, "Bob, on page five, book three, you make the following statement about semiconductors. But on the other hand in Book seven, page ninety-two, you make this statement . . . I'd like you to explain the difference." The executive didn't know how to react. He started to turn to his controller, who had put the material together, and Geneen barked, "I didn't ask *him!* I asked *you!*"

After a session like that, he would take me to one side and say, "That sonofabitch has got to go, and so has *X, Y,* and *Z.*" I would want to warn him, "Look, you can't just break up teams that way, you can't behave that way," but I know his response would have been, "Fine. If you can't do it, I'll get someone who will." So I'd say, "Yes, Hal, I'll get it moving right away." Then I'd wait a couple of days, let things cool down. Then try to reason with him. In this case, I convinced him to just demote the person to vice chairman.

Back in New York, Geneen would get back to his office and sometimes he'd, like, go completely wacky—throw paper all over the place. I was told he had not one but two psychiatrists on the payroll who he used to play off against each other. I think that was typical of his behavior. Playing favorites, and rotating favorites.

For instance, a new VP would fly into town with Geneen, and he would keep turning to the new guy every five minutes, "Joe, what do you think?" "You know, Joe, you're absolutely right"—even if Joe's comments were inane. "Joe" would last for maybe maximum six months before he was replaced by another "Joe."

The issue with a bully is *obedience above all,* and humanity has little to do with the equation:

> Geneen called me three days before Christmas. He wanted some special data related to labor relations throughout my region, and he wanted it on January 3. I warned him that around these parts, Christmas is taken very seriously. It's spent with families, sledding, that kind of thing. The information Geneen wanted had to be gotten from managing directors, other key people. Geneen got very upset. "Are you trying to tell me this can't be accomplished?" I said: "We can accomplish anything, Hal, I'm merely trying to say that we will do a great deal of damage to morale. If there's some way you can hold off for a couple of weeks, I think it would be tremendously appreciated."

> Geneen hung up on me. A couple of minutes later, I got a call from a senior VP: "You really upset Hal by telling him you don't want to cooperate." Later, I found out there was no real urgency, that there would have been time to compile this stuff later. I didn't win, by the way. My operating chairman gave me a call and kind of laughed, and said, "Well, Bill, it's your problem." My managing directors were absolutely furious. They blamed me.

The intrusion on religious or social days comes up quite often in an investigation of control-freak bullies. Let's take a moment to peek at that equally beloved Bismarck of the Boardroom, Charles Revson.

> There is the story, for example, that he once called a meeting of all his top people to discuss the problem of executive turnover. *Why couldn't Revlon keep its goddamn executives?* The meeting was called for six o'clock on the Friday of a July Fourth weekend; Charles walked in at eight o'clock; and he proceeded to tell the assembled that the *reason* they couldn't keep their goddamn executives was that they weren't *training* them properly . . . More than once he called meetings late on December 24—because to him it was just December 24. . . . [1]

[1] Andrew Tobias, *Fire and Ice* (New York: William Morrow and Company, 1976), pp. 34–35.

Once again, the issue is control. For the bully, a day without total control of his subjects' feelings, actions, and thoughts is a day without funshine.

The bully simply cannot see any issue, no matter how large and complex, from any vantage point but his own. Those who have their own perspective are not exercising their rights as human beings— they are being *disloyal.*

And disloyalty, once perceived, is occasion for extinction. And fast.

The most horrible disloyalty is the crime of being admired and loved more than the bully himself, as in this case told by Williams of ITT:

> Geneen became concerned about our operating president's popularity and authority. Let's call him Ferenzi. He wasn't flouting Geneen, he was simply doing what a good executive of ITT should do, taking decisions that should be taken. Geneen got concerned that he was losing control. A more mature CEO might have been reassured, I guess, but Hal wasn't.
>
> Geneen had his right-hand man go to our headquarters office to lay down conditions to Ferenzi. The move stripped him of 90 percent of his authority and responsibility. It was very specific. It made him a figurehead. He couldn't approve anything. Couldn't give instructions. He was to be totally bypassed by Geneen, never to speak directly to Geneen at all. He was given twenty-four hours to decide.
>
> He consulted with several of his key people, including me, and we tried to persuade him to accept Geneen's conditions. We really wanted him to stay. Ferenzi went back next day and said okay. He accepted the conditions. I happened to be in the office with Geneen's hatchetman, his emissary, who called to tell Geneen. You could hear Geneen's shout—he had to hold the receiver away from his ear— "Goddamn it! I didn't send you over there to get him to agree to these conditions! I sent you over there to get rid of him!"
>
> So my boss, Ferenzi, had the humiliation of accepting these terrible conditions, and then getting fired anyway. His successor was a guy who was a brilliant politician but useless as an executive, a guy who would do anything that Geneen wanted him to do.

Williams himself was fired when he refused to betray a confidence from a fellow manager. "There must be no secrets from Geneen," one senior manager told him before he was politely excused from office. "They make Harold feel like you don't trust him."

## I AM THE WALRUS—AND YOU'RE NOT!

This desire always to be "the central figure" leads to another problem common in bullied companies: the problem of succession. Some have suggested that they actually want the organization to fail once they have moved on, proving, "We were nothing after Jack left."

In September 1983, when Petrie Stores needed someone to come after eighty-one-year-old founder Milton Petrie, *The Wall Street Journal* wrote of Petrie:

> In 56 years, his iron rule has built Petrie from a small hosiery shop in Cleveland to a $600-million empire of women's clothing stores that stretches from Hawaii to the Virgin Islands.

> But that same domineering style has kept the 81-year-old Mr. Petrie from grooming a successor. "Milton is a brilliant person, but unfortunately he doesn't realize we're all mortal, and he isn't making plans to assure the continuity of Petrie Stores," says Gilbert Harrison, a Philadelphia takeover specialist who has tried to persuade Mr. Petrie to merge his company with another retailer. . . .

The *Journal* noted that the average age of the top four executives at Petrie was seventy-one, and continued:

> [Petrie] fired the most recent candidate, 38-year-old Michael Boyle, only seven weeks after hiring him as president and heir apparent. . . . Neither man will discuss the matter, but sources close to the company say that one of the main bones of contention was a conference room built here on Mr. Boyle's orders. Mr. Petrie thought a conference room a needless expense, says one insider, "because all the decisions are made in Milton's office."

Here again the recognizable syndromes of the boss in his bully phase rear their bald little heads: Petrie "has always reserved his harshest rule for those executives closest to him," heaping the greatest abuse on his hand-picked successor (now departed), "subjecting him to some terrible tantrums, often humiliating him in front of other employees."

The problem of succession torments all bullied companies. Take Continental Illinois, whose John Swearingen continually torpedoed all possible successors, including his hand-picked successor William Ogden. The April 24, 1988, edition of *The Wall Street Journal* observed:

> Visitors who came to the bank to see the two top men in Mr. Swearingen's office often noted that Mr. Swearingen would sit behind his desk in a big chair. And beside that large slab of hardwood, in a smaller chair where a secretary might take dictation, would sit Mr. Ogden. "The body language," said one outside adviser to the bank, was "really ugly."

Or CBS's William Paley, who, according to *Channels*, the broadcasting industry's consumer publication, "ran his network like the court at Versailles, and his pampered elite lacked for nothing—except power."

The myth of the Magnificent Bully has haunted American management for a long time. Geneen himself spawned hundreds of admiring little tyrants.

An executive I'll call Wilkerson is the retired president of a national credit corporation. "In the last two years," he says, "I was consulting with a finance company. This fellow, John Smith, was hired as president. He had previously worked for Citibank and ITT. While at ITT, he had become acquainted with Geneen's method of meeting with company presidents.

"Smith decided to run his company of two hundred and fifty employees like ITT. I told him he was making a big mistake, but he went ahead. He would call meetings quickly and run them in a style that would embarrass his managers. He would ask for reports and suggestions and then put them down *hard*. He lasted six months, because the owner of the company—it was closely held by one man— finally listened to his employees and fired him."

## TYRANNOSAURUS WREAKS HAVOC ON
## THOSE WHO LET HIM

The boss who feels free to exercise his bully muscle is not always the top guy around. Sometimes he is simply a deputy empowered by a weak and absent senior executive to make other people's lives miserable—and keep things running. Between a weak boss above and a rank of suckling sycophants below, a tough dude can get a lot of bullying done and hold an entire team of people hostage.

A guy I'll call Ronald is a high-ranking Human Resources person at a huge telecommunications company. He reports that the weakness of his supreme commander opened the door to a reign of "controlled panic" by a bully who knew how to get things done.

"Not too long ago, this company was ruled by a cruel guy, a real tyrant," he states, "a vice president who had accumulated enormous power by winning the confidence of the president, a nice guy, I guess, who found the bully a handy hatchetman for certain things that needed to be done. The abusive bully effectively ran our company. He ruled by fear. He cursed people out in the vilest language, sometimes in a two A.M. phone call to their homes. He once told me, 'If I pay someone $125,000 a year, I can do anything to him.' His subordinates ceased to be human to him. He felt he owned them." Ronald adds:

The guy was particularly upset by any sign of what he interpreted as disloyalty, which in reality could be something as minor as simply thinking for yourself. His orders were from God.

Those who could take early retirement, or find another job, left. But it was hard. In our field, there aren't too many competitors to go to. Many of the people who stayed were utterly destroyed in terms of their usefulness to the company. He punished people for thinking constructively, imaginatively. So they're unwilling to take chances.

Now, this guy in effect ran the entire show, because he ran the president. He was at the president's knee and at everyone else's throat. And he was a master at manipulating the results of the company, on paper. Our company has never been characterized by the same kind of politics and infighting you might see elsewhere. The people here are nice. So he ran roughshod over others who had no idea how to handle him, including his own boss.

He was more entrepreneurial than anyone else, he was very good at what he did. People like this can destroy an organization. This man had absolute power for about two years, and then suddenly the numbers went flat and the big boss needed a fall guy. Because he had assumed total control, and alienated so many people, he became it. If he had been in charge for ten years, well, I think he could have destroyed the company. He was building an organization that couldn't think.

Yet for all its lack of long-term effectiveness, even though *bully management doesn't work in the long run*, it continues to be pursued by those who *haven't got any idea how else to run a business*.

Bob Jacoby, former boss at Bates Advertising, was a firm believer in management by boot and fist. "There is no question in my mind that a successful president runs a dictatorship . . . a company where things happen because he or she decides they should happen," he said in a 1980 speech to the American Association of Ad Agencies.

This proud dictatorship, in practice, can look pretty ugly. "He tended to pit people against each other," said one advertising executive when Jacoby was ousted from Bates after the acquisition of that agency by Saatchi. "Loyalty was very important to him—he tried to judge people by their loyalty. He would sort of work people against each other to see how they came out. But because of that, he lost sight of everyday realities."

Bullies always do. Because, to them, there are no everyday realities. There is, in fact, no reality. Just fear and hatred and power.

A prosecutor I'll call Todd is assistant district attorney at a huge D.A.'s office somewhere south of Chicago. His boss, who himself works for a boss miles above and somewhere far away, is widely perceived as a rampant disappointment everywhere but in the office, where he holds sway with an abandon denied him in normal life. In this case, we have a complete profile of a bully in full flower: the brutality, the moodiness, the manipulative favoritism, the tiny, unattractive human hiding behind bombast and circumstance. Those who cannot stand up to the man are doomed. "He takes pleasure in degrading people, treating them like shit," says Todd. "And while he doesn't deal too well with people who stand up to him, those who *don't* stand up, he walks all over."

He's a big, fat bully. An infantile person, a sadist who enjoys making people feel uncomfortable and enjoys that, squeezing them down, making them feel small, exercising his power, which he has a lot of.

He's brilliant, I have to hand it to him. I only know from hearsay, of course, he never really struck me as anything special, but I give that to him. He took his sabbatical to teach, you know, but I don't think it worked out well, because he came back. I think students were turned off, he didn't relate well. I can see that from the way he works with junior people here. He screams. Case preparation is supposed to be a learning process, but it wasn't with him. He would tear out your pages and fling them at you, screaming.

"My first day at the general staff meeting was my first inkling of what an asshole he was," says Todd, who set the proper tone right away. "We were talking about this point of law, and he got very defensive. He challenged me, and it turned out that I was right. I won. He has a brilliant mind, but he wasn't aware of this law. He was combative. And I stood up to him, and showed my mettle. There were a couple of other senior people there, and I didn't back down. I was tough. I think that's why he and I—although we never got along—formed a sort of truce almost right away."

Those who aren't tough, who look to the bully to provide support and mentoring, endure psychological pain that can be excruciating. For loyalty is the closest a bully can get to love and friendship. And he returns that love in the only way his twisted spirit knows how— with an exercise of blunt power.

The bully's concept of loyalty is grounded firmly in the traditional "What have you done for me lately?" scenario. And there's nothing generous or classy in his nature.

Annie, vice president of a small independent production company, learned this fact in the early part of her working career.

When I got back from Charlottesville, I got married and took a year off. After that, I needed a job. The head administrator of my husband's medical school said, "There's a guy who needs a secretary. He's crazy, but it's only for a year." So I went and interviewed with him, and he hired me. After a couple of months, we began having psychological warfare because we really disliked each other. I'd rip off a corner of a piece of paper. I'd refuse to get him the Bics he wanted and substitute a generic brand. He'd call me in my office, and I'd keep the opera on so he could hear it over the phone. He'd pull Captain Queeg stuff. Get furious and yell and scream.

He was head of the committee on committees. He hired another bright young overeducated woman to be a lab assistant. She wanted to go to med school. He wrote her glowing letters of recommendation to med schools. She was admitted. She wanted to take a couple of months off before she went, and announced that sometime in May. He went batshit. Said she was delinquent in her responsibility and should continue working and this was evidence that she couldn't be a doctor. Sent letters to all of the places rescinding his original recommendation. "Remember that wonderful person I told you about? Well, she's not wonderful anymore." He wanted to be a mentor, and once he wasn't anymore, he was going to be a nemesis. He turned on her because she hadn't lived up to his idea of what a mentoree should be.

In fact, just when you think you have become his friend, he snaps the trap shut. Here's what a friend of mine, Gary M., sales manager of a television-station group, said about his bully, while their mutual honeymoon was still in flower:

> I've always worked under the principle that you can turn your boss into your ally. That's the deepest and darkest and hardest thing to do, I think. It's like going for the brass ring. I think within the limits of Lawrence's perverse, self-destructive personality, the implosive part that defeats every other part, within the limits of that, I think I've done it. By not being afraid of him when everyone else was.
>
> I said to myself, This is a very broad portfolio over here. It's deep, too. They asked me if I wanted to switch bosses during a reorganization. And I said, Yeah, I want Lawrence to be my boss. It was an abrupt left turn. Nobody expected it. Lawrence was incredibly flattered and invited me into the office and said, "You're my only reportee right now. You're mine." Six months later, he took the country. He had the capital staked out with his flag flying on it.
>
> It was like I was this sort of young, kind of fast-running horse that needed a special kind of handler, and they gave me my head, and I chose the dude they were tapping on anyway. It was a vote of confidence from the provinces, but early. And this made him a deep and lasting ally of mine. You need people like that, powerful people. I mean, only assholes and failures work in a bubble. Donald Trump. His janitor. But everybody else needs friends.

But within a year, Gary had been demoted to a smaller position in the head office, which he hated. And if you mention the name of his friend and ally now, you will be treated to a stream of invective that speaks more of hurt and loss than of simple job discomfort.

The truth is, the bully inflicts the most pain on those who get near to him. So don't.

Take this tale from the world of academia of the sick relationship between my pal Brian, now a newspaper reporter, then a graduate student, and his adviser, the head of the English department.

The pathology—and the lesson—in this story is quite clear. The bully can't effectively bully until he establishes a bully relationship with *you*. To do that, he's got to suck you in first. This honeymoon phase is most perilous, as the tyrant softens you up for the psychic kill.

When I went for my master's, I rented a small office for myself and began to write. I signed up for a workshop with a very interesting experimental writer I'll call Gold. Everything I wrote he had nothing but kudos for, and said, All you have to do is put together three or four of these and sell them. He was supportive. Then in the fall, I signed up for Gold's formal class.

I went for this pre-class interview with him, and I brought my story to show him, and he read it, and he flipped through it at lightning speed, and went, "Ah, Brian, you're good, you're real good." He whips it out of my hands, "You're good, Brian, but this isn't serious stuff, Brian." He said, "Okay, you can come to the class." And said it started on Monday night. I said, "Monday night is Rosh Hashanah. I'll be having dinner with my family." He said, "You're not religious. You're not wearing a yarmulke. I'm more religious. My best friend is a doyen of Jewish writers, and if I asked her to be at my class, she would be. So be there! Literature is your god! Literature! So be there!" He's yelling as I'm leaving. "Be there! Be there!" I felt very uncomfortable. Sacrilegious. And I always had this slumping feeling that by deciding to go, that God paid me back over the next six months.

Indeed, by agreeing to be bullied in their initial encounter, Brian had sold his soul to the power that would very shortly abuse him.

The first night we had this introduction, and Gold is going, "You guys better watch out for Brian, he's got the goods here." So naturally I didn't read for a couple of weeks. Then I did. And if he stops you, then that's it for the rest of the night. If he stops you, that's stupid writing, then you're out on the rim for the rest of the night. He's powerful, extraordinarily manipulative, and bright, and useful in his comments. But he's also as narrow as anyone on this planet. The third week I read, and Gold stops me after about three paragraphs, and says, "Stop, Brian, stop, this is dumb writing, with every sentence

BULLY

you're pushing the reader away. You're smarter than this." I was
blown away. I'd been a reporter for eight years, and never faced any
criticism as devastating as that. And everyone gets into it, a group
experience, a little cult.

He was a great note writer. He would write me notes extolling my
talent and praising me, then he'd rip me up in front of the others. It
all fed into being crazy, this terrible Oedipal kind of father-son relationship with this guy. You set yourself up to be bruised.

Don't be fooled. No matter how nurturing or gentle the bully can
be, he's after your strength, your heart, not so that he can use it, but
so that, like the vampire, he can drain it of strength to feed himself.
And it doesn't feel good to be drained of energy, of self. Brian
remembers: "I did not write for eight months or more after the
workshop. I read for the final time in the next-to-last workshop. I got
through about a page. Then I stopped and started weeping, and
cried and cried in front of eighteen people for about half an hour. I
walked home that night. I don't often think about stepping in front
of a car, but I was walking a thin line along the curb. And I don't
think I'm one of the really crazy types."

Maybe he didn't start that way. But under the heel of the crazy
bully, few can keep their lids on straight. In such an environment,
not being there to be bullied can be 99 percent of the load—and a
very good strategy.

Unless you'd rather be a toad.


## THE ATTACK OF THE SNIVELING TOADIES

To build his power and sap yours, the bully is more than brutal—he
makes brutality a virtue, a way of life, and the chief expression of *the
way he feels about things most of the time*. To make his adjustment
work, however, he's got to provide himself with the philosophical
underpinnings for his brutal approach, and then find people willing
to kiss his ring.

Take the words of this bully, as reported by my friend Harry, a
criminal attorney in a large urban law firm. "My boss Ed was very
moody," he recalls. "He had a sign on his desk that said, MY MOOD IS
SUBJECT TO CHANGE AT A MOMENT'S NOTICE, like he was proud of his
inconsistency. There was a photo on the wall in back of his desk. It

was that Pulitzer Prize-winning photograph of the mayor of Saigon blowing a man's brains out, and I asked him, 'Why do you have that particular picture up there?" and he replied, 'That's the stuff,' hitting his fist into his open palm, 'of real manhood, the moment of truth! He claimed he was capable of doing that. He admired that. The ability to aim and blow another guy away."

The philosophical commitment to brutality and unpredictability is one of his greatest clubs in a more consistently human universe. It's a weapon most effective, quite naturally, *against those within striking distance.* Harry continues:

> Because you never knew what kind of mood Ed would be in, people were afraid of him. I was uncomfortable, too, but I took no shit. As a result, we worked closely together only once. That time was okay, I guess. Nothing terrible happened. But we didn't like each other, that was clear. So now I work with *his* deputy, and everyone's a lot happier.

Just because Harry wasn't willing to play psychic ball, however, didn't mean there weren't many on hand to make the bully's solution work. The bottom line is, unfortunately, that most people need decisive leadership—even if it's decisively terrible.

In the vacuum of rationality, the bully can exercise his evil whims to the utmost—with the complicity and participation of both his bosses and subordinates.

> Ed also loves to play favorites. He does it to the hilt. He loves to show who he likes and who he doesn't and is very obvious about it. But even those he plays for favorites don't like him. Look. He's just a scumbag of the first degree. Incapable of giving praise. Respected by everyone for his mind and legal acumen. A bright man and a terrible human being.

> And the thing that's interesting is that his personality is reflected in the entire front office. Nobody there knows how to relate to employees. As long as you produce briefs, they don't give a shit if you're dying. The office manager is a female counterpart to him. She has about five sycophants suckling onto her, and it makes everybody sick. She plays favorites, too, and lets you know it. She lets out her bitterness. She'll come in and say, "You have a brief due next week." And I'll lean back and say, "Yes?" or "What of it?"

> And it kills her—she's afraid of me. Because I let my temper come out

a tiny bit and then rein it in. I never yell or raise my voice or pound my fist, of course. That would be suicide. I just acquire a note of authority in my voice and stand tall and cut to the root of what they want to say to me. They like to push you and make you feel bad and assert their power. They back down when you stand up and talk to them and let them know that you're game for a discussion—person to fucking person—on that particular issue.

To "acquire a note of authority," the bedrock of an anti-bully strategy, the employee must prove to possess enough of the right stuff to get by without the good wishes of management. That can be difficult, especially for screwups, which we all occasionally are.

For the contempt of the bully for others is wide and deep, as huge as his internal contempt for himself.

And woe be unto you if—after a strict policy of proud no sucking up—you give him a reason to strike.

For a peek at what happens when an employee isn't very effective, is, in fact, downright stupid, listen to this proud bully, a woman I'll call Margaret, the senior editor at a national woman's magazine. "I am stuck now with such an idiot employee," she moans. "I gave her a copy of a magazine that had an article in it that I wanted a Xerox of. I give it to her and say, "Here. Give me a copy of this." And she Xeroxes *the cover*. Unbelievable." Naturally, this malfeasance was only the tip of the iceberg. Margaret continues:

We got about twenty letters from clients complaining about a certain policy, and so I wrote a form letter, but I wanted it individually typed up, and at the top I typed, "Dear irate customer," and she typed that in. If I'd written "Insert name here," would she have written that? I tried to explain, but she didn't understand the enormity of the problem, she was irritated. Her attitude was, "Well, why didn't you say so in the first place?" Everything gets turned around so *I'm* the one who's let *her* down.

We have an arrangement with a drug company. So I got a diaphragm for free, and they sent it to me. I have an "Urgent" box on my desk, and this package comes saying "Ramses" all over it, and my stupid assistant puts it on my desk, and all afternoon people walked in and out of my office and here it is on my desk. When I tried to explain why I was upset, she said, "Next time you get a diaphragm in the mail, keep it in a manilla envelope." I'm only going to get one once every two years!

The bottom line is, she can't make the connection between things. I think she's really stupid. I think she also did a lot of things that resulted in brain-cell damage at one point in her life. She's a disaster on typing and filing, too, because she can't figure out anything, everything has to be spelled out, because she can't remember, or she remembers it wrong. I asked her to go through my mail and sort it, but she can't even do that. In my important file, I got a letter about the opening of the baseball season. I don't need that.

This woman can't even take a message from my husband. And half of the men who call up, she thinks *are* my husband. I had a fight with Gary, and then a guy named Barry called and she told me it was my husband, and so I picked up the phone and said all kinds of mushy things until the person said, "I think you have the wrong guy."

It's quite obvious what the bully would like to do with this particular knothead. But, in spite of her power and influence within this organization, she can't. Why? "The problem is, there have been a lot of firings and staff rearrangings here, and she's friendly with a lot of people, because she's basically sweet," Margaret says. "So I'm hoping for the big fuckup, where the reason for her firing is clear to everybody, because with all these other firings and whatnots going on, it's very upsetting to everybody, and it's hard to fire someone at will."

In other words, just because you're not a remora attached to your boss's power doesn't mean you're necessarily doomed.

On the other hand, it doesn't hurt to help out now and then.

## TOADYING IS TOUGH WORK

"I sent my assistant on this errand," says a woman bully at a software-publishing company in New England. "My husband, Brett, was going off to South America, and he needed underpants, and I sent my assistant to Jordan Marsh with my charge card, to pick out Jockey shorts. This amused her. She said it was the only time in her life when she'd have that opportunity. She saw it as a way to help me out of a jam. She perceived *her* job as helping me to get *my* job done. I sent her to Newbury Street to buy a shirt for my father, and she thought it was an adventure. She was handed two hundred bucks and told to pick out the nicest shirts she could find. My former assistant wouldn't have. She wouldn't have understood that things like that could be *fun,* and that sometimes a boss needs help in other parts of her life while she is getting business done."

This quality of *needing help* in an otherwise controlled and potent existence, is at the very heart of bullydom—and another important key to how the bully can be managed.

If you can be the one who's providing that assistance, your existence, while hard, may be relatively secure. But no one says it's going to be easy. The bully often enjoys a potent sense of *infantile entitlement,* and will have a tantrum when confronted by something that challenges that assumption. Like a baby, he expects even his unspoken demands to be met.

Brandon, manager of Employee Communications at a rust-belt manufacturing behemoth, faced this problem with his boss, and came away with a case of acute public embarrassment. He relates:

I planned and put together this executive think-tank kind of meeting, very high pressure, high prestige. And everything was going fine until we got to lunch. It was a typical Fred Smithson meeting. There always has to be one thing that Fred is upset about. This time it was the luncheon meats. There were no salads on the buffet table, just cold cuts and cheeses and breads and stuff. And mustard. No mayonnaise. That's what I ordered. And Fred comes up to the table and starts raging at me, saying, "I thought every single person in this organization knows I like pasta salads! How could you have nothing but cold cuts! I hate cold cuts!" And he was really furious. He wasn't kidding. He was on my ass about it all the way through lunch. And after I went out and had about six chickens slaughtered and turned into salad and brought in for his pleasure, he begins the afternoon session by telling the assembled executives of the company, "Our jobs are about detail and about drudgery, and a lot of you might have noticed I thought Brandon did not have what he should have had here. So I brought it up with him, and I think we worked it out. 'Nuff said."

And in that way he tried to distance himself from his display of anger. That's what I have to put up with here. Everything else goes perfectly, but there's no mayonnaise for his high-fiber bread, so he goes crazy. It makes me sick. I thought it was a very nice lunch, in fact. There wasn't a scrap left over.

In short, the bully has tremendous, immature needs. You can help meet them, when it seems appropriate. But again, don't think that by helping this child solve his immediate problems, you're going to earn any undying gratitude.

Bullies have very short memories.


## THANKS TO YOU—IT'S SPREADING!

All too often, thanks to the admiration in which bully management is held by the American business establishment, the fledgling who studies under the heel of the successful bully masters the techniques and becomes one, too.

No one ever lost money underestimating the ability of middle management to replicate the deficiencies of its bosses.

Daniels, former boss at a humongous international bank, fell from a summit of power at a young age, he states, due to his "hard-ass approach," an approach he learned at his academy, one of the largest banking institutions in the world. His professor was another Bad Caesar who pulled off the act very well.

> My first boss, whom I'll call Dick Peters, was thirty-four when he took over my group. This was quite typical of things back then, when the company would give young people an enormous amount of power and then see if they would sink or swim.
>
> I was young and naive and extremely bright. Peters was tall and handsome, about six feet four inches, with striking blond hair. He dominated any room he entered, and women literally swooned over him. He was not squeamish about the problems his physical presence created for others. He had incredible self-possession and confidence and a tremendous brain.
>
> But he was very much on the defense. You would never have guessed it. I was his chief of staff, and he was a lovable father figure to us. But he was depending on us as sycophants. He gave us recognition, promotions, raises, public praise. But the abuse he gave us was also incredible. There was tremendous pressure in our business, we were a crisis organization for years. We went from thirty-five people to more than two thousand in one-and-a-half years. We built a corner office for him with all kinds of special insulation, but when he yelled, there were times you could hear him all over the floor. People would walk out of his office white-faced.
>
> I made the mistake of assuming his characteristics with none of his

assets. He would call me in and shout, "Did you know expenses are out of control? What are you doing about it?" I would whip around and write a memo to my staff and be hard-nosed without ever thinking about the question. Expenses weren't out of control. We were growing real fast, and it cost money! But I just didn't think—I imitated.

Sometimes his willingness to do the oddball thing was the seat of his brilliance. He took risks—things no one who reported to him would dare to do. I was at one time responsible for the development of retail banking terminals that were to be placed in all branches. I pity all the people who worked with us on the project—our suppliers, our employees, our wives. I had a prototype test facility built and installed. It had a round base and was installed on masonite on the floor of various branches. Dick wanted to see what kind of physical abuse the table could take. So he walked into a big branch one noon and kicked the damn thing over. It broke the masonite and smashed all over the room.

So Dick returns to the office and calls me in and screams at me— "What the fuck! The table fell over and I almost killed somebody!" He didn't tell me *he* had kicked it over, that I found out later. I almost had a heart attack. And it was true that the diameter of the base had to be widened—Dick was right about that. It was just an unnecessarily hard way to learn it.

Dick ended up pissing off his executive peers, which really freaked him out. He got really stressful, yelled even more, told too many people what they should be doing and where they could put it. He told another executive vice president in an elevator he didn't know what the fuck he was doing. Finally, he got fired. Or left. You know how these things go.

In the vacuum created by the departure of his crazy boss, Daniels was promoted. He was now thirty-four himself.

I felt I could do no wrong. I had a company car, good money, power, respect. Then, six months after I took the job, my boss took me out to lunch and told me he was transferring me to a staff job downtown. I had lost everything. He thought my brains were scrambled. I guess in those short six months I had managed to piss off an incredible number of people. Now I'm in a full-fledged identity crisis. And I spend most of my time regrouping.

The acceptance of hard-ass tactics throughout American business is enough to have brought institutional bullydom to new heights.

Bullies are everywhere. Once established, they can move right in and create new Huns out of what were formally reasonable individuals.

A guy I'll call Tom is associate general counsel at the Chicago headquarters of a cable-television concern. "My boss, Len, was essentially the kind of guy who would go out of his way to step on an ant," Tom remembers. "He could be bland, but when he was riled, he thought screaming was the way of expressing his power, particularly when he knew he was dealing with someone who couldn't fight back":

> He'd never ask for advice and consensus. In fact, he saw staff meetings as nothing more than pure socialization. He'd call staff meetings on our own time, at eight in the morning. It meant nothing to him. He lived on Rush Street and just walked to work a few minutes early. But for us Glencoe types to get in a half hour early meant taking two earlier trains. We made jokes about it, but no one ever confronted him about it. That would have been suicide. Challenging the marching orders.

> But Len himself was a copy of *his* boss, a guy I'll call Rob Ponzini, who was a complete maniac. After several years working for him, Len started assimilating all the bad aspects of Rob's personality.

> Rob wouldn't manage with anger. It wasn't necessary. He just made an imperceptible shift in your standing. Your demise could be based on your performance, or on your wardrobe. I've heard him say, "He doesn't dress like a businessman." And the guy would work for years and years at the same job, and do a good job, and never get promoted. Most probably without being told why.

> One thing I really hated about him was that he surrounded himself with suckups and then pitted them against each other. He'd take one aside and say, "I guess I shouldn't be telling you this, but Biff Forbisher has been sticking needles in your back all week." In this way, he would foster distrust between all the people in the department, dividing them so they never would gang up on him but spend most of their time fighting each other.

> Rob recognized talent, I'll give him that. He was threatened by it. He saw it, but liked to keep it in a glass jar. He also knew how to control the entire organization. His modus operandi was to get in tight with the chairman. Insert himself as a veto person on deals. The managers who want the deal to happen then have to suck up to him. And God help you if he discovers a weakness in your proposal. He'll go straight to the chairman, not to you, and say, "Did you know that this deal will

lose the company ten million bucks?" In this way, he earns points with the chairman, and makes potential competitors look bad at the same time.

The way the bully transforms his subordinates into himself is at the heart of the organizational malaise. Tom concludes his assessment of his boss:

The longer you work for a guy, the more you become like him.

And there were times when I could see myself becoming a bully, too. When I didn't say no to him, and wish I had, and then was forced to implement a decision I didn't believe in. I'm thinking of this specific person. In the normal course of things, she would have gotten a raise. But it was decided by Rob and Len that we had to get her attention. I didn't say no, because I felt I had to go along with my bosses in military lockstep. And she didn't get it. And we had a very rough time. She improved grudgingly, never admitting that she needed to, and she got her raise in the end but was completely destroyed as a worker. All because I didn't follow my gut and take a stand. I guess I thought Len and Rob would have thought I was a pansy, and Rob in particular is a maniac and you never know what he'd do to you if you didn't go along. So I became a prick, just like them.

## BULLIES, BULLIES EVERYWHERE—AND
## HOW OUR HEARTS DO SHRINK!

All sophisticated motivations aside, your basic bully gets his jollies seeing smaller life forms cringe and fester. That's right. It's personal, and don't you forget it.

Chas, a journalist, found this out when he was a staff reporter at a major national financial publication. "I had a boss who was a zombie—everyone hated him," he says.

He loved to torture people, knowing they thought he was a jerk, and that they feared him. We had this slogan: Dick Larson before he Dicks you. My wife, Nancy, turns in an article to this guy, and she's very nervous, as everyone is when they submit one. You knew the article had made it when he brought it over to this wire basket. And you could tell by watching what he was going to do. Everyone was watching, but he acted like they weren't.

So Dick takes Nancy's story. He turns so she can't see. He puts her story underneath his blotter, takes a number of sheets of paper, blank, and pretends to read them for about five or ten minutes, rubbing his eyes, groaning, wincing. Nancy is sweating blood. He gets to the last page, crumples it all up into a ball, and tosses it into the wastebasket. Nancy starts to cry, then goes into the bathroom and throws up. Meanwhile, he goes over and puts the real story into the wire basket. He was just tormenting her for his own amusement, because he's a madman. He knew we were all obsessed with him, and he loved it.

Sane employees who wish to remain that way must never allow their guts to be manipulated by the bully, must simply play intelligent politics and wait for the thug to destroy himself. And keep reminding themselves that he *will*.

Ronald, the Human Resources guy whose weak president engendered a powerful bully-de-camp, had the satisfaction of helping his particular bully bite the dust. "I'm in Human Resources," he says. "It's my role to stop this kind of thing if I can."

So I went to the guy and said, "Look, your strength doesn't come from beating on people. Why don't you become a statesman instead? You know the job well enough." And the guy got tremendously frightened, I think because he already knew he was a little crazy. To know I saw it, too, really scared him. From that point on, he tried to get rid of me. Went to my boss, who wasn't listening. His vindictiveness knew no bounds. He tried to prevent me from traveling, blocking me on all kinds of small things. But you know, in a big company it's rather easy to go around people, and I generally succeeded in getting what I wanted.

Finally, the guy made one enemy too many: An executive vice president who was sent in from headquarters to see how we could be helped to compete in an unregulated environment. Before, as long as we were delivering our almost-a-billion dollars in earnings to the parent corporation, nobody cared. But suddenly, in a downturning environment, management became an issue. And this new executive knew all about our resident bully. In fact, he had a close friend who had taken early retirement to escape his brutality. One of the new guy's first actions was to fire the SOB. He did it as cruelly as he could, too, in front of the entire senior management team. It was great.

A happy ending. And not an enormously unusual one, either. The bully, like most crazy bosses, is in his heart a hunter of his own destruction. Eventually, his humanity catches up with him, and he goes, leaving his subjects liberated from his daily presence if not from the burden of the potent emotions he has stirred up within them.

For even when he is gone, like a bad parent, he is not forgotten, and the long reach of his tyranny can touch us from beyond even the grave. Listen to Jeffrey, a former sportswriter, speaking of a boss who was far more than just that.

I'll start and end with the late and *unlamented* Fred Barkin, who tortured me every moment of my waking life for five years, just by his presence in the same building. He couldn't brook anything about me. My youth. My hair. My mustache. My jeans. And my sort of wise-ass, bleeding-heart view of life. Sent me notes that said, "Cut the New York sociological crap from your copy. Just give us the facts."

He sent me on the road with Triple-A, hayseed, tobacco-spitting base-ball players, down to Miami for soccer, you name it. In fact, he used the issue of travel to pry into my personal life. He wanted to send me on the road all the time, perpetually, and finally I said no. "I have a happy marriage, and I'd like to keep it that way." So I go to a function, and Barkin walks up to my wife, Anne, who is with me that night, and he pinches her on the cheek and says, "This must be the reason you don't want to go on the road, huh?" It grossed us both out. Smarmy fucker.

If he didn't like my take on somebody, he'd rewrite in his corny but vile way. He said I wasn't a "professional," that I didn't have the heart of a true professional.

I clung to my hatred for him even after I left the paper because I felt he had somehow reached into my guts and pulled them out. Slowly. Taken a piece of my life, and I wasn't going to rest until I'd gotten even. I couldn't stand to be in the same room with him. It got to the point that at the Olympics in Montreal, where a staff breakfast was required, I would pass notes to another reporter who would then relay them to Barkin. I couldn't even speak to him. He knew I hated him. And he did everything he could to fuel it. I talked about him obsessively. Because he was also a convenient excuse for everything that was wrong in my life. Which I think is part of the attraction of having a serious enemy. They're sort of a slag heap for all your jus-tifications and rationalizations.

I never really got even. Over the years, once I left his employ, I felt I had to read him with even more scrupulous attention than ever be-fore. I would clip and circle the most egregious stuff in his column and keep an exhaustive file, so that sometime down the line I would be able to use it as ammunition in some imaginary battle that was continuing in my mind. I would remind him every few years that I existed by taking a cheap shot at him in print. And he attacked me for being the slowest deadline reporter that he ever worked with—anonymously. "That's the kind of guy he is," I'd say to myself. "He doesn't even have the guts to use his name."

When Barkin died, it was like a portion of my life had been returned to me, because I no longer had to obsess over him. I didn't know what to do with all that free time. So now I'm looking for new enemies. But they won't be the same, because that relationship was really larger than life. . . .

And they say that only love lasts forever.


## ACTION POINTS: THE BULLY

Now let's take a look at the short-term strategies you can implement based on what we now know about the crazy boss in his most brutal guise.

- *Be ostentatiously loyal:* Bullies demand a *visible show of fealty,* day in and day out. This means looking out for his interests and bringing matters that could cause him discomfort to his attention before anyone else does. In political struggles, it may involve conveying other people's planned machinations against him to his attention. Information is power in any workplace. The things you know, as a subordinate, are important to him. Offer him juicy tidbits of scuttlebutt as liberally and as often as you can, creating the very public impression that you and your supreme commander are one. Ask his advice often and take it literally. When it becomes necessary in hostile meetings, take a bullet that was meant for him. But make sure he sees you do it. Loyalty is one thing. Loyalty with no prospect of return is just dumb.
- *Suck up, but with dignity:* The bully doesn't want a festering, bobbing, nodding yes-man hanging around. He likes to think his guys are just two points less macho than he his. This can be delicate. Not long ago, I was complimenting my current boss on the ostensible brilliance of one of his ideas. This was fine, and he

took it with good grace. Then I went over the line. "Nobody but you could have done this, Ned," I said, realizing immediately that I was gushing. "You don't have to butter me up, Bing," he said, frowning. I won't make that mistake again.

- *Tough guys don't toady:* Never allow general, pleasant sucking up to degenerate into fawning slavishness. Ask yourself: "Do I have anything on my agenda that is not related to serving the bully?" If you don't you're in danger of falling over the line into being a nauseating slave to his moods and brutality. Work to establish function that has nothing to do with what's on his mind today. If you're occasionally too busy to minister to his needs, it wouldn't hurt. Remember, this guy wants to see you as a proud soldier in his service, not a sniveling worm ready to spit-shine his boots.

- *Provide life assistance when you can:* Bullies are in almost constant pain. They are frustrated and disappointed by existence. Anything you can do to smooth his professional path on a daily basis will be very much appreciated. If you know he likes to read the trade news while on the road in order to stay informed, see if you can get them faxed to his hotel. If he likes toys, buy him one of those little boxes that curse people out electronically. Whatever. Any *small* attempt to ease his troubled way—with no professional agenda at all—will pay off in spades. Keep it cool, however. You're not offering affection. You're offering a little bit of comfort on the hard road.

- *No love, please, even if offered:* Bullies get maudlin now and then, and may even close the door and tell you their life stories. Don't be fooled. The flip side of this bogus emotion is resentment that he has revealed his soft underbelly. He'll take it out on you later. If he or she puts his arm around you, invites you to drinks, takes you aside on the corporate retreat for a heart-to-heart, it's easy to think you've crossed over into some magical kingdom where all sins will be forgiven and life is soft and warm. You haven't. So enjoy his momentary lapse into humanity. But keep your head about you. That way you won't be disappointed later.

- *Stay out of striking distance:* Not being around is a terrific way to avoid being killed by flying shrapnel when a bomb goes off. And it will. The bully is essentially dissatisfied with life. Eventually, he will explode and take a few of those nearest into prison for torture and, sometimes, execution. Have you got a field operation out in the boonies somewhere? Another office across town where people are into production, instead of planning? Go there periodically. Establish the fact that you are at times out of the office on real business. Then get lost when you see he's in the killing vein. If you must remain in physical proximity to the bad dude (like in a grumpy budget session), establish psychological and emotional distance immediately upon noticing the darkness is upon him. In other words, shut up and speak when you're spoken to, softly. This is not the time for honesty or self-justification. Survival is the name of this game.

- *Show a little muscle now and then:* If he's not in high dudgeon about something, however, don't hesitate to push back when pushed. No, don't make it an issue of pride, or he'll squash you like a bug. Base your resistance on the facts at hand. A friend of mine was working late one evening on the eve of a vacation. She had almost wrapped things up when her bully came into her office. "Let's start planning the June meeting tomorrow at eight," the bully said. "I'm going on vacation tomorrow, Les, you know that," said my friend. The bully's brow clouded right over. "I can see where your loyalty lies," he said. There was a frosty pause. "I'm loyal, Les," said my friend. "But I need my vacation, and my work is in good shape. And I'm going on it. I hope we won't have to go to the mat on this." The two stared at each other. "Okay," the bully said, finally. "Have a good time, and let's get cracking when you come back." And that's just what they did. Once again, remember that the bully wants to bully people he respects. Once you've lost that cachet, you've hurt yourself more than you could possibly have helped yourself by any single submission.

- *Make friends. You'll need them:* This is a strategy that will serve you well when dealing with the bad manager in all his nutty phases. The only true, long-lasting protection from the cult of personality that surrounds the crazy boss is *organizational.* Keep on good terms with your peers and your boss's peers. Do work for anyone who asks you. Provide function that transcends any one individual's needs. When your crazy boss attacks you, or when he eventually goes down in flames, you do not want people to say, "Mort? You mean the wormy little guy who works for that asshole Hunsacker?" You want people to say, "Gee, I know Mort. He's okay. In fact, he's done a lot of stuff for me personally. He also knows how to hold a drink."

- *Nip the small ones in the bud, Bud:* Bullies do not bounce out full grown from the head of Zeus. They start as tiny bullies, bullying tiny people. If you're one of the tiny, and your boss himself or herself still has a lot of bosses, you don't have to put up with the same amount of crap you would if he were president already. My first boss was a woman with a foul temper who tormented anyone who would let her. When she started to yell and tear paper, I would simply say, "Excuse me, April, I think I have a call on hold." And I would stroll out of her office. Later, I would poke my head in on some pretext and reestablish relations. After a while, she learned that it wasn't as much fun to bully me as it was to make her secretary cry. So she did that instead. Meanwhile, I was making friends with her boss. Eventually, I took her job. Who says there are no happy endings in the workplace?
- *Keep on hating:* As hard as it may be to keep the fires burning, never let them smolder and die out. Sure, you may see him in his more human moments, moments full of doubt, grief, or confusion. Worse, after years of appearing loyal and true, you may eventually come to feel that way. That's natural. It's hard to live a lie for any extended period of time. But remember the basic tenet of all crazy-boss relations: he can only own your soul if you give it to him. Don't.

The complex of behaviors that characterize the bully—brutality, the demand for control, the thirst for loyalty that need not be returned—floats on a sea of insecurity that is as deep and ancient as the life of the bully itself. When the content of that sea of fear rises above the bully and overwhelms him, he is transformed into something else altogether: the same monster with a different face.

CHAPTER THREE

# PARANOID

And NUH is the letter I use to spell Nutches
Who live in small caves, known as Nitches, for hutches
These Nutches have troubles, the biggest of which is
The fact there are many more Nutches than Nitches
Each Nutch in a Nitch knows that some other Nutch
Would like to move into his Nitch very much.
So each Nutch in a Nitch has to watch that small Nitch
Or Nutches who haven't got Nitches will snitch.

Dr. Seuss
*On Beyond Zebra*

aranoia is a two-headed beast.

Anxiety and distrust are probably the sanest reaction to life as we know it. Rational paranoia is therefore endemic, a pervasive sense of wariness that every member of an organization feels when confronting the crazy environment.

The voices of the paranoid are everywhere. "I have flashes that my level of management will be eliminated," says one magazine editor. "I tell myself they won't do it. We're too valuable. But there are moments when I'm reading *The Wall Street Journal* when I get a terrible attack. It's paralyzing. I stare at a spreadsheet, and I can't concentrate because I feel that any second the guillotine is going to come down. Paranoia is my own skin."

A mid-level executive in a retail clothing concern says, "Everything your boss does becomes a test, and when he fails, or you do, you get paranoid. Is he going to say hello? Be friendly? Why didn't he take me out to lunch? I like lunch. Why did he circulate that guy's memo, not mine? The possibilities are endless."

An account executive at an office that sells TV times says, "I'm not talking about thinking things won't work out for the best. I'm talking about people who wake up in the middle of the night, drenched in a variety of fluids."

And finally, an ad executive I know: "Even paranoids have enemies."

Beyond sane fears, however, lies the land of inappropriate, crazy paranoia, which is another thing altogether, particularly when it afflicts a boss and fuels his brutality and natural suspiciousness.

Here's a good description of the classic managerial paranoid from an architect in a large metropolitan firm:

The man would sit in his office behind a locked door, and you could stand in the anteroom and hear him screaming at people. I went to a meeting where he literally picked up a sheaf of papers and threw it at everyone. We used to call him Plastic Man, because he didn't have any facial reactions. A Napoleonic weirdo throwing a sheaf of papers. He was a serious psycho case, not the run-of-the-mill neurotic, and that became obvious to everybody.

Like, he would call an 8:00 A.M. all-departments meeting, and he'd let one of his henchmen run the meeting, and he would sit in a corner like a teacher taking attendance. As you walked in, you would see him check off your name on the list.

He was a perfectionist. When we did this proposal to the city, he demanded that we hand-proof all 150 copies before they were distributed. And they were printed, you know, so every one was just like the others, which made it a pretty stupid exercise. Nevertheless, we had to do it. It took hours. Trucks were waiting to deliver these reports to city hall, and he was on the line to the printers, where we were proofing, every ten or eleven minutes. We'd say, "Yes, Bob. No, Bob. Right away, Bob," and then hang up, cursing. In the afternoon, he showed up himself, and we were all taking a break and eating sandwiches—I mean, it was three in the afternoon and we were taking a lunch break, okay?—and Bob says to the printer, who by the way he had called at 6:00 A.M. while the guy was in the shower, and screams: "Where's *my* lunch? What am *I* supposed to eat?!" He was totally off the wall. "I wanted something to eat and nobody got me anything and now I don't want anything anymore!!" It was the most amazingly blatant transformation anyone had ever seen. And stuff like that, I'm happy to say, eventually got him fired.

In this part of the larger structure of American Management Disease, a capable (sometimes highly capable) captain of industry loses his reality regulator and implodes. He is suddenly fearful, anxious, and suspicious of all around him, particularly those closest to him. This type is especially dangerous to those who have the misfortune to depend on him, because he is constantly looking for proof that his subordinates and superiors are out to get him. Cut off, incapable of analyzing situations and formulating strategies, the paranoid is, more than any other form of crazy boss, doomed to destruction. The trick is not to get swallowed in his conflagration.

The politics of the workplace function to heighten paranoia in even normal people. Barry, a corporate attorney, explains:

> You're like one of the antelope in the herd, you just have to hope you don't get some jaws around your neck. In our Legal Department, everybody is always vying for position. Like one guy was pointing out the frailties of another of his colleagues. Started a whispering campaign. The other guy he was whispering about finally screwed up, 'cause everyone does once in a while, and he was demoted, because it was almost a self-fulfilling prophesy going on. An atmosphere where screwing up was blown out of proportion. Keep your eyes open. Keep your friends close, and keep your enemies closer. I mean, you should not avoid your enemy. Then you don't know what's going on. You're in a battle whether you like it or not, so open your eyes, and get into it.

## THAT WAS NO TOADY. THAT WAS MY HENCHPERSON

Owing to their particular pathology, paranoiacs are superbly tuned to the prerogatives of power and rank—and who is in position to humiliate whom. They are sycophantic toward their superiors, and horrendous to their subordinates. In the final stages, they can attain Nixonian heights of alienation and dysfunction. In such a state, the paranoid becomes tremendously dependent on henchpeople who make his disease work within the confines of the organization.

What separates the henchperson from the kind of simpering toady who serves the bully? Just the willingness to plot, plan, scheme, and execute his loony boss's paranoid fantasies. While the toady may be guilty simply of progressive sucking up, the henchperson is the tool by which the paranoid extends his reign. Toadies are more to be pitied than censured. The henchperson must be destroyed along with his crazy boss.

Henchmen are both a necessity to the paranoiac and a liability, since a henchman, no matter how hard he tries to conceal it, is still a human being with a concept of himself that is not wholly tied to that of his boss. "The henchman is one better than a yes-man, he acts as an extension of the boss," says my friend Stephanie, project manager at a management information-systems group that consults with corporations both large and small. "The henchman lets the manager be in two places or more at one time, like a programmed clone. They're a low form of corporate life, because they have no independent judgment or power, their power only comes directly from their hench. When the hench is gone, they're an empty shell." Stephanie continues:

> A henchman sometimes has a secret fear or hatred of his boss, and you can manipulate that. With Farley, I made a direct appeal, when he was going around telling people that they were going to be fired. I told him, "We're not going to work this way anymore. We're going to be treated like human beings, and you can tell that to Alan." Farley backed down immediately and was appalled by the fact that people hated his guts as a henchman.

But bottom line, the henchman is a worm, and efforts to turn him to your side will probably be met with only limited success. One entrepreneur, a former gray-flannel type, put it quite succinctly:

> You can't really even suck up to them to neutralize them. Have you ever seen vomit neutralizer? It's something you spray on vomit to lose the smell. And it doesn't work. When someone has a fixed idea that you stand in their way, and has a malicious streak in them, a will to do harm, it's impossible to neutralize them.

Not even a working henchperson can protect the crazy paranoid forever. A fellow I'll call Alex was marketing manager at a cable-television system serving a great Eastern metropolis: "No information got to Boris unless it came through his two henchmen—Gorman and Lynn Jannes, otherwise known as Eva Braun," he recalls.

> If you had information, you had to filter it through them. You'd appeal to their sense of what's important to Boris and what's going to advance them in his eyes. And increase their own power. You'd give them a memo and they'd get it to him, but first they'd have to pass on it. They'd also do his threatening for him. "If such and such doesn't happen by three o'clock, everyone's going to be fired," Lynn liked to say. "Boris would do that kind of thing, you know."

> On Mondays, everything would be a disaster. Tuesdays were calm. Visitors would come, and Boris would smile. By Wednesday, he'd fall apart, and the rest of the week was the same. So if you had a meeting with an outsider, it had to be on a Tuesday.

> He had a direct line to all the people who reported to him. And he would sit there and jab. I was in a friend's office once, and he buzzed and she didn't answer. He buzzed again and held his finger down. You sense his frustration and meanness. People were scared of him and hated his guts. He was verbally abusive and threw things: papers, rulers, books, anything that was near at hand.

> These episodes were scary. They were tantrums.

The paranoid is always on the edge, for three reasons:

1.  It's terribly hard to live in continual fear.
2.  Henchpeople make lousy allies.
3.  Paranoids are obviously atrocious managers, a fact that becomes more quickly noticed by senior officials than other, more obscure or popular personality diseases.

"You knew Boris was going to lose his job," Alex continues, "because he had no allies in the organization. One by one, his peers began to understand that they were dealing with someone of subnormal psychological stability and drew away from him. He became totally ineffectual and couldn't get anything done. Plus he had underlings who had greater ambitions, who began to prey on his superiors. But none of his bosses wanted to be the one to fire him, because that meant they would have to talk to him to do it. When the chairman decided to fire him, he called downstairs on a Friday afternoon. Boris, with his door locked, told his secretary to tell the chairman that he, Boris, had already left on vacation and missed the call. Then he did go away, and postponed being fired for two weeks."

## I'LL GET BACK TO YOU—RIGHT
## AFTER I KILL MYSELF

The paranoid is more acutely crazy than the simple bully, although he has a similar problem handling aggression. In full-blown paranoiacs, the characteristic fearful stance can create powerful delusions that have the force of truth in much the same way as dreams. This can create a powerful sense of unreality in anyone unfortunate enough to work for one—and a tremendous sapping of personal confidence.

Lenore, a social worker at an urban agency, suffered under a paranoid who just about ruined her life. "My former boss, Carlotta, was strange and crazy," she recalls. "She accused me and others of doing all kinds of bizarre things in our offices."

Her fantasies centered around sex and dope. My office was on a separate floor from hers and had its own door, while everyone else sat in a cubbyhole near her. She became fixated on the idea that we were smoking dope and screwing in my office. What made the situation particularly frustrating was that she never confronted me directly with her crazy suspicions. She just whispered them behind my back.

I think a couple of things triggered her paranoia. I was dating a resident, and we would often have lunch in my office with the door closed. Also, some of us in the department would come back from lunch acting giggly and silly. But her response was all out of proportion. It would have been very, very stupid and unprofessional for us to have done that, and we weren't either. To even defend yourself against that kind of charge is an insult.

She was very rigid and controlling. She hates unions, and even though we were a professional unit, we were in the same union with dishwashers and others like that, people she looked down on. One of the union meetings was held at my house. After she learned that, I changed from being a "good worker," a step above everyone else. Suddenly, I was a bad girl. That's when she started having fantasies about my "lewd" behavior. She took away my office, and deprived

my clients of a place where they could get private counseling. She
didn't care. She was incredibly sensitive to any rebuff, and I guess she
thought I had, well, rebuffed her. She was real invested in the job, in
a crazier way than the rest of us. We were not so ego-involved as she
was. It came down to control. She had to have things her way, all the
time, every time.

The rational approach—Let's sit down and reason together—is a
notoriously bad solution. "At one point, she was screwing around
with our vacation schedules, and we all waited in a conference room
until she finally agreed to sit down with us to talk with her about it,"
Lenore continues. "She was pale. Her lips were tight as a wire, and
her voice broke when she tried to speak. But she sat there. After the
meeting, she canceled and rearranged a number of our vacations,
just in case we might have gotten the wrong idea."

Why should the paranoid listen to you, anyway? He's convinced,
egomaniac that he is, that all your energies are committed to a secret
strategy aimed at his destruction. And that you're probably not
working alone, either. "You can't talk things out with a paranoid,"
says one corporate doctor who has seen his share. "They can't stand
communication, and rational approaches do not work." No, the
paranoid is deep in his crazy world, and does not wish to be disturbed out of it. If possible, he'll try to convey it to you.

The fact that the paranoid is a confidence sponge should come as
no surprise to anyone who has been cheek-to-jowl with one in full
flower. "The effect on me was devastating," Lenore says. "We all
have feelings that we goof off too much. I'd think, oh dear, I talked
to my girlfriend at noon, I'm not a professional, not a good person.
It triggered an insecure part of me. I felt maybe I wasn't competent
and decent. It was only after I took a new job someplace else that I
got my confidence back."

## I KNOW YOU'RE TALKING ABOUT ME!
## AND IF YOU'RE NOT—YOU SHOULD BE!

The bully, while no pleasure to work for, is often no more than an
abnormally nasty normal person. The paranoid is far more inconsistent. Indeed, when the crazy boss slips into paranoia, nothing
works smoothly, and the worker is whipsawed back and forth like a

bug in a gale. "He's very inconsistent," says a suffering employee of her boss. "One day he'll yell, 'Why the hell don't you come in and ask me if you're looking for something?' The next day he'll say, 'I don't want you coming in here and bothering me about this petty shit. I have enough problems.' "

The one consistent theme in an otherwise inconsistent paranoid universe is the crazy boss's perception that everything in the world revolves around the destruction of him.

A guy I'll call Carl was executive secretary of a minor-league film producer in Los Angeles. "My boss Joe was a guy in his middle forties, been in the business about eighteen years, was medium-successful producing documentaries and a number of relatively well-known television commercials," he says. "I was his right hand for a while, and did everything for him."

He was kind of Dr. Jekyll and Mr. Hyde, if you know what I mean. Could be very attractive, charming, suave. Of course, so was Ted Bundy.

When he had meetings with a client, he would never allow anyone else to be involved, especially if there were any financial discussions. I found this kind of absurd, since I did the books and paid the bills. I knew who he owed money to, and I billed people. Even when Joe's wife worked for him, which she did from time to time, he never allowed her into his inner office, which he kept tightly locked whenever he wasn't in it.

I had this friend in the office, a girl from England he had around to kind of run errands and do assorted chores, you know. And we really liked each other. But he went crazy when we'd talk. Naturally, he thought we were talking about him, which we weren't, not at first. He would call me in and ask what we were talking about. He would then call her in and say, "Look, I don't want you talking with him." It was all unjustified. He would get real crazy, calling me in and giving me a lecture. He would get enraged, demand to know what was going on. And nothing was going on, which made it kind of hard to confess to anything.

The conviction that he stands alone motors the paranoid, and it can impart a psychotic kind of strength, the sort that enables a little old lady to lift the Land-Rover crushing her pet Shih Tzu.

Bruce began in sales and is now the head of a small marketing firm in the deep South. "Every time I have a hangover, I succumb to horrible paranoia," he says. "I walk around saying, 'I'm really a charlatan, I'm not one bit creative as I should be, I have no discipline, it's only a matter of time before everyone finds out what I already know about myself. I'm a fucking failure.' I'm eminently squashable. No matter how much swaggering you do over drinks or something, when you're staring into the void of truth like that, the fear is almost biblical. You know you have the vulnerability of a gnat and the bootheel of God is going to squash you flat.

"Then I get a sudden burst of energy. I go right to work. The paranoia gives me power! It's like pure, NASA-grade rocket fuel! You'll never have more energy in your life!"

Another functioning paranoid echoes this reliance on the pathology that determines his mood and rules his psyche. "I can't ignore my enemies," he says. "They fill a void in my life that would otherwise be occupied by superficial acquaintances. They give focus to my pent-up anger. By obsessing over all the terrible things that I yearn to happen to them, I spend some of my anger that might be directed at loved ones, or worse, myself."

More often than not, however, the paranoid's fear can be simply debilitating, twisting his personality into a caricature of itself as he seeks to establish his superiority over everyone in sight—even when he's arguably not especially superior. Brett, a market analyst at a financial consulting firm, is used to taking a backseat while his paranoid boss does the driving. "Our company had this opportunity to do a short spot on *Donahue*," he recalls. "It was pretty much agreed that I was a much more appealing person to be on the show than my boss, Patrick."

Such, of course, was not to be the case. For Patrick was a paranoid. Brett continues:

We had an hour of Do's and Don'ts, and Patrick got very very defensive during this session. In subsequent days, he ignored me completely, and eventually I got the word that Patrick, not I, would do the taping. I was very disappointed, but not surprised.

Not long ago, you know, I had made this very successful presentation that made a very big splash. It was on this survey that he had absolutely no hand in, and he was obviously very threatened. He froze me out. In a meeting with more than three people, he either doesn't acknowledge that you've spoken,or looks at you with complete disgust, or is abusive, saying things like, "That's just about the dumbest thing I've ever heard, don't you all agree?'' And of course everyone has to agree. He's really threatened because someone does something better, or they're getting attention, or just plain doing something he couldn't do.

I've seen people destroyed by his paranoia—like he just infected them with it and they couldn't take it. There's this one guy who now lives in Australia, which I guess is the farthest place away that he could get. He was so abused by Patrick that he couldn't do his job without feeling that the boss was going to swoop down and demolish him. So as a result he spent all his time thinking, What is Patrick going to want?, and he completely lost all sense of himself, and his self-esteem.

"The worst thing about working for a paranoid boss is that you can't be smart, or as smart as he perceives himself to be, which is very smart indeed," says Max, a senior account executive at one of the nation's big advertising agencies. "It represents too great a threat to a guy who's very tuned in to threats. To know more than him is not allowed. There's this bristling tension—and it's not a cause-and-effect kind of relationship. It's an ongoing distrust."

## THE MASTER OF A DIRTY UNIVERSE—THAT'S ME!

What the paranoid feels is a malign universe can lead to some of the behavior that makes the breed famous: excessive nitpicking, suspicious attention to seemingly unimportant detail, fear of uncontrolled factors, such as germs or foreigners. The issue here is *environmental control.*

A woman who once worked for a Washington wife who headed up a small government agency recalls:

One of her greatest eccentricities is an obsession with germs. She is one of those people who is perennially quitting smoking, who then ends up bumming cigarettes. In one incident, she asked a secretary to go fetch a cigarette for her but asked her first to go into the executive washroom to wash her hands, and instructed her that if she had to take an elevator back, she should push the buttons with her elbows.

All her staff have been dressed down for petty infractions. She berates women to tears for really minor stuff. For example, our Institute used to be a subagency of the Department of Education but has since become independent. Its stationery, however, still has "Department of Education" on it. When the staff sends out letters, we're supposed to scratch out the envelope. She yelled at one of us recently for not using a ruler to do that.

At times, the *lust for control* can attain truly weird proportions. Perhaps the most famous paranoid in American business was Howard Hughes, a man whose fear of microbes was the dramatic linchpin of his personality:

He dictated a torrent of memoranda aimed at preventing the "backflow" or "back transmission" of germs to him. In one, three pages long and single-spaced, he explained how he wanted a can of fruit opened: "The equipment used in connection with this operation will consist of the following items: 1 unopened newspaper, 1 sterile can opener; 1 large sterile plate; 1 sterile fork; 1 sterile spoon; 2 sterile brushes; 2 bars of soap; sterile paper towels." Hughes outlines nine steps for opening the can: preparing a table, procuring of fruit can, washing of can, drying the can, processing the hands, opening the can, removing the fruit from the can. . . .

When the fruit was dished onto the plate, Hughes wanted "fallout rules" in effect: "Be sure that no part of the body, including the hands, be directly over the can or the plate at any time. If possible, keep the head, upper part of the body, arms, etc. at least one foot away from the can of fruit and the sterile plate at all times." During this procedure there must be "absolutely no talking, coughing, clearing of the throat, or any movement whatsoever of the lips."[1]

When an aide of Hughes developed hepatitis, the boss's priorities were clear. "This is one case where incrimination by association is definitely to be recognized. I want this situation to be investigated to see who has been near Cissy in the immediate past and those people are to be included in the program," he wrote, although the aide in question was miles away. "I consider this the most important item on the agenda, more important than our TWA crisis, our financial crisis or any of our other problems."[2]

Ironically, in the effort to establish dominion over the complex

[1] Donald Barlett and James B. Steele, *Empire: The Life, Legend and Madness of Howard Hughes* (New York: W. W. Norton, 1981), p. 233.
[2] Ibid, p. 234.

and threatening universe, the paranoid often finds it impossible to stifle impulses more rational types can deal with. That is, he can't control *himself*. This manifests itself in compulsive behavior and also, at times, in high jinks that are irresponsible, childish, and downright amusing to just about anyone *not* dependent on him. *Newsweek* of January 26, 1987, reported:

When Democrat Michael Boyle, 43, won his second term as mayor of Omaha in 1985, some supporters touted him as a candidate for Governor of Nebraska. In the past year, however, Boyle's erratic behavior convinced most Omahans that he was unfit even for city hall. Among other embarrassing incidents, the mayor fired the police chief in a feud over traffic tickets issued to his family, and was seen tossing a pat of butter at a county official during a dinner meeting. . . . Although Boyle promised to reform, Omaha voters went to the polls in record numbers last week for a recall election. By a convincing tally, they turned the mayor out.

Unfortunately, not all nuts of this order are subject to recall. Some have been on the job for years and are impossible to unseat. Paul, regional sales manager at a consumer electronics firm, has tried mightily to deal with his: "This guy, Jerry, is very peculiar about someone invading his office," he relates.

His desk is always cluttered with material. Whenever you enter with something for him, you have to stand there with it until he determines where you should put it down, if you should at all. Sometimes he asks you to put it on a chair or windowsill.

One recent morning I had to go in and leave some material. As I entered the office, he was writing something. I saw a bare spot on the desk. I walked over and said, "I'll leave this for you." He was expecting it. As I started to walk out, he said, "What did you do?" I said, "What do you mean? I left the pictures." The boss said, "Where's my clip? I had a paperclip there." I was standing at the front of his desk and saw a jumbo clip on the floor. I said, "Oh, here it is, Jerry." I picked it up innocently. He said, "That isn't what I mean. I had that clip standing on edge. I worked for half an hour to get that clip on edge. Do you realize what you did?" I said I was sorry and left.

As I walked out, I went over to a friend of mine who I always share these stories with. I said, "I think I have the topper now," and this guy says, "The clip." I was flabbergasted. The guy said, "I was in there a few minutes ago, and he showed me the clip and told me how hard he had worked on it to get it that way. He said that proves how no one around here appreciates what he can do. "This should prove to you that I have powers of concentration that no one else around here has," he said.

Paul said that senior management permitted his crazy boss to get away with murder because "the company basically runs itself, and we all know what we're doing." But almost one year to the day after I spoke with Paul, his firm was sold to a holding company that broke it up for its asset value.


## CONFIDENTIALLY—YOU'RE NUTS!

The inability of paranoids to delegate, and their wild swings of mood and intent, make them such bad managers that the business eventually takes on their personalities and, inexorably, falls to its knees.

Lars, a videotape editor for a multimedia producer of industrial presentations, remembers the bad days under his former crazy boss:

> His paranoia got in the way of doing business, you know, when people wouldn't put up with his nonsense and nastiness. He would court the ones he was trying to impress, and be nasty to everyone else along the way if they were not obviously important to him. On more than one project, clients would insist on dealing with me, not him. But I didn't know half the things I needed to know to do what I was supposed to be doing, because he was so secretive and mistrustful, even of me.

> He was also very inconsistent and contradictory. I suppose because he was tormented by self-doubt. Say there was an insurance man trying to sell him, who called and called. He would criticize me if I said he was out, because he said people would think he was always out. But I couldn't say he was busy because he said they might get the idea he didn't want to talk with them, even though they had called four hundred times and he had refused to take their call. He just couldn't get on the line and say he didn't want any insurance.

> On the one hand, he was overly organized, like planning and planning for a big project. Then he'd jerk around for the entire day and get busy around five or six o'clock. And keep us there until all hours, till midnight or three in the morning. And he'd make us sit around all day discussing what we should do, scream at us, "You people have no

ideas! No initiative!'' And the first time a person would make a suggestion or try to decide how to get off the dime and get things moving, he'd yell at them for doing it all wrong.

Lars's boss eventually fired him when Lars had the temerity to requisition three hours of overtime pay on a day he had literally worked around the clock and slept on the cutting-room floor. The boss took this as an act of "selfishness and deceit." And lost an employee who was dedicated to the operation, and, in spite of everything, to him.

The suffering paranoid must work moment to moment to achieve some kind of comfort in the midst of his pain. And the greater the pain, the greater the compulsion, driving the crazy boss, finally, to truly magnificent personality distortions. For Loretta, an administrative assistant at a community college, it became a trauma over that most simple of daily objects: a doorknob.

Once my boss removed the doorknob from his office door so that no one could get in to see him. He had never liked people barging into his office, which he liked to keep as a really controlled environment. He had set up an elaborate structure so that only one person reports to him directly. I think this is partly so he can do nothing when he feels incapacitated. Times like that, he retreats into his hole and putts golf balls into paper cups, and spends hours reading the Milwaukee papers and typing up bowling scores for his league. None of us has been able to determine what it is in fact that he does do all day. I'm just guessing.

So anyway, he removed the doorknob from a door that connected his office with the library. He got in and out through another door where his secretary sits.

News about what he'd done traveled fast, and people came from all over the school to look at the missing doorknob. The maintenance people were upset because they don't like anyone meddling with things like that. A woman in charge of operations and procedures was upset, people were writing memos about it! Before a week was up, the dean for academic affairs found out about it, came and inspected the door and ordered him to put the knob back on. Now he has arranged to have all the coats in the department hung up on the inside of that same door so that if you try to come through, you walk into the coats. So he got his way after all.

The paranoid can't take criticism, either, which is yet another threat to his carefully constructed shell. So he must be played like a violin by those who actually want to get some serious business done. Peter, a copywriter for a direct-sales organization, has figured out how to deal with his:

> There are other times when Oliver writes a section that I don't think is good. What I do in that case—because you can't just walk and say, "It stinks," or you'll have a real resentful boss on your hands—I go in and am very apologetic; "I don't want to take up your time, or it's silly on my part, but I don't think this wording captures the true beauty of the product." And I never say even that unless I have an alternative he can claim credit for immediately. I figure I'm trying to make him as relaxed and unthreatened as possible.

The driven paranoid can also lie like a rug when need be. One of the most famous and admired American paranoids on record was our late director of the FBI, J. Edgar Hoover, a man who built an entire career on manipulating the mistrust and xenophobia of the nation. But even the tremendously powerful Hoover was canny enough to dissemble when need be. Alan Brinkley related the following tale in *The New York Review of Books*[3]:

> Hoover claimed to have truly hated few people in his life, but in his later years he freely admitted to a deep hatred of the Kennedys. He disliked their politics, surely; but what he detested above all was their freewheeling style, their impatience with established lines of authority, their contempt for bureaucratic procedures. Nothing could have contrasted more sharply with his own cautious personality; nothing could have seemed more threatening to his carefully ordered world. He grew almost apoplectic at the sight of Robert Kennedy, in shirt sleeves, moving through the FBI offices talking with agents who were never permitted to remove their own jackets on the job. He resented the direct telephone line the attorney general had installed to his office (and defiantly removed it within hours of John Kennedy's death). He was contemptuous of what he considered the President's inexperience and incompetence, as displayed at the Bay of Pigs.
>
> Privately, he attacked both John and Robert. But he was unfailingly warm and flattering in his personal dealings with the President, and he even managed occasionally to write sycophantic letters to the attorney general—which led Bobby Kennedy to conclude (erroneously) that his relationship with Hoover was "pretty good."

[3] April 23, 1987

## A NIT HERE. A NIT THERE. PRETTY SOON YOU'RE TALKING ABOUT A LOT OF NITS!

Craftiness. Fear of contamination. Mistrust of others. Manipulative drive for control. Impulsive weirdness. The final arrow in the paranoid's quiver is the cross of perfectionism—the extension of the compulsive drive to recreate the universe in his own grandiose image. One employee at a company that provides men's grooming products recalls of his former boss, "He was totally detail-oriented. He would constantly insist all people have a list of fifty objectives they were working against, when there was no way they could make ten."

Often the obsessive perfectionist's barrage contains a strong whiff of sadism, a cold-steel fury to punish those who do not conform to the Great Man's Scheme. My friend James, an actor, tells of a very famous director and choreographer with whom he has worked:

> When he's putting together a show, stuff goes in, stuff goes out—if he doesn't like something, and he rarely does, he fusses and fudges and he changes it. We have a run-through and everybody thinks it's great, and then he goes back to the original, which he hated yesterday. The stage manager can't even keep up—and he has the book containing all stage directions. You can imagine how hard it is for us. He vacillates back and forth and back and forth and does everything a director can do to annoy an actor. When you're performing, he's waving his arms around like a flight superintendent. I think sexually he's a sadist, and it comes out in his direction. As an artist, I think I have a lot of invention. He's so picky he squeezes the life out of it. I hate doing it a certain way, then he says you have to do it that way. It's frustrating, and it's not a lot of fun. I think he's the kind of guy who's into putting out cigarettes on other people's behinds.

> I think he's afraid of me because I'm a little out of control. One time he was giving notes to the whole cast and he was walking backwards and nobody said anything and he fell into the orchestra pit. We all nearly died trying to contain our laughter. He didn't hurt himself, unfortunately.

At the heart of every paranoid perfectionist is an essential coldness, an analytical lack of caring that is translated into each action, each thought. One lawyer in a huge firm serving corporations both large and huge told me:

Drew's the kind of guy who sees a dog in the street and speeds up to see if he can run it over. And when he tries to be human, it comes out real funny. Like when an attorney here was on his way out of here for good, fired with only two weeks notice, Drew called him into his office, which he hadn't done in his entire life, and says, "Hey, Lou, on your way out of the company, could you find out from the chairman if we could have secretarial help around here? And if there's anything I can do for *you* just let me know."

This kind of inhumanity seems ideally suited to the world of big business, where sloppy human considerations might tend to clutter the clean process of decision-making. Maury, vice president of development for a manufacturing company in the Southwest, has had some very strange dealings with his perfectionist:

Don, our president, had this belief that perfection is attainable, that people, human beings, are infinitely perfectible and anything that falls short of that must be removed from his presence like a bad smell. What must it be like to be him? To feel that there is such a thing as human perfection, and then look at the world around him? No wonder he had to control everything about him, like his little oat-bran muffin for breakfast, and his tiny, perfect Wedgwood plate and cup, and his immaculately clean desk.

Punctuality is all-important to him. I remember I went on this trip with him once, to Phoenix. It was very nice the whole time. We took limos everywhere, and he was more than cordial to me, he was the perfect gentleman. No temper, all sweetness and light. I was honored, frankly. It's very seductive to find that kind of attention focused on you by a guy in his position, with his experience, his power.

We went out to dinner two nights running with different groups of people, and one time Don was at least fifteen minutes late, but of course, nobody said anything. There aren't too many suicidal people in the field, most of them are concentrated at corporate headquarters in Chicago. On the last night out, he excused himself to go off to sleep at 8:30 P.M., like he always did. And the next morning, we were supposed to check out. I got in real late after about 113 beers with the boys, and the next thing I knew, it was minutes before Don's checkout time of choice—7:00 A.M.

I remember looking at the clock and realizing I had about ten minutes to get ready, but I figured, hey, no sweat. I threw everything into my bag and lurched out of there in record time. I waited a few minutes for the elevator, and I ran into the lobby all set to hit the front desk, and I noticed that the clock in the hotel lobby said that it was four minutes after seven. Big deal. I noticed Don and Jim, his gofer, standing by the revolving doors, waiting all the way at the other end of the lobby. And Jim looked even more officious than usual, and Don was looking very darkly at his watch. That kind of freaked me out, so without saying good morning or anything, I sped over to the desk, which wasn't busy at that ungodly hour, and I began the long process of getting out of there.

And I was standing there, and I suddenly feel this horrible pressure boring in on the middle of my backbone, right between my shoulder blades. And I turned around and there was Don, about six yards away from me now, just staring at my back with those piercing eyes, just staring.

I turned around and said to the guy behind the desk, "Look, buddy, just hurry up and give me the bill, please, my life is at stake here." And he gave it to me, and I was ready to pay, you know, until I noticed that I had been charged with all these towels and room-service charges I didn't deserve and stuff. I turned around and there was Don, only about a yard away now, still staring. The spot in the middle of my back was red hot. I don't know how to explain it, but it's true.

I was totally balled up. I mean, if I didn't question the bill, it would come back to me when I had to include it in my expense report, which could have left me open to charges of unfrugality, which is another thing Don hates. So I said to the guy, "Look man, you see the gentleman standing directly behind me?" And he said, "Yeah, like what's the matter with him? He looks kind of crazy." And I said, "That's the president of my corporation, and he's been waiting for me since seven o'clock," and the guy says, "Big deal! It's only five after!" He was great, though. He took one look at Don's eyes and changed the bill by hand. At this point, I was terrified out of my mind. I could feel Don only inches away, his breath on the back of my neck.

I paid, and then turned very slowly to face him. I swear to God I had to suck in my gut or I would have bumped right into him—that's how tight he was crowding me. And we stared at each other, face to face, literally, and he says, really calmly, "Maury, there are many things that distinguish a successful person in this world, but none, none, Maury, is as important as on-time percentage. On-time percentage is key. That means you've got to be there, not almost there, not fifty percent of the time, not ninety-eight percent of the time, but one hundred percent of the time. Anything less is not good enough. I want you to remember that, as you go through life."

I felt like saying to him, "Hey, Don, you were late for dinner two nights running, and how many times have I waited until two-thirty, for a noon meeting?" But I figured it would be smarter not to. We rode in the limo to the airport in complete silence, total silence. I was trying to think of something to say to sort of, you know, salvage the situation in some way. Finally, I said, "Uh, Don, I was in fact on the phone to Chicago discussing your preparation for the stockholders meeting in Dallas next Thursday. I'm not making any excuses, but I just thought I should tell you that's why I was late."

And he turned to me with those translucent light-green eyes that have destroyed hundreds of senior managers, eyes that look like he's staring right through the back of your skull into the upholstery of where you're sitting, and he honed in on me again, real tight. I think he was restraining the impulse to grab me by the lapels. And he says, "Maury, Maury, never, never once in a million years did I ever consider that, in being late, you did not have the best, most impeccable reasons for being so. That doesn't change the fact that a man's on-time percentage is his most important asset. Do you understand? Do you understand, Maury?"

I had to say I did. Of course I did. I think he had made himself very clear, and after all, it wasn't the most complicated message I ever received.

Obsessive perfectionism informs every aspect of this crazy boss's leadership. I once worked for a chairman who was deeply revered in his corporation for his vision and canny business acumen. When we upgraded our offices one spring, he decided to change the color scheme in his office. The carpet in his office was blue, since that was the general color of the whole executive suite. But Carl didn't like blue, he liked only beige. And so he had that carpet taken out and beige carpet put down. Turned out it was the wrong shade of beige, so he had another beige carpet laid. By the time he was through, Office Services had installed no less than three shades of beige.

This excruciating process was conducted during a period in which corporate layoffs and cost cuttings were happening every day. I can only wonder how hard it was for him, trying to determine which shade of beige reflected the true beigeness of his interior landscape.

The issue of control was by no means trivial to Carl. He hated anyone who was out of control. He once told me, "I would never hire anyone who smoked or is overweight. Both things are evidence of a lack of control, and the only kind of people who are able to manage other people are people who are in control of themselves. Super control of themselves. How can you expect someone to manage other people if he can't manage his vices and his waistline?"

This CEO's compulsion for the perfect extended to his treatment of the smallest details of subordinate performance, even when those subordinates were division presidents who managed billion-dollar subsidiaries. Another vice president in my company recalls, "Carl would give Brad—a very high senior VP—shit about taking a toll bridge instead of a free one. He'd pressure guys who were generating million-dollar operating profits to use the long-term parking lot at the airport."

Generally, such compulsive nitpicking generates not obedience, but rebellion. "Something like that is so ridiculous you have to find ways around it," says the observer in my company. "Like shutting off information about what you're doing so you won't get in trouble. Or eating the expense and passing it along other ways. The end is unhappy people, and restriction of information to the boss."

Far more difficult to deal with than the compulsive nitpicking is the virtually infinite reservoir of rage under the surface of iron-controlled reserve. When unleashed, it can turn the quivering paranoid into a violent one. Listen to Harry, executive assistant to the president of a national head-hunting firm.

I had been working for Bill for about three months, and while I had seen him lace into people, I always thought it was for good reason—look, he didn't get where he was by being undemanding, you know? And sure, he was weird. Very clean. Kind of obsessed about what he ate and drank, the purity of it, if you see what I mean. But I never saw him crack at all. Until one morning.

We had gotten to the office at our usual hour, just after dawn, and he was ready to go through the stack of memos and other shit that began his day, and we found that the glass door that led to the executive suite was locked, and nothing we could do would open it. It was some kind of fuckup with the electronic lock, you know. These things happen. So I said to him, "Look, Bill, you have a seat in my office, and I'll call the locksmith." And he says, "Break it." And I said, "Hm?," and he says, "You heard me. Break the damn thing." And I said, "Bill, that door is worth a couple thousand dollars, easy." And he said, "The time we've already wasted is worth more to me than that door. Break it."

So I picked up a chair and broke the door. And when other people got in that morning, they found Bill in his office and the whole front of the area smashed to shit. I guess he's not the kind of guy you want to get in his way.

As Freud observed, the fear is father to the wish. The paranoid, fearful that the sky is falling, often brings that terrible event on himself, if only to prove that his or her worldview is justified. Lewis, a paralegal for a big-city litigation firm, works for one such:

There's a senior partner here who you really have to kind of feel sorry for, except she creates havoc wherever she goes. When I pass her office, I try to go very quietly by, so she won't know I'm there and suck me into the most recent version of her paranoia—be it business, medical, personal, familial, or botanical, like when her ficus was dying. She constantly thinks that things will inevitably work out for the worst. And when something good happens, she's the kind of person who can only recognize it as something bad, since it forces her to make a judgment about whether to take advantage of the good thing. And she dilly-dallies long enough so that the advantage of the good thing passes. She gets a job offer and can't make up her mind about it because she can't see anything good in it, because anything good, in her opinion, has got to be ephemeral, can't be counted on. What a load to carry. And it makes her a bitch to work for, let me tell you. Because a person like that won't make any decisions since anything they do may turn bad. She's down in the mouth constantly because of the impending doom thing, you know. And people like her, they don't go down alone, they bring their friends and relatives with them.

## CAN SUCH A LUNATIC BE ALLOWED TO LIVE?! YOU BETCHA!

The crazy paranoid is sometimes the best boss that management has on hand. And, stranger still, a significant portion of staff may find themselves dependent on the crazy paranoid to provide a frame of reference, no matter how diseased or sorry.

For this reason, direct confrontation of even the most flagrantly bizarre boss is rarely a successful strategy.

Ted is a thirty-five-year-old social worker now with the division of substance-abuse services of a large state in the Southwest. Several years ago, he ran a methadone clinic at a large metropolitan hospital in the Great Lakes area. In this setting, he supervised services to the hundreds of methadone addicts that would come in daily for their medication. Between him and the head physician, he says, there was "an uneasy truce" about who was in charge: Ted, as head of counseling, or Marlene, the business administrator, who viewed herself with the calm and purposeful grandiosity customarily reserved for those in the medical profession. Even by those liberal standards, however, Marlene was big trouble. As Ted explains:

> Marlene ran the clinic like a teeny czar. She would not share information about patients with the counselors who communicated most regularly with them, important information such as the results of urine tests that showed whether or not patients had resumed their drug habit, or the dosage of methadone they were receiving, a matter of great concern and anxiety to many patients.
>
> Her policies deviated sharply from those enforced in other clinics around the city. For her own crazy reasons, she wanted to keep all information to herself, so she could maintain ultimate control over everybody, be the only authority. She divided the clinic into two groups—us and them. On the "us" side were the doctors. We—counselors, patients, everyone else—were the enemy.
>
> Staff meetings were amazing. She sat at the head of a long table, knitting. The staff called her Madame LaFarge. I always had the sense I was looking uphill at her. A counselor, I'll call her Gail, would report that one of her clients was progressing. Marlene would come down quick and hard. "How can you say this patient is doing well when his urine report shows he's back on drugs?!" "But I didn't get the report," Gail would say. "That doesn't matter. A good counselor should know how a patient is doing without getting reports." Then she would turn to us and say, "Isn't that stupid of Gail to misjudge the situation like that?"
>
> I think the physical layout contributed to everyone feeling childish and subservient. I suggested that the big table be taken away. And she objected on many grounds—how would people take notes? What would they write on? Where would they put their drinks? In informal talks with the staff, I knew I had everyone's support, so one meeting I put the chairs in a circle and removed the table. When everyone came in, they all hated it, and used the same objections she had—

where would they put their drinks? I knew, I mean, I suddenly saw, that I was alone in this fight. The entire organization was hooked into her madness.

I tried to tell the people up above about how crazy she was. But they already knew. One big doctor said to me, "Look, we have a lot of trouble getting people to work in these kinds of locations, and I'd rather have her there than to have another clinic without a doctor."

In short, the system worked to bolster and support the insanity that was the only management style it knew. The fact that this served neither employees nor the clients was almost beside the point. Until one evening when Ted was assaulted by a client in need of medication. Since Marlene was the only person in possession of the knowledge of how to help the addict, Ted was powerless, and became the brunt of the man's frustrations.

Ted recognized that the assault was, in fact, not on him, but on the way the organization was run. He immediately sat down and fired off a memo to his management, which said:

Yesterday I was physically assaulted by a patient. He knocked me down in anger because I told him I could not medicate him after the clinic closed. I could not arrange for late clinic, as I am not aware of his dosage and an exact procedure is not set up yet. I could not get a nurse, as both had already left the building. He struck me because I provided no way out for him.

I relate this incident because I cannot help but feel that it is a direct result of the clinic atmosphere. Staff interaction with each other contains a high degree of mistrust and manipulation. Cooperation and team approach to problems is minimal at best, and consistency toward patients is nonexistent. Procedures are changed arbitrarily, often without discussion, and staff rarely feels they are part of the decision-making process. These decisions are sometimes emotionally based, and apparently immune to any rational rebuttal. I used to tell new admissions that we were here to help. I can no longer say this in good conscience. The clinic lacks a positive direction, lacks good management, and lacks an atmosphere that provides support for the patients.

I am not one to run away from problems. My approach is usually logical, honest, and direct. I cannot ignore the roots of the problem with my clinic. While I am running a strong risk of censure by talking about what is going on, I have decided to draw the line when a patient hits me. There exists an unbreakable cycle between Dr. Marlene and the staff that simply overwhelms the clinic, and all staff is involved in one way or another. Some are resigned to it, some are resistant to it, some try to outwit it, most feed into it. Even neutrality is only a passing oasis. I now realize that any position is merely a reaction and, in effect, contributes to it.

Frankly, I am simply tired of saying no to patients. I am tired of carrying out and explaining decisions that eliminate my input. I am tired of playing silly games that tax the mind, exhaust the spirit, waste time, and have no constructive end. As clinic supervisor, I want to take the first step to eliminate the cycle, and outside assistance is essential.

Ted then went on to suggest a four-step program by which rational power could be institutionalized and patients' and counselors' rights be better served. He did not, by the way, suggest the ouster of the paranoid doctor. He closed with the following statement:

In the past year there have been many "voluntary" discharges, patients who have gone to other programs on their own. I cannot help but feel that the clinic atmosphere contributed to their decisions. I have trouble being a part of a clinic that drives patients away. I am in this job because I am committed to proper patient care, and I prefer to guide my clinic in that direction.

Shortly thereafter, Ted was forcibly transferred to a different clinic, not as punishment, he was assured, but so that he would "be happier."

Life in the old location went on much as before.

## FIGHT THE POWER—HAVE A LAUGH

Oddly enough, humor is one of the most powerful weapons employees have against the depressed, moody, scary, frightened, excessively nutty paranoid. Again and again, folks speak of the glue that can bind people together when they lay it in and let it harden.

One office manager beset by a paranoid reflects on the impact her boss's assumption that "everyone was talking about me" had on her and her co-worker. "After a while," she says, "my friend and I found it hysterically funny, because after a while we *did* find ourselves talking about him . . . though we tried to do it when he was out of the office."

It's true that, more than any other boss, the muttering, grumbling, raving paranoid, is, well, funnier than his crazy counterparts. "We were all young and liked each other," says another employee of a paranoid boss, "and Linda always suspected we were plotting against her. And after a while, we were. We were obsessed with her, frankly. Her behavior knitted us tighter. We became more support-ive of each other—uniting against the common enemy. Which didn't do us any good. But it did make us feel better."

That's a lot. What is often incompletely understood is that, when people suffer under a crazy boss, the issue for them is not only *job preservation;* the issue is *psychological survival.*

A marketing manager I'll call Davidson tried that approach and failed miserably. "I would try to make manly jokes, locker-room jokes," he remembers, speaking of a former and hated boss. "My mistake was that it was an Irish old boys' network, so I would say something like, 'Ach, what a heartburn I got from that,' and I'd just get blank looks. It became a matter of pride that I wasn't going to let them back me down. And they didn't. My theory is that if the person doesn't have a sense of humor, it's my duty to hammer away at them until you get a thin smile. That's what I was doing with this guy, Doyle. I figured I just can't be as earnest and serious as they are, so I'm going to try to humor my way through. Unless I'm amused, I can't work in a place. I just put my head down and ram it through the wall. So at least I made things entertaining for myself."

Still, the quality of laughter, no matter how strained, can save the toiling employee from total desperation. "He's very, very moody," says one of the afflicted about her boss. "He never says good morn-ing. If you should meet him in the hall and say good morning, he will answer, 'Fuck you, too.' The way we survive is to look at the hu-morous side. By sharing the stories and problems with each other, we are all able to take it a little better. If there were even a shred of sanity on his part, I think it would bother us more."

## AND THEN, OF COURSE, THERE'S WAR!

Duplicity, subterfuge, and sabotage also work, but can be more dangerous. A paranoid is uniquely susceptible to concerted, subter-ranean, dirty fighting, preferably done in association with others. He already thinks you're doing something like it. Why not live up to his expectation?

My friend Fletch, editor of a national men's magazine, has his methods:

> Because of their complex and sinister psychological makeup, these guys take joy in seeing other people fall on their faces, this alone makes them feel they succeed. These are the guys you have to attack. You have to make sure greater and greater numbers of people know that they're as nutty as a fruitcake, and undermine their credibility. Always refer to your passive enemies as "that nut" or "that fruitcake." You want to build up the sense that the person is a walking time bomb. You have to attack, and you can take great joy in it, because they're psychologically so fragile that their defeat can be utter. Someone who wants your job can be rational. But someone who is just after making you crazy for no particular reason is paranoid, that's all.
>
> And you can play on their paranoia. These people need to be totally destroyed on the battlefield. You have to win the war, not just the battles. Conflict is a natural component of human behavior, because we are political animals. So wear away at him, and stay cool, because he wants to disrupt you, and thinks he can conquer you, but I believe in the long, protracted struggle. Deal with the crises right away, but if you maintain a holding pattern and get your defenses shored up, you can undermine your opponent. Don't dwell too much on the enemy's strategy—that means you're playing his game. You've got to play on your own home court.

That home court is *sanity*, sanity created by *job performance based on rational strategy, not personality.*

Thanks to the depth of dysfunction wrought on this boss by his disease, the paranoid eventually begins to offer ever-diminishing returns to the company he serves. The astute and patient employee will assimilate his superior's responsibilities, duty by duty. And, as Fletch suggests, will continue to politely wear away at the credibility the crazy paranoid enjoys with his superiors.

As he putts those golf balls, twiddles his trembling thumbs, torments his subordinates, and concentrates more completely on all matters associated clearly with his illness, his turf will be increasingly vacant, and fair game for you.

Unless he gets you first.

## ACTION POINTS: THE PARANOID

The paranoid can be managed just about as well as his bully counterpart, which is to say: with great and enduring difficulty. Unlike the bully, he is profoundly hard to read and predict. This leads to a different set of approaches and strategies:

- *Expect inconsistency:* As we have seen, the paranoid is swept by a powerful sequence of conflicting fears, grandiose hopes, despondency, and outraged perfectionism. Each of these potent emotions is exquisitely real to him *at the time,* and he is unable to perceive them as arising from within himself—it's the world that makes him feel this way. Actually, the fight is taking place almost solely within him, as his pathology battles to make sense of an existence that does not meet with his expectations. This stance places him constantly at odds with the world, continually striving to establish equilibrium in the face of the supposed onslaught from without. As his employee, you'll be whipped back and forth by these tempests unless you establish an internal sense of priority and control not tied to his demands and emotions. Realize that his swings have very little to do with you. Do not take them personally. And work to establish solid routines and standards for yourself not based on his demands. Sweet bun at your desk at nine. Paperwork and trade reading until ten. Meetings independent of his agenda until eleven-thirty. Check in with the boss and listen to him fulminate for a while. Maybe he even yells at you. So what? At noon, off to lunch with someone nice. More meetings. Then perhaps a bizarre session with the boss again, quietly listening to him fulminate about how he plans to skewer his enemies sometime real soon. A little more paperwork and some phoning. Before you know it, it's time to go home! Have a drink on the train. You've earned it.
- *Don't be a good little employee:* Paranoids respect bad people, not good ones. So don't hesitate to be thorny, tough, dense, and obstinate, as long as the paranoid doesn't perceive your behavior as a *direct challenge* (see point below). Being a nasty boy or girl is quite possibly the quickest way to a paranoid's heart. A friend who works for a suspicious and contentious theatrical director (he's a stage manager) says of his leader: "If there's one thing Henry hates, it's a sweet little kitty cat. I learned very early that

if I'm going to get his attention, I have to be just a little bit less surly than he is. The first time I worked with him, I was really polite all the time. He treated me like shit. One morning I lost my temper and sulked for an entire day. After that, he was a lot more relaxed with me and actually treated me with a sort of respect. Well, as close as he gets to it." Sheepish acceptance of bad treatment may earn you points in the short run, of course. But in addition to its hurting you daily, you will get nothing from it in the long run, either. Your dubious acquiescence will be repaid with betrayal. Bet on it.

- *Never directly challenge him:* This goes without saying, but I'll say it anyway. The guy believes that others are out to get him, and that he is the one perfect entity in an imperfect and infuriating universe. Line yourself up on the other side of his Me vs. Them scenario, and you will lose. Be crafty. There are hundreds of ways to finesse things.

- *Silence confounds paranoids. Use it:* It's very hard to keep on dribbling a basketball that refuses to bounce. Self-justification at length when he's in your face will prove ineffective. Countervailing argumentation on the silliness of his fears or accusations will only make him suspect you. Displays of rage or resentment on your part will only give him what he wants—control over the interpersonal dynamic between you. It's far better to nod and look thoughtful until the storm blows over. Inconsistency has its positive side, too. The guy eventually will exhaust himself and kick you out of his office (for the time being) when he senses that he's not getting the return on emotional investment his outburst called for. If you absolutely must comment on a particular raving, think of something blank and relatively noncommittal. "Gee, Irv. I had no idea things had developed along those lines" should do nicely. Look for an opportunity to glance at your watch and look concerned, as if you have an upcoming meeting of extreme importance to *him* and *his* agenda. Paranoids respect the desire to be punctual, even in other people.

- *Establish your own style, early and firmly:* Naturally, you can't be as wonderful as he wants you to be. If you could be, you'd be him! No, you're not as neat as he'd like you to be. You leave little piles of paper while he likes a desk so clean you could perform surgery on it. Still, you've got to work the way that works for you. Ultimately, the paranoid wants only two things from your work habits: crack professionalism and on-time delivery. If you can deliver that with that cup of soup seeping onto your blotter, go ahead and slurp away.

- *Well, shut my door!* Paranoids in their gestating phase often retreat into the quiet of their office while their internal battles rage. Do not attempt to break through the door unless you have a very specific piece of business—brief and to the point—to conduct. The last thing you want is to enter when he's looking for something to flog. Best of all is to wait until you have a number of things that require nothing more than a signature. Do *not* descend to the stupidity of slipping important communications under his door, even if other people do so. It's unseemly. If something remains undone that she asked for, a polite "Sorry, Cheryl, I was waiting until I could get to you on this" will demurely convey the message that it was her closed door that held up the works. If asked, "Then why the hell didn't you just slip it under my door?!," you may reply, "Gosh, I really hate to do that. Suppose it got kicked under your credenza or something." When you've got something for the paranoid, simply knock briskly, wait until you are admitted, and state your business. Get it done. Leave. Do not look for any personal contact. You'll be sorry. If *you* have a door, by the way, don't hesitate to use it unless you are directly told not to do so. He does it—why not you? It's amazingly nice in a closed office, especially with all those unpleasant vibes emanating from the corner office. It's your door. Use what you've got.

- *Make friends and influence henchpeople:* As we've seen, a Haldeman or Ehrlichman type most probably stands between you and the paranoid. Two points here. First, being a henchperson is no fun, so don't try out for the job unless you're intent on taking a lot of shit along with the resulting power rush. Paranoids, like many other crazy bosses, are meanest to those within striking distance. Of course, if you want the job, you probably deserve being victimized. Lord knows you're most likely victimizing a lot of other, more innocent people every day. If you're a functioning individual, however, point number two kicks in: You'll have to do some pleasant, lightweight sucking up to the paranoid's henches. Nothing heavy. Just recognition of their influence, that's all. "Say, Jerry, I wonder if you could give me a hand getting to Murray on the Finster issue" pulls them into the mix and makes them feel

like players. That's what they want to be: respected members of
the team in their own right. Make them feel like they have via-
bility outside of the boss's and you'll have an untrustworthy
friend—which is a whole lot better than an untrustworthy enemy.
Under no circumstances, however, give over your job duties and
important projects *in toto* to the craven henchperson. He wouldn't
know what to do with them anyway—for him, work is just a way
to either build up his own credibility or destroy yours. Your work
is the one thing that keeps you sane no matter who your boss is.
Never lose sight of that.

- *Don't let it get you down about yourself:* You look marvelous!
  You're talented and smart! Nothing the guy heaps on you can
  change that or diminish that—unless *you* allow it to! Right? Of
  course! Now go out there and feel *good,* okay? Okay. I know it's
  not easy when someone is piling suspicion and negativity in your
  ear all day long. It's easy to let it get down deep and make you as
  crazy as your boss. But your own emotional makeup is probably
  the one thing that you *do* have some control over in the wacky
  world of the crazy workplace. When you've lost control over that,
  you've lost the war. So keep in touch with the real you. The one
  inside that outfit you wear each and every day to the battlefront.
  I suggest several things to keep you reminded that you are a real
  individual who exists outside the mind of your paranoid:

  —Lunches with friends who have nothing to do with business.
  —A small tape player in your office, cubicle, or work location
    that can play music that keeps you in touch with yourself.
  —At least one walking tour of your workplace daily, hobnob-
    bing briefly with the folks who seem to be human.
  —Use of the phone to escape into the more pleasant portions of
    the present and, possibly, the past.
  —The establishment of "mental health days" when the pres-
    sure is starting to make you forget yourself.

  Think of your own solutions, but do *something*. A self is a terrible
  thing to waste.
- *Establish different fealty if you can:* As with other crazy bosses,
  you must assume that the paranoid will ultimately spin away
  from your orbit and spiral into the sun. Be on a continuous look-
  out for senior off·ers who might like you enough to save you

when this happens. It's not impossible. I've run through no less than four crazy bosses in ten years. Each time, I was protected when the change of power took place above me by the friendship of a variety of those in the six-figure club who appreciated all the tasks and projects I had accomplished for them while working for the variety of mad fools they assigned to head my department. Today, I'm the mad fool who heads my department. It's a good feeling.

- *Laugh, Clown, laugh!* The power of human amusement should never be underestimated. In all my interviews with people who work for paranoids, there is one common theme: after a while, employees simply have to get together and have a good laugh at the expense of the nutty, festering dork who's making their lives miserable. That laughter may be the most powerful weapon in their ongoing fight to maintain sanity. When you do laugh, however, make sure to do it carefully, out of his hearing. The last thing you want to do is confirm his suspicion that people are laughing at him behind his back by laughing about him in front of it.

- *Destroy the monster with his own craziness:* This is a delicate tactic, but perhaps the most powerful of all. If you can play it well, it may serve to destroy the paranoid who depends on you more quickly than any other thing you do. Here's how it works: When he aerates a fear, corroborate it. "I bet Lazenby is just waiting for me to fuck up on this," he may say. "What I hear," you could respond, "is that he's in there with the chairman every morning, whispering in Doug's ear about how we don't know what we're doing. It makes me sick." Note two things. First, the story can never be checked without your paranoid going to the chairman and risking his neck. This he will not do. Second, the use of the word *we*. Working this line, you must establish your membership in the Us camp, as against the horrible, detested Them. Never get his dander up against the small and defenseless. Always bring him fetid tidbits about those he cannot control or bully. Engender few new insights or stories. Just gently feed and water the ones he already has. You can be instrumental in driving him from a low boil to volcanic heights of irrationality. Get busy. Life's a-wasting.

CHAPTER FOUR

# NARCISSIST

Got to be good-looking,
'cause he's so hard to see.
John Lennon

eyond the vale of bully violence and paranoid fear within
every crazy boss, there lies a distorted idea of who, exactly,
he may be. This definition of self, like every other part of
his persona, is out of whack—either too large, too small, or
both.

Sociopathic narcissists have ruined a number of perfectly successful industries in the last couple of years. Televised religion is
still in shambles after the Bakker-like excesses of the 1980s (and
let's not forget Oral Roberts's huge tower to God in the middle of
Omaha). The city of New York and the Office of the Attorney General of the United States were both stripped clean to reveal truly
smarmy undercoats of self-interest, greed, and fraud. And in at
least one case, a genuinely spooky narcissist seized control of the
nation's foreign policy and the hearts and minds of most of the
nation as well. That was just the eighties, and the young 1990s
already have given us a president's son waist-deep in the S&L
scandal, federal housing abused to benefit those who knew the
right Republicans. And so on.

Yet while the issue for the working stiff is not the famously amoral
crazies, but the quiet, unsung narcissists who never make *Business
Week* or *The Wall Street Journal*, it is still those humongous Meeses,
Caseys, Boeskys, Milkens, Keatings, D'Amatos, and—still!—Nixons
who set the moral tone. And the mess they made of the 1980s
resonates to this day, as we spiral downward into recession.

## A Healthy Self-Image

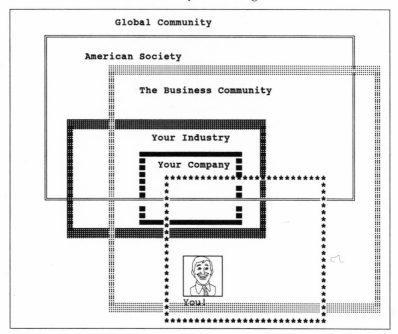

Boesky is the best example of narcissist rage to plunder run amok, the man who leveraged the entire state of corporate capitalism, with the help of many fish both smaller and larger. Yet it almost seems like a waste of time to attack him. This most famous inside trader was such a smug, bloated miscreant, his crimes so vast and blatant, and so much ink has been spilled excoriating him. In his sinking wake, he dragged some of the best fresh blood that Wall Street had to offer. This was no accident. It took smart, bold men, unencumbered by the sensitivities that hold smaller men in check, to evaluate the ultimate implications of the process that is now laughingly known as Democratization of Capital.

The greed was there, as it always had been, but more important, the acceptance of greed as a respectable driving force became and has remained a healthy assumption far and wide. It was a short step between making deals happen and using information to help make them happen. Only the really big narcissists, the ones with great conceptions and the energy to pursue them, stepped over the line in the irresponsible environment and became downright criminal.

But their deeds didn't have to be criminal in order to be wrong.

## The Narcissist on a Bad Day

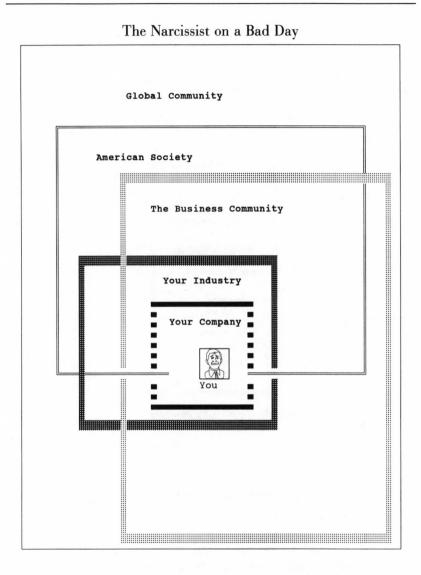

And the damage they did to organizations wasn't always outside the law, which may explain why some of the terrorists are still walking around granting interviews and looking svelte.

The well-publicized crimes of Boesky, Milken, Siegal, Levine, et al., were merely the most obvious evidence of the pervasive illness that has attacked the American business organism. Through the structure of our financial establishment, narcissistic economic hedonists are wielding their fantasies to get things done.

## The Narcissist on an Average Day

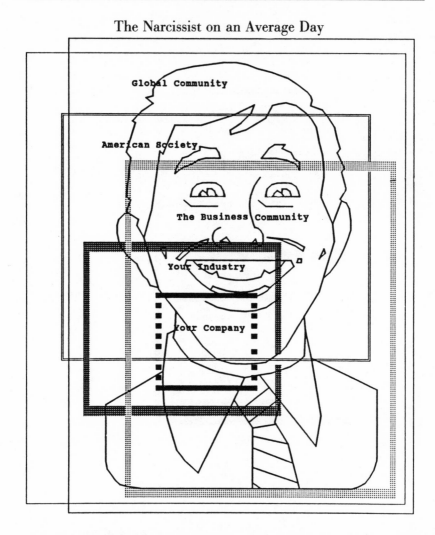

The bottom line is: manipulating works. The criminals merely give us a peek at what less courageous men are doing every day, more carefully. And for the most part, less successfully.

What Boesky and the other double agents of eighties-style greed taught the business community was where the line was drawn. Now the good boys stay on the right side of it, and the beat goes on, and on. Naive crusaders talk about teaching the narcissist about ethics, but the ability to see other people as real is not something that can be taught to anyone past teething.

The key to understanding this aspect of his behavior is to know a very simple truth: when the narcissistic glow is full upon him, Large Marvin doesn't give a fuck. He's on the road to greatness in his own mind. While you travel along in his parade, you may be afforded a junior measure of the same freedom he reserves for his fine self, as long as you don't step on his blue suede ego.

## HURRAH FOR THE RED, WHITE, AND SELFISH!

The cowboy spirit is celebrated throughout American culture, always has been. Consequently, the guy who believes he's a lone redwood standing at the edge of the bold frontier can be found in every business that employs more than one person. We're all guilty of this convenient personal myth, to a certain degree. Who really believes anyone else's life is more important than his? Gandhi, maybe, but maybe not, either. This boss takes his self very seriously. To him, it's his religion.

In today's business environment, the narcissist will most likely be an entrepreneur, a role few people succeed at without a sense of mythic self-confidence. As a people, too, we tend to like the cocky streetfighters like Lee Iacocca who have the initial nerts to tell Ford where to shove it, then go on to set the world on fire.

The media loves the narcissist almost as much as it admires the bully. The *Times* calls H. Ross Perot, the bee General Motors paid $700 million to bail out of its bonnet, the guy who was nearly given the job of running the United States Post Office without bidding on it, a "Pesky Entrepreneur." Now, Perot certainly calls 'em as he sees 'em and all that good stuff. But if this guy is merely "pesky," I'd like to see someone truly dangerous.

Throughout the nation, entrepreneurs are admired because of, not in spite of, their huge commitment to act selfishly. Michael Milken, before his troubles, liked to quote—why, look!—Harold Geneen. "Milken recalls a talk he once had with former ITT chairman Harold Geneen, who used to hold review sessions with ITT managers on weekends when he ran the show," *Forbes* wrote. " 'Harold Geneen told me he knew it was all over when they had those meetings on Thursday and Friday instead of the weekend,' Milken says." Right. How dare they forget about the boss for two whole days! Beyond that pale lies organizational madness and, eventually—freedom!

Rather than viewing such aberrant behavior as an illness, we've made guys like Perot (crusty, entrepreneurial, and legal) and Milken (bold, innovative, and illegal) national institutions. "Alan Gaines knows he's the type of Wall Streeter that chief executive officers love to hate," *The Wall Street Journal* wrote back in 1987. "He's the fast-talking head of an investment firm, lives in a Park Avenue townhouse, drives a Rolls Royce and earns more than $1 million a year. He also doesn't hesitate to tell American CEOs how to do their jobs." In this jolly and quite congratulatory vein, the *Journal* continues:

> Two years ago, the youthful Mr. Gaines flew to Houston to tell Tenneco Inc's silver-haired chief executive, 56-year-old James Ketelson, to restructure the $15-billion oil conglomerate or risk a takeover.
>
> "I walk into his office in Houston and Ketelson is like Mr. WASP, Mr. Proper. And here I am, a 32-year-old kid making more money than he does, telling him how to run his company. What would your reaction be?"
>
> Neither Mr. Ketelson nor Tenneco will comment, but Mr. Gaines says the advice was spurned. Not that he was surprised. He's used to what he calls the "anti-investment banker, anti-New York, anti-little rich kid" attitude of big company executives.
>
> He in turn sometimes holds a disdainful view of Main Street. "You go out and visit these CEOs who talk very slow, very deliberate. 'Well, sir-r-r, we're ve-ry interested in long-term valuuue,'" mimics Mr. Gaines, the head of Gaines Berland Co. "I want to say, 'Come on, guy, spit it out. Talk. I want to get home by next year.'"

*Brrrr . . .*

Narcissism was defined by Freud as a state in which "the satisfaction of the instincts is partially or totally withdrawn from the influence of other people." Meaning he's having fun whether you're there or not. In fact, the whole concept of "you" is very hazy to him. He's focused on himself. Or herself.

That power of concentration can be very seductive, if you're the focus of it for a time. A guy I'll call Todd, senior editor at a book-publishing house, was nearly seduced out of his job and into one he didn't want by the persuasive power of a beautiful narcissist. "She came in reeking of power, with her luxuriant mane of hair, lashing people as she walked," he recalls of his almost-boss. "She was carrying a shopping bag from Gucci, I swear, with manuscripts in it. I thought, wow, this is the ultimate of pretension." At first, the narcissist had taken the familiar gambit of any superimportant person—she'd played hard to get, even though she had been the one who had initiated the getting:

> She'd canceled four times, and the last time the assistant called, finally, I said, "Gee, I really hope Betsy can make this in Calendar 1989. Friday is my last available day this year." But then of course, I'm thinking Big House and lots of zeros at the end of the check, and she beguiled me into agreeing that it might be a good challenge to go up against the heavy hitters in the nonfiction best-seller division, so I found a little voice in my head saying. "What are you doing? Are you out of your fucking mind?" And in the meantime I hear myself saying, "Sure! I could do that!"

> By the end of the drinks, I was talking in the third person We, Us, and then she said, "So, what I really need is for you to sit down and *bang out* ten big blockbuster ideas. Send them over tomorrow." I was really pleased with myself until the realization hit me like a wrecking ball on the side of my face that I had committed myself to do a ton of work pursuing a job I don't want. As if *she's* ever *banged out* anything. It dawned on me about thirty seconds after she sashayed down the street that I had made a catastrophic mistake by showing enthusiasm. She sent me a note afterwards saying "Looking for your ideas." But I never did send them. I don't want to work for her.

A lot of very self-centered people seem to be attracted to journalism and show business, fields where a big ego is viewed as a badge of creativity. There's the tale of the theatrical director who sat in a corner at all cast parties (attendance at which was mandatory) taking notes on the social behavior of his working actors. The next day, at rehearsal, critiques were given. No rebuttal was allowed. This is the same individual who, after a terrible fire had wiped out the offices of this Boston theater company (as well as the homes of those who lived in the same building), was heard on the street, screaming at firemen, "I've got a five-thousand-dollar Rolex in that goddamn building, and I'd like to know which one of you guys is going to go up there and get it!" It isn't that such a boss is inconsiderate, exactly. It's just that he's not thinking about *you*. Unless you have his Rolex.

The crazy boss on a narcissistic binge can be a lot more pleasant than the same guy in a bully or paranoid frame of mind. In this aspect, he's immensely confident of his own judgment (if not of yours). He's dynamic, charming, and pleasantly ruthless in pursuit of his goals. Above all, he feels free to show the kind of selfishness only those with very young children will recognize.

And like a child, he can be kind of likable when he's at his spoiled worst—for a while. Unless you're his mommy or daddy, though, the kick can wear thin quickly. Randy, vice president of operations at a consulting firm that helps to elect—and advise—political heavy-weights both domestic and international speaks of his CEO:

> It's his firm. He's the king. But sometimes he acts like a three-year-old child. Recently, we moved into new, plush offices right in the heart of the city. At breakfast yesterday, we're sitting in the new conference room and talking about drinking coffee. "I'm trying to give it up," the chairman says. "I'm trying to drink water instead." He turns to the president of the firm, the guy who reports to him, everyone else's boss, and says, "Jack, I don't see my glass on the table here. Where is it?" It was a total reprimand. Jack says, "Gee, Les, I think it was lost in the move." For the rest of the day, the entire firm looked for that stupid glass. We never found it. It's still missing. I think somebody stole it, just to see how crazy Les would get about it. If so, they weren't disappointed.

The rewards of working for a jerk of these proportions are excitement, high stakes, and, possibly, great money. But if you want to make a quiet living, no one could be worse. In his mind, he's the Great One who created the business, knows it better than any tiny mortal, and will brook no contradiction about what's best for it. He's also not too good about listening to advice.

## FAST FAST FAST DECAY

The narcissist who is unable to "come down" from his unrealistic plane is likely to implode in the near-term rather than the long-term.

When the company is on the way up—in the green days of its original leadership—the Me-style may work quite well. It is only when the time comes for team action, or for institutionalization of roles—which it does, if the company is any kind of a success—that the entrepreneur is most often unable to create a team that will run without his large, rotating ego at the hub. Nor does he want to. The Company *is* him; he has writ his name large upon it.

The price for the organizational dynamism and centralization of power is constant turmoil. Without turmoil, the guy doesn't know what to do, can't really *feel* himself at work.

We are consequently treated each day to stories about courageous narcissistic entrepreneurs who acquire corporations, or build them, only to be booted out when the time comes for serious, daily operations. Steve Jobs, wunderkind of Apple Computer, is a good example of the entrepreneur constitutionally unable to function as an operating officer. George Westinghouse bit the same dust earlier in the century, when he was forcibly ejected by his middle managers. "A great inventor. A genius," says an old hand with the company. "But he didn't know beans about running a business. They had to get rid of him if they were ever going to move into the twentieth century."

In short, the talents necessary for building a business may not be the same as those needed for running it.

In the building phase, the Lone Wolf's narcissism rewards sycophants who try to mimic him—down to the pinstripe on his suit. This is the land of the Yes-Man, the inert barnacle on the executive office. No one feels secure enough to disagree with the narcissist, or to give him news he doesn't want to hear. For those unable to bow, scrape, and nod without interruption, it can be a degrading, irritating, and fearsome environment.

In the plateau phase, the company is established and continuing to grow nicely. The boss is on top of the world, and possible acquirers are sniffing the wind around the executive suite. Now is the time to carve out some turf, if any is to be had, in the areas in which the Lone Wolf has little interest. This is the only insurance of outliving his tenure.

During the next phase, the corporation grows beyond the need for his entrepreneurial skill, and may jettison him, if it can. Healthy companies identify certain necessary, less flamboyant men who can take over while the macho man is floating downward on his platinum chute and more sober business-as-usual becomes the name of the game.

These career bureaucrat types may be boring and predictable, but they're a hell of a lot more fun to work for. It's nice to avoid a useless trip to the Pocatello suburbs on some executive whim without being called a traitor, laggard, or weak sister who isn't in touch with every single one of the emperor's momentary needs.

After a couple of years with a boss who is predominantly a narcissist, the average worker may find himself yearning for a good old bureaucrat with a tendency toward paranoia.

Everything is relative, including occupational misery.

## I'M OKAY—IT'S OKAY!

The narcissist's self-orientation translates—depending on its power—into anything from mild sociopathology to outright criminality.

"For a while, John De Lorean's dream seemed to come true. But suddenly the man who had done everything right found everything going wrong," wrote *The Wall Street Journal* on October 22, 1982. "Sales of his sleek new sports car dried up, debts began to mount and the British government forced his lone manufacturing plant in Northern Ireland into receivership. De Lorean began a desperate struggle to avoid failure, a struggle that ended Tuesday with his arrest in Los Angeles on drug-trafficking charges." The *Journal* continued:

> Friends and associates of the flamboyant auto executive paint a picture of a man who changed drastically as he became increasingly desperate in his attempts to rescue the company he had founded. From the coolly brilliant GM engineer, he became increasingly erratic and dictatorial. . . . He lost trust in close advisers and began to concentrate in his own hands more and more of the campaign to save the company. In the end, the swashbuckling entrepreneur may have become a victim of his own myth. . . .

In his guts, the Big Dude *believes* in his life story, and central to that construct is his own divinity, his feeling that he is Law unto himself, that if he wants it, *it is right.* Driven by that sense of righteous mission, he goes forth to make sure the world conforms to his expectations.

## ANGER, YES, BUT ONLY WITH ARDOR

A lawyer I know worked overnight on an injunction, while, of course, her narcissist boss went home to his supper and end of business as always. She relates: "The boss came in the next morning, and said to me, 'What are you doing here?' He said, 'Didn't you hear? We settled. I got the call just before I went home. Didn't anybody tell you?' " At that moment, blind with exhaustion and rage, the poor droid just snapped. "I took a little bottle of whiteout and threw it hard, and it smashed all over his door," she says, smiling. "He didn't clean the door. He had it removed and threw it away." My correspondent further notes that from that point on in, communications between the Boss and staff improved.

Similar displays of anger will be effective only if the supreme self-image of the narcissist is not threatened. Indeed, all attempts to thwart the narcissist must be conducted simultaneously to ongoing ministrations to his ego. The Me serpent appreciates only the kind of service that glorifies him, does honor to his name, and he has no problem manipulating others to suit his ends. One employee in the PR department of a big company tells how he was pressured continually to churn out flattering news about the chief executive. "Every issue of the company magazine had to have at least two or three mentions of him," the executive recalls. "If his name appeared only once in an issue, he would rail against it, tearing it apart, but he wouldn't directly confront the reason why. After we added a few more details about the chief's activities, however, he was satisfied." The magazine had three editors in seven years.

## THERE'S NO BUSINESS WITHOUT SHOW BUSINESS

This effort to deliver high kudos to the Big Balloon bears no relationship to the actual success of the Boss himself, because the size of the guy's ego can make him very credible to other inflated bosses up above. In other words, a crazy boss is often defined and revered for the size of his failures, as well as his successes.

My friend Mel is a middle manager in a humongous communications conglomerate that delivers information to America via every media from paper to satellite beam. His boss's career has been marked by the strange amalgam of failure and promotion.

> There's a guy here whose title is president of the Magazine Group. He's the number two, reporting to the chairman. In his forties. Generally given credit for the multimillion-dollar loss at [names magazine].

He's the most vilified manager in America today. Makes an enormous amount of money, and as far as anyone can tell, he's never done anything well. There have been no successes here. He got promoted after his last humongous, expensive failure. There's one of the mysteries in the organization. Why does he keep getting promoted?

He's an extremely forceful, dynamic person with a lot of social graces, a hail-fellow-well-met, who creates the illusion that when he's around, he has control of the situation and good things are going to happen. Unfortunately, no good things have happened, but no one seems to have caught on.

He's one of those people who has a job not because he's demonstrated that he's smarter, or more competent, or delivers more, but because *he gives that impression*. He fulfills the stereotype of what a successful corporate executive should look like, act like, and even think like. He knows how to conduct a meeting.

He talks to no one. Has no instincts for the business in which he's supposed to be a leader. It's like the Charge of the Light Brigade. He's leading the company in a series of dashing charges into the mouth of the cannon. And he looks great doing it.

Since appearances are all-important to the narcissist, sometimes this type of crazy mind can produce behavior that is very dynamic, when the crazy boss's vision of his personal destiny is stoked to a fever pitch. John is a producer at a number-one network-affiliated television station somewhere in this nation's breadbasket. He reports:

My boss Bob came out of a top Ivy League school with, I think, a master's of something or other unrelated to our business. He had a very swift career in publishing, and attained a lot of power before he was thirty. He was fired from that job within two years—there was a virtual staff mutiny. The guy is extremely ambitious for power, per se. Irrationally competitive. Respects no one or anything. No respect for talent, or for experience. Extraordinary obstructionist. Puts down all suggestions and ideas so that no one likes to tell him anything. Physically, not much: a small man with a large desk. The day after he was fired from here, he appeared at the office in shirtsleeves, ready for work, as though nothing had happened. I guess he couldn't accept the fact that he had been fired.

Like many bosses on a narcissist trip, Bob is blithe about his effect on other people. Because he's unable to concentrate on anything other than himself, he retains very little beyond what has just transpired to him personally in the last five to seven minutes. John continues:

> He's the general manager of our entire television station—a really big job, but he has the attention span of a three-year-old child. He'll cut programming and acquisition budgets, and then he'll ask why there's no development or acquisition going on. And if, as usual, he has expressed contempt for a program, and it succeeds, he'll immediately adopt it as his own. But he has no real commitment to anything. Except to power.

## DON'T BOTHER ME, I'M TOO BIG TO COPE

The problem with very self-centered people—before they hit the rocks of reality—is that they live in a dream. If the dream is a busy dream, they get busy. If the dream is in deep REM, however, absolutely nothing happens anywhere. Deadlines are blown, opportunities decay, while the executive senior VP is behind locked doors musing on which lucky businessperson will be favored with lunch that day.

Vanity can be aggressive as well as passive. A woman I'll call Lucille was the chief arts administrator for a small nonprofit organization that served an inner city on the East Coast. Her job primarily involved fund-raising, but she fancied herself a patroness of the arts, according to one of her employees, a hardworking performer I'll call Chet. "Her management style was so odd as to be nonexistent," Chet says. "We're a small organization where one-on-one communications is all-important. But you'd have to make an appointment to see her. It was hard to get one, too. She couldn't stand to talk to anyone below a certain level. She basically didn't know most people existed. She had no idea who I was, and I supposedly reported to her. She had a reputation for being charming, but I think she reserved that for the rich and famous. She's horrible to her own employees." What was the woman doing while she was ignoring the mundane? Chet knows:

> She had her hair and makeup done every morning before she came to work. That was her style. Some days she would come to work with an unusually bad blond job—almost platinum frosted. She thought it was great. The blonder the better.

Behind the narcissist's self-absorption is not a vacuum, however. As Chet found out, there is a viciousness there, too, that the narcissist must eventually act upon.

> She wanted to firmly establish that she was superior. She did that by being cold and inaccessible and remote and unresponsive. She was absolutely horrible. The turnover was incredible. I think she fired almost all of the people from the previous administration, the ones she hadn't chosen in her own image.

### YOU—LOOK—MARVELOUS!

My friend Curt works for a magazine editor, one of the most highly respected in the business. "Here's a guy who's surly and gruff, he's pompous-looking and never loosens his tie, no one has ever seen him remove his sports jacket or roll up his sleeves in public. The kind of guy who looks like he sleeps in his suit and it still isn't wrinkled. Looks like he and his suit get dry-cleaned at the same time, with him in it."

This hatred of "mess" is typical in the narcissist crazy boss. If you're one of the people who can keep the messy details or sloppy human incidents at bay, you may have a niche in the organization, if that's the game you want to play. "I used to work with a woman who needed hot cups of tea all day long," says my friend Sally, who is an assistant manager at a retail store that sells an inordinate amount of wicker and scented candles. "It had to be a particular kind of tea, and it had to be in her own special china cup, and had to be on a little tray, with a particular kind of spoon, all like that. And that got pretty persnickety. All I ask of my assistant is that he just run and grab me a crummy paper cup of coffee now and then." Sally reports that, eventually, the boss's assistant, in a fit of annoyance while being bothered during a genuinely important task, requested that her boss get her *own* tea. "The woman said, 'Fine, you're fired. You drive me crazy!' I think the boss really feels that it helps her function. A sense of order, style, is important. And it's a formality that quiets her down. This is a person perched on the brink of a nervous breakdown, but aren't most of us? When you get to a certain level, your job is really tense. I don't know anyone who doesn't have to deal with making large decisions, and we're put on the line all day long. You need someone who can keep you informed and anticipate your needs. Make it possible not to go nuts."

In his favor, it must be said that your narcissist is likely to be kind, even generous, to those who contribute to his sense of well-being and do not go out of their way to threaten him. And his easygoing largess can leave subordinates a lot of turf to farm with no fear of reprisals.

Best of all, he's not into details. Details are something outside yourself. They take *attention*. Ooh, that hurts. "With Doris, the best tactic was to say yes, and then not do it," says my friend Anne, vice president of planning at a large broadcasting and cable company. "Almost immediately, she'd forget. She was really reliable in that way. Anything she really wanted had to be done within twenty-four hours or she'd just—lose consciousness about it. So the half-life of any project was twenty-four hours, and then it disintegrated into nothingness. If you got by that window of vulnerability, you were okay."

This quality of *living in the here and now* makes the narcissist a great maven for the short-term details that pertain to conception of himself. Marlo is the administrative assistant serving the former chairman of a large electric-equipment manufacturer. "They asked me to fill in for this girl when she was out on the first vacation he'd allowed her to have in two years," she says.

> I was to arrange the great man's transportation from the airport, make sure the limo got there on time, that kind of stuff. And when he would land, he would call, that was the arrangement. So the phone rang, and I said, "Mr. Kogle's office." And it's him, and he says, "This is Mr. Kogle." And I said, "Hi, what's up?" And there's a pause, and then he says, "I'll be in about four o'clock." And that's it.

> His secretary comes back about a week later. And she takes me aside in the ladies' room and says to me, "Marlo, Mr. Kogle wanted me to tell you that if you ever answer his phone again, you are under no circumstances to say, 'Hi, what's up?' That's not the way he likes to be spoken to. He doesn't feel it's proper." So I figured okay, if he wants to live with a stick up his ass, it's fine with me, and I referred to him as "sir" from that time in. And he's gone and forgotten around here at least ten years before I'm due to retire, by the way.

## MARGE—MY TOYS!

Give him his autoerotic office paraphernalia and he'll be happy. Chief among these is the telephone and all the playthings that go along with it. In fact, the best way to spot a narcissist is by his

trinkets, doodads, and geegaws. Arnold, copywriter at a Chicago
advertising agency, reports:

> There are a lot of guys in advertising who like a speakerphone. They
> see it as a sign of success or status. These same guys generally like to
> take a call when you're in their office, and stay on while you watch
> them talk. That's infuriating. Typically, I just sit there and fume. It
> conveys the message: "You don't work *with* me, you work *for* me."
> It sets up a hierarchy.

A press agent who spends a lot of time on the receiving end of
narcissist phoners says:

> The speakerphone is horrible. People who think they're important but
> aren't as important as they think they are. They want you to think that
> you're talking to some exalted personage, and so they put you on the
> speakerphone. The most insulting thing is when you're on a speak-
> erphone and the person's in a car. Hollywood agents do that, or at
> least the second rung. They let you know right away. They say, "I'm
> calling from my car, because blah blah blah. Whoops! I'm going into
> a tunnel!" Who gives a damn?

Many egophone jockeys seem to reside in the world of show business, where the instrument is more important than the typewriter.
Sheldon is a subagent at a bicoastal talent agency whose name I will
not utter because they may at some time like to represent me. Sheldon works for a guy I'll call Levine, a Supreme High Agent whose
phone tactics are an integral part of his narcissistic style. "He is
definitely the person in control of any phone call," Sheldon says.

> One way he asserts himself is to never take the call, but always call the
> other person back at his leisure. He developed a reputation through-
> out his career of never calling people back. That is his foremost at-
> tribute. What started to happen is that slowly but surely his clients
> started going elsewhere to find an agent who will return a phone call.
> It's actually an industry joke. The gag goes, when he dies, his tomb-
> stone will read: HERE LIES MAX LEVINE—HE'LL GET BACK TO YOU.

> Legend has it that one day one of his assistants had been out to lunch
> with him, and they came back, and Max picks up the list of phone
> messages, and says, angry, "This is terrible. Are these the only calls
> I've received? I could legitimately return all these calls!" So he pro-
> ceeds to return not one of them, goes into his office and starts playing

backgammon with his assistant. At which point the head of a major studio calls, urgent. Max says, "I'll call him back." Just to impress his assistant, to show he's still not returning important calls. "I'm still not returning the big ones," that kind of thing.

I'm sure he has a tremendous sense of power over people on the phone, because they're afraid he's going to hang up, or go away. At the same time, his client list is shrinking.

On the other hand, a guy who sees the world in terms of electronic playthings can be sort of fun, if you don't have to depend on him. Molly, a playwright I know, has her own fond memory of getting good phone from that same Max Levine: "His male secretary placed the call, and says, 'Will you hold for Max Levine?'"

Of course I'm going to hold! So anyway, I'm kept on hold for about two minutes, and then Max comes on and says, "How are ya!?" His voice was jovial and friendly and took me off guard that he was so nice, and concerned about how I was. He kept me on the phone for about two minutes, but in that time I felt really, really good. Then he hung up. He was kind and sweet.

Nice. Yet remember—while he may love his phone, he doesn't have any respect for yours. Melanie, a researcher director at a network news operation, recalls an incident with her boss, a tremendous meisterphoner:

He yelled at me. I was talking to a very important source on the phone, and he came over and started shouting at me. "Melanie! Melanie! Get off the phone! Hang up the phone!" He did it until I hung up. It was really rude. He said, "I can't be having you make these personal calls during work." And I said, "It wasn't a personal call, it was professional!" And he said, "Whatever." And I said, "What was it you wanted, anyway?" And he said, "Nothing. It can wait."

The issue, as always, is control. Of information. Of power. Of you. And ultimately, of all the credit that flows anywhere in his neighborhood. For the narcissistic personality is into receiving acclaim for anything and everything within his grasp. And if you want to survive, you'd best let him have it. Fighting a narcissist on the prestige battlefront is hopeless. You're threatening the one single thing he cherishes, and he'll turn you into anchovy paste if you stand in his

way. Vince, a project manager at a manufacturing concern in Pitts-
burgh, says:

> Joel takes credit for all the good ideas at the meeting. You say some-
> thing and he ridicules it, and then, weeks later, when things pan out
> fine, he'll say, "So I guess it was a good idea I thought of, huh?" And
> I'll say, "Excuse me, Joel, but it wasn't yours, it was mine," and he'll
> say, "Sure it was mine." I guess I'm stupid to make an issue of it. But
> I just have to. Every now and then I do come up with something that
> I can claim publicly. And of course that pisses him off, because he
> wants to take credit for it.

The greed for *ownership* is central to the guy who is building a
cinematography for himself. It extends to everything that confers
affection and widespread regard, from a contract to a witty comment.


## GOSH, HERB, YOU'RE SO DARNED *FUNNY*

A laugh is a precious thing, especially in the workplace, and the
narcissist wants to control that, too. "If Gary makes a joke, the lower
you are on the ladder, the louder you have to laugh," says a public-
relations manager at a food company in the Midwest. "The higher
you are, too, maybe, but I'd hate to think that's true."

It *is* true. "When I can't make a subordinate laugh, I feel I'm in
deep trouble with that person," admits Rogan, an honest narcissist
who runs an accounting department of forty souls for a great preening peacock who sets the tone. "It feels like I've just crossed the void.
If I can't get them to laugh, we don't share a sensibility, and it's
going to be very difficult to get them to do the work I want them to
do. I'd suggest that any employee of mine laugh at my jokes. I do the
same for my boss, and we get along splendidly."

While insincerity isn't easy, it is necessary, and those who can't
muster it might be working for the wrong guy. Of course, there is
that sensation, when you leave the office after laughing at four or five
unfunny jokes, of needing to take a shower. "I do tend to have that
existential feeling that Sartre described as nausea," states Rogan.
"You feel alienated from yourself. But it goes away, and yearly
promotions and raises compensate for the existential problem. I personally feel nausea until I get into my new sports car."

Appreciation for the boss's ostensible humor is one of the best pathways to his high regard. Luke, a salesman for a radio station, is used to stroking his sales director for fun and profit, and, if not profit, at least continued employment. He does so in a very technical and specific way, by affectionately teasing the narcissist. It's a dangerous game. "There are only a couple of guys who can get away with it," he relates.

> He always felt it was innocent with me, which in fact it was. In every movie, you know, the king usually has his jester. The role is to dissipate tension, make small symbolic nicks and cuts in the boss without actually drawing blood. That satisfies the court that the guy has a human side; if he can take it a little bit, they can give him credit for being humane. Imitations of him were always good. Growling. He was so quick, a little bit of sarcasm was his tool. He could zing you. When Mosconi made a joke, you could moan and stuff, because bad jokes are a way of showing self-abnegation. The boss makes a bad joke and you moan. It's as good as a laugh.

Managing a sick manager in his narcissist stage is a lot easier than handling him when he's feeling a little bully, or chattering with paranoia. Manipulative narcissists are people who take circuitous routes to express their aggressive impulses. This means they are likely to be, at bottom, more in touch with the doubts and insecurities that afflict sane people. Tap into those insecurities, gently, bolster his ego and make him feel nice, and the narcissistic boss will be a puddle of goo beneath your feet. Or you'll be that at his feet. Either way, you're a winner, you big suckup, you.

## FIRST SUCKUP, PART ONE: WHAT IT LOOKS LIKE

A fellow I'll call Warren is a senior editor at an immensely powerful newspaper in one of the largest American cities. "If the public knew the level of egregious ass-kissing that went on at this highly respected bastion of news excellence, it would be appalled," he says. "Fortunately, all this sucking up went on out of the public eye." The worse excesses were demonstrated by another high senior editor Warren calls Fred, who reported to Henry, the editor in chief. "Fred was one of the all-time greats," Warren states.

They were at a meeting during a discussion of something and Fred turned to Henry and ran his hand along the crease of his pants. "Nice fabric, Henry," he says. It was a little private moment between a serf and his preening asshole. About eight people were there. We were grossed out. After Henry retired, Fred was gone, I mean gone, almost immediately.

Henry demanded that kind of grooming. I was in attendance at a meeting when the paper inaugurated a new metropolitan section. I was invited to a meeting, the only reporter there. One of the other editors held the meeting to elicit responses on this new idea. Twelve editors there trashed the idea. As the last person, who was Biff Green, the culture editor, was just finished trashing it, Henry walked in. Henry slams his fist on the table and says, "It's a fait accompli, I'm so thrilled about it. Now I'd like to hear what everybody has to say," and to a man, every single body praised it, and Green, who had been badmouthing the idea up and down, said something like, "Sure there are problems with it, but I don't see that they can't be overcome. I like it."

Henry required it. And Fred did it all the time. One thing that Fred always did was kill any story that Henry didn't like. I remember writing a story as a guest observer on whales, and Fred killed it based on the rumor that Henry didn't like downbeat stories about nature. And I got so mad about it, and I went in to Henry and he said he'd said no such thing, and located Fred at the airport and chewed his ass out.

People felt Fred was an oily character who had no mind of his own, just a suckup. That was his only purpose. Henry was the real editor of Fred's section. There was also some thought that Henry liked him there, even when he made horrible mistakes, that somehow this enhanced Henry's reputation, because he could whip him. That was the reason Fred was there. And to protect Henry from criticism.

Other guys did the same thing. Allen Horst's whole career was made sucking up to Henry, and the minute Henry left, Allen started saying he and Henry never saw eye to eye. A couple of hours after Henry left, literally, and Allen is saying he was a lot closer to Wes Kunkle, the new editor. But Fred would kill things or change things because he'd heard ten years ago that, for instance, Henry didn't like certain table lamps, and this accumulated to the point where no one could say anything in Fred's section, because as he would read things, bells would go off in his head and he'd have to recall if things were offensive to Henry. His whole world centered around pleasing Henry.

It was institutionalized. You knew who was in what position and who it was necessary to preen. There was an underlying feeling that everybody's open to that kind of thing. That it never hurt; it paid. You'd think, He must be nauseated, but he wasn't. You think or hope that the boss is smart enough to see through it and think the suckup is an asshole and that he's doing this while he should be working, but my experience is that these kind of bosses don't see through it, and you are better off just doing it and hanging around.

*Hanging around* is a very important concept. In more than three separate cases, I received reports of subordinates *waiting for the boss to hit the men's room so they could share with him some quality toilet time.* "People were timing leaks to when the boss went," says a source in advertising. "They figured you might not have a chance to come face to face unless they did. They'd see the guy go down the hall and make a point to get a chance to cross streams."

But those who wait by the bathroom door do not go unnoticed by their enemies, competitors, and other office friends. A guy who works in the New York headquarters of a large multinational corporation reports:

I got a reference call about this one guy that used to work here, and the first thing I told them was that he had this uncanny habit of leaping up from his desk and going to the men's room right at the precise time he saw Pietr headed in that direction. I think he got enormous work done in there. He had Pietr's ear there. There is no way you can have a door slammed in your face in there. It's a captive audience. Just small talk. Hi. I think the Frebish Project is the most synergistic thing I ever saw. That kind of smut. That will militate against you down the line, because who likes someone who always has their nose up someone else's heinie?

Nobody—but the boss, that is!

## FIRST SUCKUP, PART TWO: A STRATEGIC RATIONALIZATION

Bootlicking. Ass-kissing. Brownnosing. Apple-polishing. Buttering up. Toadying. Fawning. Tuft-hunting. All names for the game Fred was playing with Henry. "I like the term bootlicking the best," says a corporate politician, "especially with a woman boss. I imagine her in thigh-high black boots, spikes. I'd start from the back and work forward."

The art of sucking up is useful with the bully, helpful with the paranoid, but absolutely essential in narcissist management.

Is greasing the golden goose so bad? Some, especially the cool of blood and cold of heart, don't think so. My friend Brewster has parlayed his knowledge of corporate politics into a decent income as management consultant. His analysis of the phenomenon of sucking up would do a courtier in the Borgia empire proud. "I think it's the stuff that makes the world go round," he says.

> Who's to say that being married isn't an extended brownnosing extravaganza, or getting a woman into bed, or anything you want. It's about fixing that smile to your face instead of saying what you really think. Come to think of it, saying what you really think isn't valued in any polite society I can think of.

> What you have to do is what great criminals do, which is mask their emotions and make as if you're not committing the act even as you're doing it. You do it, but you don't. The obvious suckups are guys whose actions are charged with desperation. Desperation is what rears its ugly head, and when you see that, that's what nobody likes. That's what everybody means when they say they don't like it.

> I try to pursue it as a calm policy. Think of it like the ABM treaty, you have to adhere to it, you don't necessarily like it, and maybe something better will come along, but until disarmament arrives, you have got to stick to it.

Does sucking up involve loss of self? Brewster continues:

> You have to maintain your own personality's location in your body. Don't be a chameleon, don't alter your personality grotesquely to fit certain social circumstances. If you and I were in a fascist mansion in Buenos Aires, we'd make snide comments, shake all the hands around, and get the fuck out of there before they put us in a prison camp.

> You've just got to make them come to you. In other words, if you maintain your center of gravity, you know you're a reasonably okay guy, proceeding through this mortal coil in a reasonable way, why wouldn't the president want to come over to you? If he can count on a couple of jokes, a little lively conversation, as opposed to some boring shit about your third-quarter profits, he's going to want to come over and schmooze a little bit, shoot the bull. It is sucking up, because you wouldn't ever really talk to him unless he was the president.

> You gotta think like a fucking spy all the time. Calculate the approach. Apply the smarm. And get the fuck off the premises before they find out about you. On to the next victim. You have to be brutal

about this shit. If you brownnose with any sentimentality, you're dead meat. You have to use cold, surgical cruelty. You're a dentist. You have to apply the grease and then move on down the line. It's like you're in a tropical environment and the sun is beating down, you wipe the grease on top of his head. All he knows is his head feels better and you were around when it happened.

In other words, it's not an art that reaches into your soul. It's a game that, like all great games, can be played by the professional for monetary advantage.

That's how I choose to see it, at any rate.

## FIRST SUCKUP, PART THREE: MORE OF WHAT YOU NEED TO KNOW

All narcissists think themselves unique and special, so they try to find unique and special ways to grease the tops of their tiny heads.

Female narcissists are subject to unique pressures on their neurotic pride, and so must be stroked in a very calculating, efficient, and delicate way. Ian, a junior broker at a firm that markets mortgages, has become practiced in sucking up very subtly to his attractive, recently divorced CEO. No, it's not what you think. In fact, it's the exact opposite.

"Women are extremely sensitive about being regarded in a businesslike fashion, and anything you say that pushes them back into a social role can be seen as less than respectful of their standing, their stature," he says. "That's dangerous." How does one suck up in this case without offending, presuming, casting aspersions, diminishing, or otherwise serving up an affront? By stealth. Ian continues:

If you have something tasty for the boss, you don't shovel it in there loaded with turkey, you slide it in sideways, across the table a nibble at a time. It's a family, babies, all that personal stuff, and you remember her children's names and ages, and then from time to time you drop a question, "How is Suzie doing at Choate?"

At the same time, when talking to women bosses, remember that they prefer to discuss things in much more esoteric terms than men. Male bosses tend to limit the intellectual content of their stories. I think women are much more comfortable with the idea of discussing the larger issue at hand, or the societal relationships, and they appreciate talking about them. And I think I've probably used that more than anything else in sucking up to female bosses. In other words, women like to talk about big issues. Get them started and they won't quit. The ability to listen is tremendously valued by women, especially in men, especially women in a managerial position who want to be listened to by men.

Come to think of it, nowadays men can talk pretty good, too. Last week I had a great conversation with the vice president of Finance about infant farting. We almost bonded.

But beware: even if the guy is a humongous personal mythmaker, he won't appreciate an obvious sleazeball shoving table scraps in his face. Sherman, a friend in corporate advertising, remembers:

There was a guy who once, you would think, had figured out the consummate suckup scam. At that time he was facing a crisis in his career—I think he'd been offered another job someplace else. He knew that the boss was very religious. So he went into the boss's office and laid out the job issue that was facing him, and then asked the boss if he would get down and pray with him. And the boss did get down and pray with him, and then canned him a week later. In my mind, that incident stands out as the difference between the suckup and the fuckup.

Bottom line on the big suckup question? If you're not careful and discreet, you can get busted by the toad you're trying to toady. For some reason, narcissists love to humiliate friends even more than people they feel neutral about. In one particularly gruesome case, a guy I'll call Ed spent some fruitless time sucking up to Benny, his former boss, a Me-person of the first order at his old law firm. Frank, an attorney in Ed's former firm, picks up the gory details:

So I happen to know that Ed was in the middle of a salary negotiation with his new boss, at his new firm. And in the middle of that, he sent Benny a long memo about recent court decisions he thought worthy of note that should be brought to the attention of all associates at our firm. This memo arrived right in the middle of his own salary negotiation at his new company. See? Think he wanted to come home? Maybe he thought it might be good fodder for his meeting with *his* senior guy. It didn't go down too well. For weeks after, people were talking about it at my firm and laughing about it. Benny actually showed everybody the memo and was chuckling about it.

There was no explanation beyond my friend's need to nuzzle a surrogate father. He wasn't getting that from his boss, so he went back to his former boss for it. It was kind of like the child negotiating for a better deal between his two parents.

Thanks to its dangers, and the fact that unless it is done perfectly it can backfire, there are those who forswear pandering entirely. Brad, an ad sales manager for a national TV sales group, knows the risks of seeming too much the toady:

You have to calculate how you're regarded by people at your level. If you're going to do it, better be subtle, because you'll be alienating a lot of co-workers, and never count on them as allies when you're putting forth your cause. You're putting all your trust in your boss. They'll always be critical of you after they've seen that. It's very difficult. When you see a friend do that, you feel bad, nauseated. I've been in a situation where I've seen someone I liked turn into a different person. Then I think . . . "Do I really want to be this person's friend?"

These are intelligent men, but their lasting memory, their heritage will always be linked to the fact that they were suckups.

## YES . . . BUT . . .

Refusing to truckle to a narcissist can be great for your integrity but devastating to your career. So if you're not made of sterner stuff, stay out of his way and accept that fact that you're *never going to be on his A-Team.*

The very last thing you want to do is puncture the delicate balloon of fictional grandeur that insulates his perilously inflated ego. My friend Neil was a performer in a successful national theatrical touring company. His boss was a megalomaniac I'll call Louis who eventually triumphed over the honest, straightforward actor who stupidly believed in the power of honesty. If my source here seems bitter, I think he may be forgiven.

Louis was a malicious son of a bitch when thwarted. A revisionist. He is the co-founder of the company, the business manager, but he's rewritten history so he's the only founding father. I can't talk about him. He's the worst enemy I've ever had. I despised him.

One time Louis ordered the company to participate in a photo call in support of a book he was writing. That wasn't in our contract, and there was no extra money involved. Now I have to tell you, we were making about eighty dollars a week and working ten, twelve hours a day between shows and rehearsals. Anyway, doing publicity photos for free really got under my skin.

So I got up at rehearsal in front of the company and objected. Louis wasn't there, and I just expressed my feelings. I said I have nothing against this book, but this is not in our contract, and shouldn't we be paid extra money for this kind of thing? It was a mistake. I should have asked for a meeting.

Anyway, Louis came. A company spy ran and told him, he came in—"Neil, I want to talk to you"—and he takes me out and he's screaming like a little baby, all red in the face, and pacing back and forth to keep people off guard, acting all noblesse oblige, screaming stuff about loyalty and "What are you, a locker-room lawyer?" That kind of stuff. I said, "Listen, you have no right to order us to do something that's outside the contract," and he went on in his rage, and I said, "You're the Great White Father, leading us around like sheep." He became apoplectic. He said, "Go home! Don't come back today!" I said, "Oh, I see, you're punishing me like I'm a little bad boy." I turned around and walked away.

Later, I issued a typed apology to the company to the effect that the time, place, and manner of my objection may have been ill-considered, but the content of my message I took pride in. That drove him nuts, which I'm thankful for.

He fucked all the pretty women of the company, or tried to. I have no proof of this, but I also think he screws around with the finances. He sees the company as being himself. He won't permit the actors to unionize. The company is his fiefdom. And he treats the kids like slaves.

And when need be, he can do more than just rant and rave and act childish. He can assert himself all over you, firm in the knowledge that he could cut your throat without a first thought, let alone a second. For, as we have seen in each of the grand felonious narcissists of the 1980s, conscience about the implications of their actions on other people's lives is not one of their big strengths. And they don't like to have their supreme wisdom questioned too closely.

"Failure to bend and scrape ultimately destroyed my relationship with my boss, Fritz," says Mort, a database manager at a direct-marketing firm. "Fritz is a capricious guy who has total power."

My inability to just say yes about everything destroyed my relationship with him eventually. He took me out to lunch, about two years into the job where I was, like, the number-four guy. And he lambasted me. He said, "Do you want to keep your job, do you like it? Then why are you thwarting me? You don't do what I ask you to do." He said, "You're becoming just like Ken," a guy who was a complete brat and totally negative. And as he was telling me this—that "people didn't like my attitude" and so forth—he interjected, "Are you finished with your potatoes?" (which I hadn't touched), and I said, "Yes," and he said, "Great," and ate them. And he said, "You know, when I hired you, I had great hopes for you, but if you continue to be so negative, I don't know whether there's any future for you here," and then he said, "Have you finished your steak?" and I was sweating bullets, my heart in my throat, and I said, "Sure, Fritz, I'm finished with it," and he finished my steak. And after that, the last time I said no to him directly was the time I told him I was leaving the firm.

In any event, and no matter how charming he may look in his new ascot, remember that, more than any other crazy boss, the Very Self-Centered is not to be trusted. He's slippery, and he has no idea of good or evil outside of whether something is good or evil for him personally.

## THE EMPEROR HAS UGLY UNDERWEAR

Underneath the bluster and fustian is a well of poisonous jealousy of any success that is not his own. My friend Jessie develops marketing plans for new projects at a large entertainment company based in Los Angeles. She has a "dotted line" reporting relationship to a vice president of Sales at the company, one whose piggish narcissism has blossomed over the years.

This person, Babs Berrigan, is the kind of boss who pretends to work real collegially with you when all she really wants to do is knife you in the back, because she wants to be a Queen Bee. The sweetness quotient is key.

She's the only person who I've worked for whose guts I really hate. She likes people to think she's looking out at the world with sweetness and light, but inside all is green with envy. And she's constantly trying to figure out how to get the best from you and make it her own. We used to work on projects together, and then, before I knew it, she put her name on it and I was erased from the face of the earth. And you feel like a wimp going around people saying, "That's my work!," because you work in a corporation and we're all team players and all that.

When there was dirty work to be done, like beating on the production company, she was happy for me to play the heavy, but when there was an industry awards contest, before I even knew what was happening, she had submitted the company's application with her name on it, and she was right up there ready to accept when we did win.

Another time, we were about to start a big meeting, and people were milling about and lining up, and somehow the subject of children came up. And Babs said, looking up at me with awe in her eyes, "I don't know how you manage to take care of your children and your house and still have anything left to give to your job. I mean, I just give my all to my career, and I don't see how you have anything left." I could have killed her. Every vice president in the company heard this. There was an assemblage of senior doohickies. To me, it was such a way of saying "You're a mommy, and I'm a full-time employee." I probably stared dumbfounded. I was aghast at being slotted as a part-timer. I murdered her in my heart, though, on the spot.

It's an interesting profile. She's a true organizational parasite. She will attach herself to one source of power, and derive as much energy from that source as she can, then move on to a new source of light. And it sort of reduces you to your meanest qualities, 'cause you're always forced to toot your own horn and demand credit for what she's already claimed as her work.

From the big Boeskys to the tiny, selfish middle managers that dot our organizations, the key ingredient that binds all Me-people is a systemic inability to apply general moral laws—which they understand when they are applied to other people—to their own behavior.

The knowledge that the narcissist is empty of values and totally self-serving can confer a kind of serenity on the employee who needs to manage one. In the abandoning of hope, there is power.

Those who expect nothing cannot be disappointed.

## ACTION POINTS: THE NARCISSIST

Due to his massive *unconsciousness* about anything not himself, the
narcissist may be more easily manipulated than many other types of
loony. You're unreal to him, simply a projection of what's going on
inside his personal cinematography at that moment. Keep his little
personal motion picture running smoothly, and you've just about got
him where you want him. Beyond that general rule, observe the
following precepts:

- *Maintain his comfort level:* Keep things neat for him, emotionally
  and physically. Deal with all the obnoxious details he doesn't
  want to. Personal ease is the most important thing to the narcissist. When he's uncomfortable in any way, it damages his sense of
  divine entitlement. So moderate your emotional climate. It should
  be neither too hot nor too cool, but just right. Even if something
  is truly grievous, allow him to delegate the better part of the
  remedial action to you, if you can. The less he is encouraged to
  deal with the day-to-day details of work, the better. He's not
  suited to it. His gift is for demeanor and mood. Allow him to
  establish a generally upbeat tone and a pleasant working environment and he's done just about all that can be expected of him.
  In keeping him temperate, you are opening up vast new vistas of
  personal responsibility and power for yourself. "You'll take care
  of that, won't you, Danny?" should be just about the most frequent observation the narcissist offers during his reign. Especially
  if your name is Danny.
- *Spread that grease but don't get greasy:* The narcissist will take
  as much blatant, disgusting sucking up as you can dish out, and
  if you're not careful, you'll end up with a reputation as a simpering yes-person. You don't want that. As always, your independent credibility is your greatest asset. That said, in private
  you can tickle him as much as you want about personal matters.
  Compliment his new shoes. Look him directly in the eye and tell
  him how much you liked his remarks at that industry panel on
  deregulation. Don't worry. He won't suspect that you're being
  fatuous. He'll think you're just a person of incredible discernment
  and taste. Don't let your sucking up slop over into blanket appreciation of his business decisions, however. Your greatest value
  to the narcissist may be to give him some teeny bit of perspective

on operational issues. If you are able to tell him when he's heading down the wrong path—gently and respectfully—you'll find that he's likely to ask your advice more and more as time goes on. In his darkest moments, when nobody has pumped up his ego in the last couple of days or so, he knows he has no ideas. Let him have yours.

- *Keep his show on the road:* Narcissists are all about appearances. They want to look like they are managing. They want other people to see that they look like they're managing. Your job, as you go about assimilating his work and his operational power, is to keep up that front. Absolutely everyone in the organization will thank you for it. Those above the narcissist want their management structure to look like it's functional, not insane. Those below the narcissist will appreciate the way you keep him basically restricted to figurehead duties. And you'll be happy, too, because he will consider you, after a time, a critical beam in his interior support system, one of the lovely things that keep his grand and dangerously attenuated infrastructure propped up.

- *You've got to give him credit:* Be prepared, however, to watch him eat your ideas and work and claim them as his own. That's what it means to work for a narcissist. Nothing you produce for his office will gain you any notoriety if he has anything to say about it. That doesn't mean you won't get any, by the way. Most people are aware that the preening dude can't really do any work that requires detail and an attention span of more than five minutes. It's obvious that the guy rushing around with the furrowed brow is the one who's really sweating, not the one with his name at the top of the memo. But get used to the notion: all glory you do earn will be reflected. Don't waste any bitterness on it. The bright side is, you've got plenty of good work to do while he's gazing in the executive washroom mirror. And when the time comes for what are referred to these days as "operating efficiencies," senior management will often opt to keep the guy who's more substance than flash. That's you!

- *Hang around:* In managing your narcissist, never ignore the simple power of *being in the vicinity.* Sometimes he doesn't know what he needs. Sometimes all he needs is company. Great lords in the Middle Ages had people who simply were *in attendance* on them. Except for secretaries, nobody does that job anymore, and a secretary isn't always the right person. They tend to want to get back to work, or back to conversation with those who don't want to work, either. So take a moment in your busy day to stick your head into his office and show him you care. Invite him to lunch now and then on the spur of the moment. Walk with him to the train station at the end of the day. Be nice. Be there.

- *Petulance is acceptable:* Since comfort is his central requirement, the narcissist can't handle anger from the Lilliputians who, in his mind, exist to serve and glorify his name. On the other hand, a little gristle and bristle can help him sit up and take notice, at least for a moment, of the fact that there's a real, breathing human being in the room. Injecting that sense of reality can be a valuable service for you both.

My friend Wooten, a sales manager, used to serve a horrendous narcissist who thought the sun rose and set on his priorities. One evening when Wooten was just completing a particularly large contract and had his hands full with several other important matters for the morrow, his boss sauntered into Wooten's office on the way to his postwork workout at his club. "Make sure you have the 1992 sales projections on my desk tomorrow morning," he said. "Well, Ivan, I'm *not* going to have them on your desk tomorrow morning unless you'd like me to drop the Gladstone contract and my dinner with the folks from Positron and several other things that you said were top priority earlier today!" Wooten snapped. "Well you don't have to shout at me," his boss replied, somewhat hurt. As he turned sadly to go, he added, "And if you'd like to hire a temp or something to take up the slack, just let me know." Wooten hired that temp the very next day.

Remember, the narcissist wants to be beloved by others as much as he is beloved of himself. Once he's convinced you have affection for him, he won't want to lose it. So convince him that you have affection for him. Go ahead. You sort of do, now and then, don't you?

- *Be insincere—and laugh!* Speaking of insincerity, don't forget to laugh at his jokes. If he's your basic Me-person, he's periodically in a jolly mood, and eager to share that sense that all is well with those he believes love him. Workplace laughter is easy to generate. Just take in a bushel full of air, then smile in any way you can manage and let out the air in a series of snorts, chuckles, or, in large meetings, hoots and guffaws. Even a garrulous, "Really not funny, Irv!" can do the trick. Keep in mind that people generally consider those with a good sense of humor to be those who laugh at their jokes—not those who themselves make funny remarks, just as "great conversationalists" are generally the best listeners. Sure, he's not funny. But he's trying. Give him the benefit of the doubt and make him feel good about his dumb self.

- *Don't get cocky:* Just because the guy is a preening buffoon, don't get lulled into the idea that he's benign. He's not. When cornered or threatened, he's likely to be as nasty as a rabid ferret. Narcissists make horrible enemies due to their comprehensive *l'état, c'est moi* worldview. Keep in mind, too, that *he has no conscience.* He'll do anything in the belief that it's right simply because it's he who is doing it. So don't go directly into his face with something that will displease him. In doing so, you're not only taking a big risk. You're also ignoring rule number one—upsetting the poor wonk.

- *Wait until it blows over:* If you have difficulty with your narcissist, withdraw and do your own thing for a while. He has an attention span of a three-year-old, and a memory that extends only as far as his last major mood swing. I know one guy in my company who was fired by our former chief executive. "You're fired!" Russ screamed at him one morning when the numbers he had to report were particularly terrible. "Pack up your shit and move out!" My friend went back to his office and had a good cry. Then he started throwing things into boxes. A couple of minutes went by. His phone rang. "Hi, Willie, this is Russ! Can you have the draft of my Denver presentation in my office right after lunch, please?" Willie was flummoxed. "Russ!" he yelled into the phone. "You just fired me!" There was a thoughtful silence on the other end of the executive line. "Oh, that," said Russ. "Well you're hired again. See you at two!" This principle extends not only to unpleasant blowups, but also to orders with which you don't wish to comply. It's amazing how many rotten things simply disappear if you depend on your narcissist to follow them through. Patience.

- *Play up his insecurities:* Your greatest tool against this individual is the secret, lurking fear that burbles down deep inside him that he is not what he believes he appears to be. In essence, grandiosity is simply a defense against a crippling sense of inadequacy that cannot be borne. That deep-down, childlike conviction—that at heart he's a dork—drives the narcissist to protect his aura of invincibility. But you know him. You work with him. You can very gently press up against that tiny internal blister and make it hurt when you want to. You've got to be careful. You've got to be shrewd. But it's the thing that makes him tick, and it's at your disposal. "Word's out we can't make our number," you might say. Something simple like that can plummet this kind of guy from the top of the world into a toilet of despondency. I can't tell you what his hot button is. You're there on the scene. "I'm worried about whether this vision thing is going to sell to senior management," or just, "Are we up to that challenge?" can spin him into a welter of self-doubt, if you launch it right. You have power, you know, once you understand his pathology and how to play it. Use it wisely, but use it.

• *Don't trust him:* It's every man and woman for himself or herself, and don't you forget it. He's in it for Number One. You be, too.

# CHAPTER FIVE

# BUREAUCRAZY

"You are old, Father William," the young man said,
"And your hair has become very white;
And yet you incessantly stand on your head—
Do you think, at your age, it is right?"

"In my youth," Father William replied to his son,
"I feared it might injure the brain;
But, now that I'm perfectly sure I have none,
Why, I do it again and again."

Lewis Carroll

hen I first entered corporate America back in the beginning of the 1980s, I worked for an acutely crazy individual I will call Chuck. After a background in the military, he had moved into a large electrical utility in the Midwest and worked his way up to the position of vice president. He then joined my company, a division of a larger corporation headquartered in the Southwest.

Chuck had worked hard to get where he was, and he believed that his success to that date was almost wholly due to his understanding of procedure. For this reason, all our paper had to be perfect; all our conversations with individuals both inside the corporation and without had to be documented; all criticism and apologia had to be produced in multiple copies and routed through the entire chain of command.

When it came to promotions, he would tell me, "I had to work thirty years to make manager, and here you want it right out of the box." I pushed, however, and to his surprise his bosses showed no resistance to the idea. "I don't get it," he told me, "but you can have it if you want." I wanted. He did, however, hold me to the 3.5 percent raise mandated by the policy manual. I was the only one in my peer group to be held to that criteria, but Chuck wouldn't budge. I didn't hold it against him all that much. Without the rules, the snaillike creep through protocol and procedure, the man was lost.

Perhaps this *modus operandi* made sense in his prior corporate culture, but ours was rapidly changing, moving ever closer to the informal, management-by-walking-around mode that became synonymous with excellence in the late 1980s. This form of management left no trail at all. It was heavily reliant on the telephone, and light on the need for overwhelming consensus. Such a style creates its own problems, but they were not of the sort that Chuck had to worry about.

People began to laugh at him, to route his painstaking memos back to me, folded into paper airplanes and stuff like that. "You'd better watch out," one senior pinstripe told me at that time, "or everyone will think you're as big an asshole as he is."

Chuck was no dummy. He knew his reign was moldering. But the greater the pressure he felt, the more locked into the nuts and bolts he became. This was the only way he knew to handle crisis, and so he stuck by it, even after he was demoted, forced to report to another vice president. He became a madman for form, requiring me to document virtually every hour of his waking day, generating pages and pages of single-spaced memos justifying his every move. He was paralyzed, but he didn't know it. He thought he was managing.

In the end, it was pretty gruesome. They hired a new senior vice president for him to report to, someone ten years his junior who lunched with the power brokers of this city. Chuck refused, absolutely, to deal with his new boss, stating that he had been hired by the chairman and told at that time he was to report to the chairman and therefore would continue to report to the chairman until told by the chairman that he was not to continue to do so. The chairman, about to be "retired" himself, had no time for Chuck. And the new VP, after trying hard to make things work, gave Chuck the door.

He stuck around for two painful months, "straightening up his paperwork," and "putting his files in order." One day he was finally

gone, and we threw away every piece of paper he had so meticu-
lously categorized and saved.

In the four years I worked for Chuck, I saw him display a lot of
crazy personalities. He was a bully, a suspicious and Queeg-like
paranoid, a strutting narcissist who held his nose so high in the air
you could see his bald spot when you walked behind him down the
hall. But in his tiny little heart, all those characteristics were off-
shoots of the one root problem that shaped his persona. Chuck was
a wimp.

Deep in the core of this crazy boss was a timid worm who was
unable to provide leadership but instead depended solely on the
exercise of official authority.

Chuck was a bureaucrazy.

## I THINK WHAT YOU THINK, J.D.

There's a difference between leadership and authority, and while the
wimp can squeeze out some of the latter, he knows nothing about the
former. To lead, one must be willing, occasionally, to risk the dis-
favor of others, particularly the boss. The only way to avoid this is
to tell everyone very decisively what they want to hear at all times,
and to evade responsibility for any decision that is in any way con-
troversial or risky. While this may be a viable route to national
candidacy, it is not the best way to manage a business.

Caroline is the former fashion editor of a large magazine targeted
to a female audience. These establishments, often ruled by a bully
with an iron fist, customarily suffer from a tremendous confluence of
wimps in middle management. She relates what life was like for
writers who dealt with her bureaucratic power structure.

One of our best freelance writers, Betty, turned in a piece, and Jane—
her editor—read it and called her back two days later and said, "This
piece is wonderful! I wish I could put payment through, because it's
exactly what we wanted! Of course, we have to go through the
formality of showing it to the other editors as well as Arthur, the
editor in chief, but thanks, it's terrific." So Betty was very happy.

The piece was then routed. And Arthur's comment went something
like, "This is a total disaster." So Jane calls Betty back and says—I
mean, this is how she starts the conversation: "Hi, Betty, I'm wondering if this piece is even *do-able*." And Betty says, "What do you

mean?" And Jane says, "I don't think it works at all, and I'm wondering if it can even be done." And so finally Betty says, "Well, Jane, what about all the stuff you said last week!?" And Jane says, "After seeing Arthur's comments I've rethought it, and I'm seeing it differently now." In other words, she totally wimped out and hid behind her "professional" function.

In professionalism and formality lie the wimp's best hope. That's why he needs to cover his tail with paper and protocol in every situation, no matter how trivial, and is fond of delegating every decision up to and including what he's going to have for lunch. This behavior is generally found and welcomed in large organizations where flawless procedure is valued in its own right—like the military, large urban school systems, and television networks.

The bureaucrazy is fearful of the personal implications of the authority he wields, and seeks to spread responsibility for his every action so thin that blame cannot be fixed on him. As Crozier has observed, "A main rationale of bureaucratic development is the elimination of power relationships and personal dependencies—to administer *things* instead of governing *men*. The ideal of bureaucracy is a world where people are bound by impersonal rules and not by personal influence and arbitrary command."

The bureaucracy is a social structure that creates Good Germans: a system in which following orders is the highest good, and responsibility is spread so thin that no individual need worry about his personal share of it.

## THE TWO-FACED FACELESS MANAGER

In business today, this loathing for responsibility creates two separate managerial phenomena: the pure wimp and the organizational fascist. Both depend on the structure to confer power, eliminate challenges, and negate individual accountability. The wimp finds personal action fearful and difficult. The organizational fascist finds comfort within the exercise of his function, and free rein for the manipulative and sadistic impulses that rage within the breast of every deeply insecure person.

These are two faces of one beast. The fascist is simply a wimp who has found an ideological shield behind which to hide.

## THE PURE WIMP: THE BUCK STOPS NOT HERE

Before a definitive step can be taken, the wimp must ascertain that it was the only conceivable one, and feel he can prove that to others; so every decision is agony. The bureaucrazy staggers under the fatal need to control every detail, so that each may best fit into his rationale. Ultimate decisions—if they are ever made—require support studies, memos, committee meetings, and other tools that effectively cover his back and diffuse responsibility. Many large organizations encourage this kind of approach.

The man in such an organization doesn't really need to have a vision of the future, or a strategic plan to implement. All he needs are the pressures of the moment. They take all his attention.

The wimp's solutions are always based on what has succeeded—and not got anyone in trouble in the past. Lloyd, a New York screenwriter, tells how it works:

I was called by a development person for one of the big studios. She's about twenty-six, tops. She's in from L.A. for a couple of days, and tells me, "Hey let's meet at six on Friday, up at my office." It's an inconvenient time for me, but I figure okay, this woman could make my career. On the phone, she tells me, "I'm looking for something truly original, something with a very quixotic stamp on it, something that will really shake people up." So we talk about a story and everything's "Great," and I write up what I think is a pretty good treatment based on our conversations and fax it to her. I'm very enthusiastic. I mean, this woman could pay me $100,000 for turning in a script that's never produced! It's enticing. So anyhow, I go to this office on Fifty-seventh Street and up to the top floor, and there's nobody but us up there, and here's this very attractive woman who's ten years younger than me, and she's wearing one of those sleeveless T-shirts that Stallone likes to wear and a sports jacket over it that costs maybe twelve hundred dollars and jeans and high cowboy boots, and man, she's sharp. And I'm feeling like, hey, this is a cool person and ready for the whacky stuff I'd like to write about. And she pours me a drink and she's name-dropping like Barbara Walters or something about Jack and Eddie and Kris and whatever, and then she leans forward over the desk and says, "You know, I'm sorry to say that your treatment is not really what we're looking for."

Who's *we?* I think to myself. I mean, I've been talking to her so far. I thought she's the one who's making the decisions.

"No," she says, "your treatment is unlike anything I've ever seen before." Now she looks really disappointed. "What we're looking for, and I really think you can produce this, is something between *The Big Chill* and *The Breakfast Club*." We talked for a couple more minutes, but that was about it. It was the first time I'd ever seen originality positioned as a bad thing. But since then, I've noticed that every time I talk high concept with certain film people from big coastal studios, they always tell me about why a certain project is *like* a hundred others that went before, and how it's a *cross between* two or three other, more imaginative projects. And when I hear that shit, I know I'm peeing on the wrong tree.

In place of creativity, which carries with it certain risks, the wimp elevates formal procedure, a love of antecedents, and the aggressive picking of nits. It sure beats relying on your own judgment. In his heart, he's deeply fearful of human contact that may reveal his inadequacy, for good reason. That fear of being "found out" drives his need to rely on organizational formalities—and his own superiors—for strength and validation. A friend who works for a bureaucrazy complains:

Dick demands that we document every single phone call into and out of the department. This means filling out special "Communications Reports." He then puts each report in a special binder, in chronological order. At the end of the year, he throws out the binders. It's ridiculous.

In certain industries and individual firms, management by weakness is the only means for survival.

The wimp survives in such an environment because, in the course of a lifetime, he takes so few risks.


## MY ASSISTANT WILL GET BACK TO YOU
## WITH WHAT I THINK IMMEDIATELY

A senior executive vice president who used to work at my corporation was famous for his ESP in regards to positions that our chairman was purported to have. Walter would call around the company several times a week, and debrief subordinates from New York to Houston to Atlanta to Los Angeles on what comments they might have heard the chairman pass at meetings, during phone calls, in personal memos, you name it.

"What's Carl thinking on the deregulation thing?" he'd ask. And you would tell him, because he was your boss, and even if he was not, he was so many people's boss that in any event he should be told.

Walter would then wait until the proper moment at a big executive meeting, and parrot Carl's opinions back to him at great length, with tremendous passion.

"My, how smart Walt is," Carl would say quietly, to anyone who would listen. And people would almost, but not quite, barf.

Then one day a very critical strategic planning meeting was called very hastily, involving every single senior manager in the top echelon of the company. I was there. Actually, I was not there, but the incident that transpired has attained so much fame within our walls that it's one of those happenings where you can say you were there—along with about seven hundred others—even if you weren't.

So at this meeting, Carl is pontificating on his belief that a strong advertising budget was necessary to "project world-class performance within our local constituencies." And everybody is zoning out, Walter included. Halfway through his sermon, Carl turned to Walter and breezily asked, "That's enough from me! What do you think about it, Walt?"

Walter, it is said, looked intensely uncomfortable, bobbing and weaving back and forth in his seat and pulling on the tiny mustache of which he was excessively proud. After one or two seconds of torment, he shot back, as a pure reflex action, I am sure, "Well . . . I think whatever you think, Carl."

What a drag to be such a person! Always apprehensive about the reaction you're having on people, calculating and gelatinous.

Those who work for a wimp may find themselves making the decisions he won't make, taking the risks he won't take. This has its bright side. A dynamic subordinate, willing to act decisively and cover his ass with the requisite paper, can thrive in the vacuum. If the work is necessary, there are likely to be clients lurking around, looking for a reasonable person to talk to and deal with, instead of the trembling weasel in the big corner office.

In fact, any subordinate willing to state a clear position is appreciated by those in search of forward momentum. Pete, a mid-level executive at a large banking concern in San Francisco,[1] describes the personality of his boss:

> Jason was devious, he would never answer a question directly. Basically, I think he doesn't want to communicate. I think his theory is that if he talks this way, he will appear to be wise and smart. He would do this in front of clients. Some bought it, others didn't. For example, if a company had a complex financial problem that required clarity to solve, Jason's solution would be terribly convoluted, it would require several steps.
>
> Often the simplest way would be straightforward, but he had no use for that.
>
> He'd come into my office, sit down, ask me a question, fold his arms, smoke his pipe, then listen to my answer, get up and leave without saying one word. He held meetings on Friday ostensibly to get ideas, but they would end up as long lectures from him. One day—all within the course of one meeting—I watched him talking and at the same time carefully taking out twelve aspirin from a bottle, *chewing them,* and swallowing them.
>
> He got very erratic toward the end. He was under the impression that a more "hands on" manager was needed—which was true—so he began to write seven to twelve memos a day. "Pete," he would write to me on formal memo paper, with a cc: to himself. "I see you spent $150 on dinner last night with Kosnofski. That is excessive. Jase." I would write back, "Kosnofski had three martinis and insisted on expensive brandy after dinner. Best, Pete." Half my time was spent answering those stupid memos while a lot of necessary stuff got ignored.

In the face of such organizational paralysis, any player who actually generates work will be recognized. Eventually, the rumor that you get things done will drive you upward, and the wimp out into a job where his talents are needed—in the corporate headquarters of a huge multinational, for instance, or the public-relations department of an electrical utility.

But for the most part, a wimp is a terrible burden for those who work beneath him, capable of prodigiously manipulative behavior and cowardice that poisons a normal employee's ability to function

---

[1] Banks—and other places that regularly deal with a great deal of Other People's Money—are notorious haunts of craven bureaucrazies.

and to enjoy the exercise of his or her own authority, talent, and energy.

## I WANT YOU TO LOVE ME!

Central to the wimp's pathology—driving his impulsiveness, excessive timidity, and above all, inconsistency in thought, word, and deed—is the neurotic desire to be liked by everybody, no matter what. This manifests itself in a pathetic desire to be "friends," a desire that would be touching were it not based solely on the power conferred by his status as a senior manager. And it plays hell with one of the central tenets of decent management: the establishment of consistent policies that apply to everyone.

My friend Laura is a primary-school teacher who worked for an insufferably wimpy administrator.[2] Here is her story:

> I worked under Carole for two years. She was director of the lower school here. The hallmarks of her administration were inconsistency and lack of policy, lack of ability to set policy and keep to it. She'll make decisions based on whether she likes you or not, or whether she wants you to like her.
>
> Her aura is that she's very giving. When the staff were all old-timers, she would celebrate everybody's birthday by buying some cake and displaying a sign saying HAPPY BIRTHDAY. I guess there was a very confused line between friendship and professional relationship. She wanted friendship, and couldn't handle the role of manager at the same time, not being the peer. She was evaluated every year by the staff, and her ratings were horrible, because she was a bad boss whether she gave you a party once a year or not. You don't fall for that kind of stuff when you've been wanked around the rest of the time.
>
> Different people get different results on the same issue, which is bad. If one teacher is asked to do some extra work, and that teacher has the sense enough to ask, "How much will I get paid for it?," that person will get a fee. If another doesn't ask, then that one won't get anything. Then the first person will be asked to keep her mouth shut.

---

[2] Bureaucrazies are pandemic in the world of academia, where indecisiveness and subterfuge are a respected way of life.

Here we have one of the wimp's most reliable ploys: playing people against each other, feasting on other people's weaknesses as if they in some way mitigated his own. Laura continues:

> She would talk about teachers behind their back. Play favorites. She just made everybody nervous because if she talked to you about somebody else, it was safe to assume that sometime, at some point, she'd be talking about you.

Undermining others is key in the wimp's approach, because *strength in other people is something that cannot be tolerated.*

> She's forever undermining your authority. I'm librarian, and she said, "There are going to be parents working in the library while you're not there." And she asked me to take the time to talk to them, prepare them. I just found out this week that another parent has been working in the library for more than a month, and nobody told me. It doesn't make any sense.

From deviousness, the wimp may quickly flip over to manipulative meddling. Turf—the real estate of a power other than his own—has little meaning to a manager whose perception of his own limits is lousy. And the criteria changes moment to moment, as the wimp works to please whichever person is in his face. As Laura complains:

> She tries to get involved and manage everything and everybody. When I first started the library, I wanted to change certain rules of the school. For instance, we'd lost a lot of books, so I wanted to make a rule that kids can only take one book out at a time—and that parents could not take any books out of the building at all. Since we can't afford to replace them, that made sense to me. So the day after I announce this new policy, a mother comes to me and says, "I'll be in here a lot," and she starts to take out a bunch of books. I told her no. She hit the ceiling. Went up to Carole with her kid, right that minute. After school I saw Carole—she didn't even seek me out, by the way— and she says to me, "Oh, incidentally, Mrs. Gruber is allowed to take out books." I really got pissed off, and said, "How do you justify that? It doesn't make any sense!" I said the only reason to have a policy is if you stick to it. Even that concept of consistency is something she doesn't get. She says, "Mrs. Gruber told me she wasn't going to discuss it with anybody else." I asked her, "Don't you think this kind of undermines my authority?" And she says, "I'm really sorry, but

there's no way I can anticipate that, but things aren't cut and dried, and there have to be exceptions to things . . . if I have any further problems on this, I'll just refer them to you."

It's almost as if she has a learning disability when it comes to policy.

Why not? The only policy the wimp finds worth pursuing is the policy of self-preservation and global ingratiation.

## IT'S NOT ENOUGH THAT I AM WEAK! OTHERS MUST BE WEAKER!

In his attempts to control through weakness, the crazy boss in his wimpish frame of mind will also work to undermine power relationships he cannot directly control. In doing so, he is rarely willing to go *mano a mano* with anyone who enjoys even a modicum of power. He's far happier diddling with little people.

Jorgenson, a friend who works for a snack-packaging company, got a new boss not long ago. "JC was new to the organization, and had just been given this department, and the fastest way he could put his stamp on it was to reorganize it and realign the allegiances and grab some loyalty for himself," he says.

We found ourselves sitting next to each other on the airplane, and he began to share with me his very sketchy and preliminary plans and thoughts about the department. He was just thinking out loud. And part of those plans included moving my little tushie from my current seat to a more elevated one in charge of a whole new area. I could immediately tell that this was *his* plan, and had never been discussed with my immediate superior. Which immediately set my interests and those of my boss at cross purposes. I think it was, in part, a genuine desire to expand the department's coverage, but I also think he was trying to break up a working team and grab some allegiance for himself, since I would supposedly have been immensely grateful for the promotion. In the weeks that followed, that's exactly what happened. I began to feel as if good things might come from him, rather than from my boss, and to chafe at the reporting structure, which had previously been a source of pleasure.

I told my boss about the plan, and she tried to convince me that her dislike of the plan was based on an objective understanding of the situation. She gave JC an opportunity (over lunch) to reveal his plan, and this time he kept his mouth shut. He never discussed it. Which left the suspicion in everyone's mind that I had dreamed the whole thing up out of my egotism. As far as I was concerned, he'd made a tawdry little grab for my loyalty, and I was a bit chagrined at my willingness to go for the bait.

This story demonstrates two things:

- Gobbling up other people's loyal subordinates is a fast and cheap way for a crazy wimp to build a power base.
- Never believe anything a wimp tells you, especially on an airplane when extended conversation makes the mouth of any ingratiating fool run fast and loose.

Passivity and lack of spine can almost be a relief when compared with the wimp's actual management abilities. Very often, the wimp functions to make whatever anxiety you might be feeling increase a hundredfold—*to bring you up to his level of fear, where you can keep him company.*

Harvey is a salesman for a company that, he states, "makes widgets. Say I sell widgets." So Harvey's company sells widgets. What is important is that he sells them.

When I joined here, they told me that every May the person in my position was expected to set up a schedule of visits by individual buyers from large department-store chains. I did. I was also told how much time was given to each sales conference. A half hour. We were to take an entire day off from our usual round of business to conduct these special meetings. We were relieved from staff meetings for the purpose. I scheduled my client interfaces very carefully.

On the day of my client meetings, I stepped out to the men's room while my boss, Geoff, was inspecting my office before the clients were due to come in. When I came back, my desk calendar was gone. I couldn't remember where I put it. I went frantically running around asking everybody, "Did you see anyone take my desk calendar? My life is in that calendar!" Finally, I found Geoff, and he had my calendar. He said, "You can't do this. You've only allocated one half hour per conference. You should allocate an hour." I said, "That's impossible! There's only eight hours a day, and I have about twenty of these to do!" He said, "I'll relieve you from your daily duties one extra day if you fill out the requisite forms. But you really have to redo this schedule."

To do it that way was horrendous. I was nervous enough. Then he made a lot of criticisms of my office two minutes before my first conference. The month before he was very avuncular, very benign, saying, "Don't worry, you'll do just fine, you're making a big deal out of this, Harv." He had millions of opportunities to talk to me. And then he just walks in and criticizes me. It was bullshit. I asked him: "You had so much time to talk about this, why are you undermining me just a few minutes before the buyers come in?" At that point, I was really red in the face, totally upset. "I'm sorry, Harv," he says, "but I'm even more nervous than you are," he says.

Aha! An honest answer.

## I'M AS NERVOUS AS YOU ARE

The wimp is insecure because he's convinced of his essential *lack of fitness*. Consequently, he believes, with some justification, that if he were strong, people would see the havoc he would create and hate him. And as we've seen, that would be worse than anything else to the wimp, who desperately *needs to be liked*.

The good news is that this pathetic craving for acceptance makes the wimp extremely vulnerable. Alex is the business editor at a newspaper in New England. His boss, Dewey, was not trained to lead. He was born to it. Which doesn't stop him from wanting to be one of the boys. "Dewey is an aristocrat landowner, who thinks it's important for him to be one with the serfs," Alex says.

He never worked in a corporate office in his life. The post was due him through divine right. But he has no training. To compensate for that, he tries to be friendly to everybody, make jokes. There's no way *that* can succeed. He'd make an awkward bon mot in front of you and you were forced to laugh. And to reply. And what can you say? It makes it awkward for everybody. Like if you said, after Thanksgiving, "Morning, hope you had a nice weekend," he'd look at you and say, "No, it was a turkey," then look at you with his eyes filled with anticipation, and expect a reply to this witticism. Of course, there's no answer to that.

These aristocrats—if they're considered by their people as geniuses, then it works fine. But unfortunately nobody thinks he's qualified for the job. So therefore you have this situation that's totally awkward.

There are sycophants around him, three or four people who have the ability to talk to someone like this. They immediately rise to the top not because they're any good, but they're the only ones that he can communicate with. It's a wonderful opportunity for people with bizarre verbal skills to get ahead. If by some fluke you can communicate with this socially autistic boss, then you've got an inside track. Of course, getting along with that kind of boss has nothing to do with doing a good job. Working for a boss like that is like every day having a blind date that's ugly. What do you do?

## THAT'S RIGHT—TOADIES AGAIN!

His pervasive weakness encourages those around the wimp to engorge themselves. But unlike the bully, who generates bully toadies, or the paranoid, who produces craven henchmen, or the narcissist, who gives birth to humongous suckups, the wimp begets teeny-weeny little wimplings who do his bidding. Often it's the smallest work units in the company— secretaries—who assume the role normally taken by the manager himself. One idea jockey for a Hollywood studio observes:

These guys' secretaries take over and become the person they serve. They're not secretaries, they're the VP in charge of taking care of the big guy. That's fucked up, because it strips *you* of *your* power with him. There's tons of these types. They get power-mad and start doing things for themselves as if they were the boss.

Too often, this aggrandizement of subordinate function allows the wimp's secretary to decay into a crazy miniboss himself or herself. As an extension of his function, she or he literally has carte blanche. One corporate attorney recalls:

Jack's secretary was a complete schizo. A crazy person. Her only goal was to serve Jack, which was great for him and bad for anyone else. She'd interrupt meetings to find out if anyone had a paper clip on them if he wanted a paper clip. She'd make everyone else frantic because he made her frantic. The thing I liked least was that she wanted to be a singer, and every time you walked by, she'd be practicing a tune to herself. One week it rained for five days in a row, and for the whole week she was warbling "Singing in the Rain," and I had to restrain myself from strangling her. I was depressed about the frigging weather, okay, and she thought it was great. She fucked everybody else up.

Leaving aside distinctions between leadership and authority, the average wimp can no more manage his secretary than he can manage higher-level subordinates. One extraordinarily wimpy vice president relates:

We had a day where I was supposed to edit the entire annual report, and I said to her, "Look, I've never asked you to do this, but could you possibly get me a sandwich?," and she cried and cried and cried and, like, people had to come over and comfort her. She was so insulted that I had asked her. I think I'm basically happier without a secretary. I'm a sixties person, and it gives me no sense of accomplishment to have one. To have someone call and say, "Will you hold for Mr. J.?" I hate to ask people to do things. If I even ask my boss's secretary to Xerox an article for him, she looks at me like I should do it. It's dreadful.

Unable to manage up except through excessive consensus and a glut of paper, powerless to manage downward by his fear of human interaction and the possibility of being disliked, the wimp is the crazy boss at his most dysfunctional.

## OOOH. I LOVE IT WHEN YOU STEP ON MY FACE

The worker who knows the right buttons to push *and is willing to ally himself with friends* will find that the wimp—more than any other crazy boss—*can* be terrified into acquiescence and eventual self-destruction. He needs you. And his ultimate respect is given to anyone who shares his low opinion of himself. So be a little mean to your wimp. He'll love you for it.

My friend Bruce is a news producer at a TV station in the Rocky Mountain states. He knocked off one of his wimps several years ago, and he tells me it was a gratifying experience. "Now this was a guy who could be *intimidated*," he says.

Here we have this small news department, and they'd made him the sports editor temporarily. He was assistant managing editor, and the

Olympics were coming up, and this guy could be intimidated by al-most anyone on staff. The worse he was treated, the more he would do for the people who treated him bad. The people who worked hard and treated him with respect, he developed contempt for.

So he allowed himself to be bullied by people. It was an unhappy department, full of washed-up people, excluding me, of course. There were certain people who would intimidate him by screaming, insist-ing, and generally being out of control. It was like a classroom where the kids have taken over. He knew people were running all over him, but he didn't know how to deal with it. He took the people who were hardworking and conscientious, and he would treat them with con-tempt. Pass along the contempt that he was receiving. We would take it. In my case, he really disliked me, and I was the best worker on the staff. We went out to the team softball game, rode on the hottest day of the year for about sixty miles, and he wouldn't put me in the game. We didn't have a pitcher, and I'm sitting on the sidelines. We're getting killed. I'm warming up with bullets, and he wouldn't put me in the game. Finally, I quit. He was eventually taken out of the news-room, and kicked back up to his real job where he had even more responsibility, but less contact with people directly.

This fate—solitude with great, undefined duty—just might be the ultimate wish of the working wimp. Come to think of it, you don't have to be a wimp to appreciate that job. In fact, let me know if you see one posted.

Be that as it may.

If you can say no to a wimp, there's a pretty good chance he'll roll over and actually love you for it. For he is deeply fearful and re-spectful of anyone who can articulate a critical thought. One man-ager in an electronic publishing company reports:

I found that by saying no to Lance I almost went up in his esteem. He responds to people who won't go along with him. It makes you always want to say no to him, just to see what would happen. He's cultivated this gruff exterior to get what he wants, but inside he's just a bunch of mush that will turn over with the slightest provocation to give what you want.

A slow, inexorable resistance may also be effective, as Hank, a former associate of mine in Purchasing, found when dealing with his boss, the vice president and controller. "When I was busy with my

normal duties, and Arnie asked me to fill in on something menial—
which he liked to do—I said no and took a lot of shit for it."

> I said I was busy and what I was working on was important, and Arnie
> would try to persuade me that his was something I had to do, saying
> stuff like, "If you expect to get ahead, you can't refuse work." I said
> I was trying to discriminate between work *anyone* could do and the
> work *only* I could do—which was to manage client relationships and
> pursue new business leads.
>
> I was trying to create a long-term image for myself, so eventually they
> would think, Hank's too valuable to do diddlyshit stuff. So even if he
> was annoyed with me over any specific resistance, it began to create
> a drift in the right direction.

## IF YOU BUILD IT, HE MAY COME,
## BUT THEN AGAIN HE MAY NOT

In short, yes; the wimp can be pushed, pulled, and squeezed into
some shape that you find pleasurable. For a time.

But the problem remains: the bureaucrazy views you not as an
individual human being in need of guidance, but as a functioning
piece of the great machine that orders his days and shapes his
dreams. And he's not above manipulating your existence to make
it fit in better with the operation of that structure. Remember: he
is not *just* a wimp, although that is his primary complaint—and
yours. He is also a narcissist, somewhere down deep—and you
have little reality to him as another living human being. If you
want something inconvenient for him, it's tough noogies on you,
and he will use the structure of the organization to make things
work the way *he* wants.

And make no mistake: he wants what he wants just like any other
crazy boss. He's just too chickenshit to do it out in the open.

Ted is a senior vice president at a large financial-services organization. Not long ago he was offered a presidency at the corporate
parent of his subsidiary. It was a job he wanted a lot, had, in fact,
been working his whole career for. He said yes.

As a courtesy, the chairman of the parent approached Ted's current boss, Rob, festering wimp of the first order, and asked for his
blessing. The wimp at the top of Ted's present division thought

about Ted's promotion for about five minutes. He considered the way Ted made his life so much easier by sweating the details of his operation day to day. Then he said no. Ted relates: "On the day in question, the chairman of the parent corporation went down the hall to Rob's office, and then, about five minutes later, he goes back the other way and *doesn't stop in to see me*. I see the whole thing then very clearly—Rob said no, and that's that." Unwilling to breach corporate etiquette on the issue, the parent withdrew its job offer, and Ted now continues to languish where he is, filled with anger and regret. "I feel that it inhibits your ability to make good decisions— the desire for revenge," he says.

Just because he was screwing over a loyal subordinate, however, didn't mean, as a wimp, that Rob didn't want to be *friends*. Ted continues:

> So after his meeting on my future, Rob calls me in, and I figure he's going to tell me what's up, but instead he says, "My daughter and I have tickets to the Knicks game, you want to come? Michael Jordan will be playing, it should be a great game." I say okay. But I'm baffled. I don't hear from anybody. Now it's five. We go to some bar, and he sends his daughter away, and he says, "Look, I'm not going to let you do it. I'm the president of this company and I need you to be number two." And I said, "Yeah, but look, I want to do it!" And he says, "Yeah, I know, but it's not good for you." It was a great game. The Knicks destroyed the Bulls.

> After that he was very nice, I'll give that to him, gave me a lot of credit for the stuff I was doing. And the next week he kept on saying stuff like, "Nothing's for sure, anything could happen, but being president of this company is what you should be working for." And I'd say, "Well, good, because that's what I'm working for," and he says, "Great, because that's what I want, too, but I can't give you any timetable." He did tell me that he was going to get me a consultancy at the division he'd prevented me from working at. So the next day, after he's just told me I'm the next president of the company, he comes in and he doesn't say a word. Not about the job he blocked me for, not about the consultancy.

> I go over and talk to the head of development at my company, and I mention the consultancy that Rob had promised he was going to help set up, and the guy, who is a very nice guy, says, "Hey, he has no right to do that. You have to talk to the chairman of *that* division, he's the only one who can set that up." And it turned out Rob had absolutely

nothing to do with setting it up. It was all smoke. And I felt . . .
misused. For being . . . you know, taken in.

Ted shouldn't blame himself. It's hard to deal with a guy who's
willing to make promises he knows he has no intention of keeping.
Most employees have the *need to believe* such horrible trolls in order
to keep their sanity while they report to them.


## NO DETAILS, PLEASE, WE'RE TOO SQUISHY INSIDE

Like the narcissist, the bureaucrazy is also often incapable of attending to details, because they take a commitment to process that
is beyond his capacity.

This leads to a currently popular symptom in American management, one that tends to be highly respected as long as it gets no one
in trouble: delegatitis.

The most famous carrier of this pathology was former president
Ronald Reagan. Now that the counterrevolution that bore his name
is history, and we are all suffering from the excesses of greed and
fake freedom it generated, it might be possible to spend a few moments reliving one incident that reflected the tone of those glorious
years for American management. It's an incident that stripped bare
the way the great man worked.

*The New York Times*
February 21, 1987

REAGAN CAUGHT IN FEUD BETWEEN WIFE AND AIDE
. . . The dispute is about whether Mr. Reagan should be resuming a
full load of activity as he recovers from his prostate surgery last month.
His wife wants him to strictly follow doctors' orders that he take it
easy, and some sources say she is angry over Mr. Regan's insistence
that the President resume a normal work schedule to deflect attention
from the Iran arms scandal.

Donald Regan, consummate White House politician and wimp-
master, whose power had grown and engorged during years of flaccid
delegatitis, had found himself jowl to jowl with the de facto president, First Lady Nancy Reagan. A week later, Regan was ousted and
replaced by party regular Howard Baker.

*The New York Times*
February 28, 1987

. . . Mr. Reagan announced the change a day after a special Presidential review commission harshly criticized his detached style of management and blamed Mr. Regan for "chaos" in the White House after disclosures of the secret Iran policy.

. . . Nancy Reagan, who had led a three-month private effort to oust Mr. Regan that had become increasingly acrimonious, said she was pleased about the replacement. . . .

In the gap created by the Gipper's minimalist style, the president's wife grew and flourished. "Nancy Reagan is now far more powerful, more confident and more politically involved than at any point in the Reagan Presidency, and she intends to remain so for the rest of her husband's term. . . ." the *Times* wrote as the president's popularity hit new lows.

The former president not only embodied the worst of the nightmare delegator. He was also, above all else, an idealogue who believed that any action taken by his administration and its supporters was justified.

## HOW FAR IS THE OLD IDEOLOGUE IN?

The infrastructure of dogma did not limit itself to the chief executive, but transmitted to all within his organization. Within an organization run by wimps and cowardly delegators, it is the ideologue who is valued and promoted, simply because, unlike the pure wimp, he *believes*, and is willing to act on those beliefs personally and dynamically. The bureaucracy is the breeding ground for those who yearn for dynamic, totalitarian excellence.

*The Wall Street Journal*
December 31, 1986

When young Naval Academy midshipman Oliver Laurence North suffered severe knee and back injuries in a 1964 auto accident, he returned to his home in tiny Philmont, N.Y. to recuperate for several weeks—and spent the time jumping off the roof.

The idea was to toughen his body for the return to Annapolis. "He was always jumping off his roof and his garage," recalls Howard Rhodes, a neighbor. "He said next he would take a survival course where he would have nothing to eat, no matches, that kind of thing."

Even in those days, Oliver North was full of dreams and guts and glory . . . In the years since, he has thrown himself at projects with the same daring and ferocious intensity that once propelled his body off the roof.

North was also commended by his high school track coach as the kind of "selfless team player" who would join the relay team—forgoing the glory of solo events—for the good of the school.

That's the kind of employee who's valued in a large organization. Add to that the willingness, if necessary, to take the blame for things that others ordered you to do, and you've got world-class middle-management potential.

When the fire of political belief lights up a bureaucrat, the results can be devastating to a professional organization.

*The New York Times*
December 12, 1986

NBC HEAD PROPOSES STAFF POLITICAL CONTRIBUTIONS
The president of NBC has urged that the network start a political action committee and that NBC employees who refuse to contribute to it "question their own dedication to the company," according to sources at NBC . . .

Later in the week, trade publications revealed that Mr. Wright had labored in midnight solitude over this heartfelt memo. As new boss on the block, he had ignored all organizational structures that could have set him off his chosen course, perhaps injected a bit of industry reality.

The plan was shot down later, after considerable embarrassment to both Wright and the company of which he was trying to become a part.

The seething *need to instill belief* is typical of today's worst wimp, the wimp who moves into the void created by his passive masters, the guy who isn't happy, until you're converted, the man who's building more than just a business, goddamn it, a man who's *building an idea!*

## THE ORGANIZATIONAL FASCIST

Wimps love consultants. They provide instant credibility, cost lots of money that justifies the importance of the executive who hired them, and defray the need for action perhaps indefinitely. Best of all, the consultant fills the wimp's incredible vacuum of ideas with any number of attractive fads. These fads come bearing a "new" management philosophy to transform the culture and make the trains run on time.

Since the early 1950s, we've been managed by objective, managed in one minute, Theory Z'd; plumbed niches, spun matrixes, woven grids; slaved over PERT charts by the light of late-night fluorescence, hammered ourselves into hard-networking intrapreneurs, sat in stupefaction before lanky lay preachers hollering, pleading, exhorting us to go home and *be excellent*! One friend who attended a lecture by the leading excellence merchant, Tom Peters, observes:

> It was amazing to me how much money you could make out of purveying common sense. The businesses he feels so evangelical about are simply better than anyone else at giving the customer what he wants. Making the customer feel wanted and happy and satisfied with the product and service he's paying good money for. It's sad, in a way, that you have to elevate that good business judgment to the status of preaching. There's nothing bullshit about the idea that quality makes good business sense. What's bullshit is the idea that you can distill from that a roadmap, a set of rules, and if you just follow those rules closely enough, bingo bango, you've got a good business.

Passing by the environs of greater Excellence, we've sought Quality and Productivity. Some of us have even found Wellness. Employees are willing to give each new creed a chance, until its priests begin torturing the innocent into false confessions. Which, by nature, they're only too willing to do.

A senior manager in the office of a San Antonio real estate developer describes the chief financial officer of his company, and it is a profile that adequately sums up the curriculum vitae of the organizational fascist:

> He was such a bullheaded asshole that he'd do anything to anybody out of his fanatic pursuit of what he thinks company needs are. A

corporate nazi. He would do things without involving other people in
the company. He was not an ally. He was an island. There are those
who do not recognize the importance of combining efforts. He could
have embarrassed me many times. He could have gone down the
road of something dangerous—doing something I should have known
about—without telling me. He was sneaky. Got people to go along
with him by involving them in discussions that are sort of blindsided,
saying, "Of course, I've discussed this with people on your staff, they
tell me this is okay," when he hadn't. Either your staff was consulted
without your knowing about it, and was given advice circumventing
you, or you're disagreeing with them. So he pressures you into being
his ally. You're left thinking he's an asshole, with tremendous resistance to what he has in mind, but going along strictly out of fear of
doing anything that could get him pissed off at you.

For some reason, the guys put in charge of forging the mandatory
new culture aren't usually the Mother Teresa type, filled with reason,
charity, and gentle persistence. A friend who works for a vice president of Participative Management describes her boss:

He surrounds himself with clones who all laugh and show their teeth
and nod at the same time. He asks for diversity of opinion, but when
it comes, he shuts it off like a bad smell. Either he abruptly changes
the subject, or denigrates the person giving his opinion: "Well, that's
silly," he says. "Let's move on to something else." And we do, of
course. His word is law in this particular participative setup.

The odd thing is, when the right idea is given the chance to
mellow, spread and ooze deep into the culture, it can actually do
some good. Unfortunately, few corporations are willing to let a culture change take that natural course, relying on jackboots to implement the transformation instead. A financial officer in a factory that
is trying to eliminate all defects as well as many of its people observes:

Most fad managements of today are based on the assumption of
long-term planning and the assimilation of a new culture, whereas
the whole business environment is up for grabs. So you've got two
movements at cross purposes. Cynicism is natural. Can you imagine
the future career path of Joe Schlub who gets up and tells his new
bosses, who have just taken over the new company, about quality,
when the new culture is lean and mean and screw the customer? All

this stuff about long-range planning went out the door when the company got sold. Everybody's getting sold. Maybe a handful will escape that, but they'll get it in the next decade. You reinvent the corporation long enough to redesign the corporate brochure, then there's a new name on the door. That's what makes them fads, because there's no time for them to mellow into corporate culture.

Even when the idea is right—which it rarely is—most corporations still get it wrong. "You can go back to Management by Objective,[3] Son of Management by Objective, Management by Objective meets Appraisal and Counseling," says E. Kirby Warren, professor at the Columbia University Graduate School of Business. "Most of these fads would have some real value if senior management took the time to ask themselves: 1) How do I adapt the idea to our culture and business? 2) What has to be changed to reinforce that thing we're talking about? and 3) Are we committed to staying with it long enough to make it work?"

But in today's overheated business environment, most firms are too desperate to wait for results. "When we're facing intense competition from Asia, and money is relatively expensive, and technology is available and moves rapidly, it's not surprising that people reach out for a way of getting a handle, and what they tend to reach for are what you call fads," says Professor Joseph Bower of the Harvard Business School. "If you take almost any one of them and discuss it with the author, it's a perfectly qualified view of how a set of ideas can run a company. But if it's treated as a kind of cookbook, as a single tool carried to an extreme, you get nonsense."

The nonsense is often rigid and, to the untrained eye, stupid. Listen to Hope, a marketing director at a textile-manufacturing company, as she describes her company's reliance on what are known as PERT charts, very detailed chronicles of milestones to be reached on the way to some mythic performance standard:

The PERT chart takes on a life of its own. You end up planning the document and never do anything else, never produce anything except

[3] Management by Objective is described by one who was forced to live under it as follows: "You take a piece of paper at the beginning of the year, and you write down the objectives you will seek to achieve, and chances are that you never look at the piece of paper again. It really comes down to whether you have a view of the world in which you believe that in order to get anywhere in the world, you have to know where you're going. It presumes that life is a roadmap with recognizable signs along the way. It takes intuition and serendipity out of the process, whereas I think those things are what it's all about."

the chart. Somehow, senior managers feel better when the chart has been done, never questioning whether the product itself will ever come to pass. Nancy, our director of Quality, for instance, spent maybe six weeks doing a milestone chart for our project that was as big as a door, and then we never looked at it again. It made her feel good that things were structured.

Then there's the other kind of manager, like me, who sort of lumbers forward with some vague sense of deadlines and schedule, and somehow, miraculously, things still get done.

There's a software program that you can buy which you plug yourself into and then spend a lot of time hanging ideas onto decision trees. But the trees never bear fruit. Lots of lines with arrows and dotted lines and time lines, and they're abstract and reductive. They boil processes down to words of ten letters or less. And then they are supposed to govern your actions. I don't believe that anyone ever made a decision based on a decision tree.

Still, when the guys with liver spots get that nutsy gleam in their collective eye, the average employee has to snap to. Doing so can be good for your career. One mid-level person in a Quality-oriented culture observes: "Take a shnook like Larry Stivers—a second-rate general manager in a third-rate line operation. Under ordinary circumstances, his name would no more be recognized by the chairman than the janitor's. But because of his association with Quality Improvement, he'll have a chance to press the flesh of his betters, and I do mean betters."

Yes, the anal-retentive graphs and rah-rah lingo may seem absurd, but those who wish to survive will develop some instant naiveté on the subject: more than one astute corporate critic has been mailed overnight to the district office in Elmira for being too irreverent. "It's a religion," says one worker currently being garroted by a Quality Circle. "To question it openly or be overtly cynical about it—you're more than grumpy, you're an apostate."

The rationale for philosophical pursuit of Wonderfulness is now dogma not only within large organizations, but in the consultancies and business press that serve them. ORC of Princeton, New Jersey, has been conducting human-resource research since 1950. A spokesperson articulates the corporate line on fad managements quite well: "A lot of employees are getting the message that we've got to get tough," she says:

The people who are the low-cost producers are going to be survivors. I think that now people have gone through that sort of storm of cost containment, changing the attitude toward work itself, I think that now people are saying that management is not so bad after all, people are gaining appreciation for the problems that management is facing.

Once employees have bought into the program, they start to feel that management may not be so bad after all. That they're a part of this whole scene. That they, too, impact the bottom line. They do imply a long-term commitment, but they also imply that the fat is going to be cut, and that the lean and mean and efficient processes, as well as people, are going to remain. I think what business and industry is facing is a challenge—get lean and mean or we can't continue to support you. The chairman and founder of Fed Ex, just the other day I heard him speak at a meeting—Frederick W. Smith, head of Federal Express—he basically said to the audience, some fairly senior execs, challenged them, said, "Each one of you is costing your companies at least five hundred dollars a day, if you guys can't contribute at least five hundred a day on the average, then why are you here?" So basically what he's saying is that every employee has a responsibility to that bottom line. It's almost like the consultant industry—we ask *how much are you bringing into the firm?* Basically, what he's saying is that we have to get that mentality into corporate America, if you're pushing a pencil or a broom, you have to contribute to that bottom line.

This search for organizational solutions to industry problems arises from the basic inability of management to function in traditional ways. A good new credo can pump life into an ailing culture, true, but the average worker has simply endured too many passing executive fancies to take the next new one seriously. Resistance to joining management cults is therefore very strong among employees who feel that professionalism might be religion enough. Wes, a senior counsel at the hub of a large broadcasting network, is one who objects. "This Management-by-Objective stuff is total garbage," he says.

At the beginning of the year, management is supposed to set out objectives; report those objectives to your superior, and then live up to them. Anybody who's in the bonus pool has to do it. And at the end of the year, you see if you've met your objectives. Naturally, that means everybody sets down objectives you know you could meet.

And your superiors accept those objectives. It's a silent conspiracy. No one sets hard objectives, because they'll only come up against you at bonus-review time.

It's totally fucked up. How does a lawyer set objectives? What do you say? I'm going to win so many cases? Stay out of the following number of lawsuits? How do accountants set them? PR people? It's not applicable.

What we'd do is take a Xeroxed copy of last year's objectives, change the date on the top, and attach them to the cover sheet. Say things like, "To aim to facilitate coordination between different divisions," or "assist management in attaining maximum synergy between various operating divisions." Synergy is a very big word around here. That's the way the performance-appraisal system works. Wait a minute. I think Performance Appraisal may have taken the place of Management by Objective, but I'm not sure.

Once a year, I have to write this bullshit, and then at the end of the year I sit down for an evaluation. The review takes about twenty seconds. My boss says, "You did good this year. Here's your raise. Here's your bonus. Thanks a lot and good-bye." The objectives don't deal with reality.

Why do organizations go through this folderol? Wes speculates:

Upper management gets a hair up their ass and thinks this is going to improve worker productivity or something. The bottom line is that everybody knows who's doing a good job and who isn't. No matter how you evaluate anybody, it's subjective. There's no framework, and neither you nor your boss wants to deal with it. I find it hard to believe these fads and schemes will work—whatever the current management trend is. Either they truly believe it, or they have a hidden agenda. No matter what personnel kick you're talking about, it's all the same. When they first come out, there are meetings people have to attend. You don't get your raise or your bonus unless you go and take part. There are reams of memos from senior management saying how important this is. For a while it's hot, and then the real work of the company sets in. If the company has problems, the fad is ignored. And if the company is doing real well, the fad is ignored, too.

It becomes the subject of jokes, and the only people who take it seriously are nerds.

You go to work, you sit down, and you do what you have to do. You don't have time for that Mickey Mouse crap. You know you're working hard. You might give it a certain degree of lip service. But it's the Soviet system. And it doesn't work so good over there, either. These people create scenarios in academia, and it's impossible to translate into the real world. It's the mark of these systems to try to put controls on human nature. To control behavior. Limit the tendency of people to be informal at their jobs.

That quest to eradicate informality is at the heart of the wimp's mentality, whether he's a pure wimp or an organizational wimpy fascist. To get troops marching in lockstep, and offset the strong feelings of people like Wes, the organization must find a leader capable of instilling zeal, and, when necessary, fear. For motivation by a crazy boss is a lot cheaper than giving people the tools they need to do a job. One manager remarks:

For the creed to work, you've got to have not just the idea but the resources to put it in place. On the West Coast they were told, "You will answer phones by the third ring. The fact that they had an obsolete phone system that had to be replaced was, to management, irrelevant. In other words, Quality is great, but don't spend any money on it. Quality is capital-intensive. I don't think many managements understand that. They'd just rather you learn the anthem.

Underneath the warm and fuzzy participatory lingo, the songs written to be sung in unison, organizational fascists crave obedience and, worse, love. But while they have power and ideology on their side, there is one huge weapon available to employees: the power of rebellion.

Eileen is vice president of Promotion and Public Relations for a telecommunications company where the management decided everyone should Get Culture. Almost right away, a series of touchy-feely gatherings on the subject began. "You had a concept that was totally amorphous, to be implemented by a task force that was infinitely diffuse," she says. "The result was a lot of misty meetings and soggy sandwiches." Pretty soon, however, the bureaucratic machine started to roll. "Every department had to have its chart, and graph its progress in a public place," Eileen recalls. "That was one thing that always made me feel uncomfortable. I mean, I love the idea of teamwork, but I don't like putting it up on a wall." In charge of the process was a typical organizational fascist.

The greatest proponent of Quality within the organization was himself extremely uncomfortable about inviting his lieutenants to participate in a true, free exchange of ideas and really participate in
planning. Consensus was great, as long as it agreed with what he
wanted to do, and if it didn't, he would get tight-lipped and grim, and
shoot daggers at the troops who presumed that quality participation
included disagreement or diversity of opinion. You couldn't express
open skepticism with impunity. Bart had been so glorified by the
organization that you were clearly holding up your hand against the
person who had been designated as a power broker.

One of the darker moments was a meeting of our district sales managers at last year's sales rally, when Mike, our Quality Czar, asked
everyone to sign a petition he would put on his wall. I told him I had
sworn off petitions after the Vietnam War. I think I left the room while
the piece of paper was being passed around. I had the sudden need
to go to the ladies' room, and stayed there a good long time until the
signing was over. I was never punished, either. Although I think they
saw me as less of a team player from then on in.

If you're lucky, persistent, and smart, however, rebellion may not
be necessary. The crazy jerk, if given the opportunity, may just take
care of himself. Most do, over time. Like kamikazes who worship
their own madness, they all seek an incandescent end.

The trick for the concerned employee is to spot the pre-meltdown
symptoms, and, if possible, discreetly, tastefully, and humanely as
possible, push them over the brink to the disaster that they are
seeking—and deserve.

## ACTION POINTS: THE BUREAUCRAZY

The organization nut can only be cracked as a stone is worn away—
with the incessant, patient drip of your technical proficiency. On the
one hand, you've got to be *good*. Good at all the little jobs that
eventually add up to a career. On the other hand, you've got to
pursue your real activities well out of the way of his stupid, bureaucratic obsession with form over content. There's plenty of room
outside his direct view for you to maneuver, and therein lies the
heart of your strategy, which should be more direct—and even
simpler—than others. It's built on courage and hard work. You can
do that.

- *Take the heat:* While he's as hungry as the Me-person for credit, the bureaucrat is totally unwilling to risk taking responsibility for actions before their success is proven. That means you can accept accountability for major decisions, strategies, and projects all the way up to the point where they enter the public eye. That's a big piece of turf. As you go about developing a piece of business, you're likely to come into contact with a wide variety of people who see that it is *you*, not your boss, who's attending to the messy realities of working life. That way everyone will be quite clear that your fearful wimp's true interest extends only to the paper surrounding the event. In time they will come to expect that, after they pay him all the superficial cordialities of rank, you're the one they must deal with to get anything done in real time. With that functional power comes risk—but you don't mind that. You're not the wimp here, are you?

- *Manipulate the paper:* At the same time, you're going to have to become superb at the technicalities of covering your butt. In some organizations, this may just mean a few discreet phone calls to all the appropriate parties, including your boss. But phone calls are unlikely to satisfy the true wimp. He may need documentation. This can be more than just a pain in the neck. This can actually protect you if something funky comes down and the wimpish quisling that is your manager tries to wriggle out of his share of the blame. When that happens, you can merely whip out the piece of paper that bears his signature and remind him that you were in this together. Paper, in short, is not simply the triumph of form over substance. At a certain point, it becomes all the substance you may need to trace a decision path and stay alive. Don't disdain it, even if it does seem like bullshit when you're pounding it out at close of business.

- *Talk straight:* Your wimp has a terrible habit of taking one thousand words to say what could be said with one. This is just as annoying to his peers and managers as it is to you. They need action and bold momentum from him, no matter what your company does or what your function is—nobody needs a windy blowhard weaving around the point and wasting the chief currency of the workplace, i.e., time. You've got a huge opportunity here. If you can communicate clear instructions, needs, and answers to those who require them, you'll once again be stepping into the breach formed by the bureaucratic lack of spine.

- *Think of prior solutions, and if those don't work, think of ante-cedents:* No matter what you're doing when he's not around to wring his hands, you'll occasionally have to sell your wimp on the ideas and plans you're putting forth in your daily commerce with other people. To succeed here, be prepared to dress up your good, original thinking in plain old brown paper wrapping. That means taking your innovative proposals and coming up with things that have existed before that bore some similarity to them, things that succeeded and brought glory to the boss who okayed them. He doesn't want to hear, "Nobody's ever done anything like this before, J.B.!" He wants to hear "When they tried something exactly like this over at Omnivore, it went like gangbusters, Milt! The company went private not long thereafter, and they all made out like bandits!" The wimp is deeply disturbed by anything new and dangerous. He's against risk, no matter how advisable the gamble might he. Don't ask him to be anything other than his entrenched self—that's true of all crazy bosses, no matter what stripe.

- *Show him how much he is liked when he does what you want:* Remember that the wimp wants to be liked by positively every-one. That includes you. Never holler or denigrate him, of course, unless you're righteously pissed off about a real slight to your dignity. But make it quite clear to him that when he's a good wimp you like and respect him a lot more than when he isn't. He wants to putter around with you and waste time with stupid detail. That's his meat. If you grant him that pleasure only when he accedes to your agenda, you'll be one step ahead.

- *Balance detail with mid-range thinking:* The wimp is an expert at long-term posturing and postulating. He's also pretty good at planning seating arrangements for today's staff meeting. But he's a lot less able to come up with coherent, achievable goals and ways to accomplish them over the course of the next quarter—which is the heart and soul of all business activity. Your chal-lenge: think in three-month parcels. Assemble a list of your "customers" both inside and outside your company who will rely on your product or service during that time. Keep in touch with each to establish their level of need. Set deadlines. Meet them. The problem with wimpy management is that it is not customer-driven. It's management-driven. It exists not to serve, but to perpetuate its own existence. Rise above that and become a champion of those for whom you provide function. You'll be applauded far and wide and, eventually, promoted.

- *Smooth his teeny toadies:* Like all other crazy bosses, the wimp has his sycophants who hang on to his professional body the way remora cling to a great white shark. The wimp's toadies are smaller than most. They're incredibly timid, and they have no teeth, just little oral apertures that extrude pleasant noises. Don't be annoyed by them. They're not the vicious henchpeople who wait on the paranoid. They're not the great horned amphibians who clamber around the feet of the bully. They're not even the fawning yes-men who dance when the narcissist says boo. They're just weensy little miscreants who are looking for someone big to cover their tushies. If you're nice to them, and decisive when you need to be, they'll be happy to toady *you.* Let 'em. It's kind of agreeable if you don't get overly dependent on it. Give them the job of listening for you, and they make mighty fine spies, too.

- *Offer your bogus friendship and expect exactly the same in return:* The bureaucrazy—in either the wimp or the organizational-fascist flavor—can be a jocular fellow. Like all crazy bosses, he will demand loyalty and even a show of affection. At times, he will seem to give some back. Enjoy it when it's offered, but don't be a chump. The guy is a fine ally and pal when things are running smoothly. But when the firestorms start, he'll be looking for anyone to fry in his place. And if you're the easiest and nearest around, you're toast. This doesn't mean you can't be pleasant. Superficial amity between boss and employee is a lot more comfortable than truthful distrust and suspicion. But while you're smiling and trading box scores, keep your rear covered with paper and real, operational friendships. In any reporting relationship, it's easy to give your heart. Don't misplace your love in someone who does not deserve it, and who will abuse it.

- *Expect no advancement that you have earned:* The sad truth is that the wimp seeks his own promotion and views you as a tool, nothing more. He is capricious, and will elevate those who do not merit it. If you work hard for him, and make his career look good, you'll be sure to keep your present job and may look forward to that generous 3.5 percent raise every year. Next fall, when a good position opens, you just might find a fair-haired boy recommended by the chairman gets the slot you've been promised. He'll stroke you and promise future goodies for you, of course. But he has no intention of making good on his promises. Why? Because, as a bureaucrat, *he sees you in a certain role*. Unless you break that perception in some way—sometimes by kicking and screaming—in that role you will stay. He respects the sense of place more than he does any mythic notions of gratitude or fairness. Your career path will be what you fight for, nothing more and possibly a lot less.

- *Scare him when you have to:* In his heart, the wimp is frightened and nervous all the time. When it seems appropriate, don't be shy about conjuring up all the bad things that could happen if "we" screw up. Like the narcissist, the wimp has a kernel of self-doubt and terror lurking under the compulsive need for form and order. Play on it. When he expresses a concern, do not assuage it. When he's tortured, feed his internal beast. Ultimately, he will see your terrorism as truthfulness, and will come to depend on you to solve the emotional problem his character has wished on his terrified self. Then, if the time comes when he must be destroyed, withdraw your assistance and watch him drift slowly out to oblivion on his solitary raft of dysfunction. Yeah, it sounds brutal. You want to play in the big leagues or not?

CHAPTER SIX

# DISASTER HUNTER

I don't like it when things are too peaceful. I really enjoy seeing people squirm. I like to live life as though I were living on a cliff. If I feel myself pulling back too far, getting too safe, I deliberately manipulate things back to the edge where it is exciting.

A Disaster Hunter

nd what could be more exciting than actually *falling off the edge?* Possibly nothing, especially when you've been so crazy for so long. When the thrills get harder and harder to find, and the pain gets tougher and tougher to take . . . enter the disaster hunter.

The collective weight of the crazy boss's neurosis cannot be supported for an indefinite amount of time. After a while, it crushes in on him, pressing on him from within while the pressures of business compress him from without. For as long as he can stand it (which may be longer than you can), he is in critical condition, terminal, because he's addicted to something that will eventually kill him. It could be adrenaline, or the taste of his own gall, or booze or pills or blow or sex or no sex ever. He needs the hit and can't do without it.

He's in trouble, and he's going to fall. He knows it, somewhere in his crazy heart. And, deep down, he doesn't mind the prospect of his eventual demise, not really, because in addition to all his other obnoxious pathologies, he is also a wounded beast seeking an end to his pain and torment. Part of him, in fact, is going about the task of actively creating that final solution, hunting his own disaster with all the energy that his madness imparts. And that's a lot.

Not all crazy bosses become disaster hunters, but a gratifying number do. With a little early diagnosis and help, you can do your part to make sure that your boss is one of them.

Let's look at the quiver of terminal problems suffered by the crazy boss nearing the end of his rope.

The disaster hunter is out of control. The demands of his daily existence have totally flipped him out. Virtually every aspect of his life is affected. He is brutal, silly, oversexed, drunk when he should be sober, sober when he should at least appear to be drunk; he lies almost more readily than he tells the truth; he seems inexplicable to the people who thought they knew him. What does it look like? Remember Gary Hart? Let's cut through for one brief moment the cultural amnesia that afflicts us all.

*The New York Times*
May 8, 1987

HART WILL REPORTEDLY QUIT RACE FOR PRESIDENCY TODAY
IN STORM OVER PRIVATE LIFE

. . . Mr. Hart's campaign began to crumble after the Miami Herald reported that he spent part of last weekend with a 29-year-old model and actress, Donna Rice.

Mr. Hart repeatedly denied that he had had any sexual relationship with Ms. Rice. Friends said he had been worn down by the attacks on his character and feared further articles about his personal life, including reports of romances with other women that would challenge his insistence that he was not a "womanizer."

Hart's inability to control his limbic impulses was only part of his conflicted personality. Tremendous achievement and intellect on subtle matters on one side; utter, heedless stupidity and willfulness on the other.

*The Washington Post*
May 8, 1987

. . . As they watched his public self-destruction this week, many of the people who went through earlier campaigns with him, especially the one in 1984, were struck by a sense of déja vu, but this time with a pestering—some said terrifying—final thought: Perhaps they had been wrong to suppress, or silence, their doubts for so long. "May-be," said one, "despite everything we love in and believe to be admirable about this man, he had a death wish. Maybe he didn't really want the prize. . . ."

Turns out that back in 1984, Hart reacted to questions about his name (Hartpence?) and age (not what he had claimed) with a torrent of evasion and self-aggrandizement. "It had a messianic quality then," a friend told the *Post* in 1987, "and even more so now." Hart's reaction to the Rice affair—an attack on the integrity of his attackers—"rang too many danger bells from the last time," another friend stated.

Larry Smith, his administrative assistant during the early 1980s . . . quit just before the race began. He told staff members later that he left in large part because he had become convinced that Hart had a dangerous sense of being "divine and above the rules."

What we have in Hart, as in Nixon before him, is an *excess of terrible self*, a persona that cannot be denied or modulated. "Only half of me wants to be President," Hart told a friend in the latter days of his campaign, "but the 50 percent that wants to be President is better than 100 percent of the others."

Hubris! And a delusional belief that the truth can be molded to the Great Man's need, that the Huge One can sustain risks and stupidities far beyond those of mortal men. Perhaps he could, were his stupidities not so huge as well.

## DOWN THEY GO, INTO THE WILD BLUE YONDER . . .

Throughout politics and business, we see the specter of disaster hunters melting down in their own craziness, stalking the destruction that will put them out of their misery.

*The New York Times*
December 5, 1988

NABISCO BATTLE REDEFINES DIRECTORS' ROLE
. . . The board's decision last week to sell RJR Nabisco to Kohlberg, Kravis, Roberts & Company for $24.88 billion—the largest corporate transaction in history—completed a story of missed opportunities and a slow but serious souring of the board's attitude toward Mr. [F. Ross]

Johnson [Nabisco's chief executive]. His position was undermined by the large rewards that he planned to take for himself in the deal, his unwillingness to guarantee employee benefits after the buyout and his stated aim of dismembering the company.

And this from *Business Week* of February 16, 1987:

When William H. Bricker stepped to the podium to answer questions from the press on February 2, it sure seemed that he had some explaining to do. Diamond Shamrock Corp. had just announced that Bricker was stepping down as chief executive officer after launching the floundering company's third major restructuring in less than three years. . . .

During the years Bricker was on top, *Business Week* points out, he had forged a number of deals that, by the late eighties would "come back to haunt him."

Despite the financial pressures on the company, its layoffs and asset sales, Diamond's lavish executive perks seemed immune from the cost-cutting. One example: Riverside Farms, the company ranch outside of Hamilton, Tex. Bricker defends it as typical of the hunting camps favored by oil companies. But Riverside Farms is far more than that. The local tax assessor values the sprawling ranch and its spacious lodge at $9 million. . . . Regular visitors included Sir Richard Musgrave, a professional shoot manager whom Diamond flew in regularly from Ireland to organize English-style pheasant hunts.

Diamond Shamrock's problems were resolved when, under assault by T. Boone Pickens, Bricker resigned and the rescued company was disassembled by its savior, Prudential.

According to one insider, Bricker asked the bankers to estimate how much his staying on would affect the value of the deal. The bankers told him the company would be worth more if he resigned.

And in early 1990, word came that Frank Lorenzo, the ultimate symbol of 1980s leverage, who had previously been stripped of his right to run Continental by a responsible board of his peers, had been bought out, achieving a tremendous personal profit not shared by either his workers or his stockholders.

He was gone, at any rate. As so many of our crazy bosses are.

Today, throughout the world, in companies large and small, established and entrepreneurial, crazy bosses are metastasizing, spreading out beyond their boundaries of place, hunting their own very personalized disasters, destroying themselves.

*Forbes*
June 29, 1987

THE ULTIMATE FAMILY FEUD
Seen from the street, the one-story brick offices of Horvitz Enterprises, Inc. of Cleveland look about as interesting as, say, a motor vehicle department. But enter the magazine-strewn lobby, stroll past the bouffant-coiffed receptionist at the switchboard, open the door to the executive offices beyond, and you enter a world like no other in business.

Here executives scream obscenities one minute, then glower at each other the next. There is an occasional fistfight, at other times eavesdropping.

Who are these people? Who else but the heirs to one of America's largest family fortunes, the $700-million newspaper, cable television and real estate empire of the late, great Samuel A. Horvitz, one of the meanest, hardest-drinking sons of the Buckeye State. . . .

In the end, of course, there was no choice but to sell. . . .

Yes, yes. Sale, divestiture, restructure. It's the cure for everything in the world of American business. And even across the waters, in the land of the rising investment, the cost of crazy management is finally coming clear, as retribution slams down on the disaster hunter.

*Business Week*
April 7, 1986

THE HIGH PRICE THE JAPANESE PAY FOR SUCCESS
. . . Stress is taking its heaviest toll on men in their 40s and 50s who have devoted themselves to Japan's postwar industrial push—often at their own and their families' expense. . . . Suicides among males aged 35 to 59 jumped from 4,429 in 1975 to 10,128 in 1984, more than doubling at a time when the overall population grew by just 8%. Meanwhile, trouble at work caused a sharp rise in the number of men who left their families and companies behind to begin new lives under aliases. Police records show that 6,527 men disappeared for work-related reasons in 1975; nine years later, 12,339 vanished.

Bottom line, worldwide, the man is doomed. He'll see to that. You've just got to wait it out and understand the symptoms. Look for ways to guide him gently into his happier future. And you know where that is: Away from you.

As you go about the job of unseating the crazy boss, look for the tiny fissures in his personality that foretell his eventual collapse. And have no fear—thanks to the severity of the situational madness around us today, *most will*. Especially when they have a loving and well-meaning subordinate like you to help them go down in dignity, or possibly without.

Look sharp and closely observe your disaster hunter:

## IS HE HYSTERICAL?

A formal functionary in a federal regulatory agency describes her old boss:

> She used to primal scream in her old office. Unbelievable. In a major government organization she would close her door and let out a yell that could be heard around the building trying to release her tensions.

The first symptom of the crack-up to come is a tendency to be really and truly "nuts" in the traditional sense; running, jumping, screaming, worrying, spreading pressure and anxiety that the boss can no longer contain within the boundaries of his suffering self.

This hysteria is quickly transmitted within the normal working environment. Marty is executive assistant to the president of a conglomerate located in the New South, whatever that is. His boss is in the process of tipping over in his canoe. "I think half of the problems my boss Brent has with *his* boss, the chairman, are due to the fact that the chairman overhears Brent screaming intimate secrets about the business into the phone. I've told Brent about this, but he just can't contain himself. Nobody knows who the fuck he's talking to when he's screaming like a nut, and he makes bets with his bookie, for chrissake, other real indiscreet stuff, and it's mind-bogglingly insecure—in the intelligence sense. That's what you're dealing with here when you have a person of his importance talking in public with his door open, with intelligence in both senses of the word. And the phones and the office aren't *secure*, that's the only word I can use for it."

Public insecurity. That is the question. And you can't really blame the crazy disaster hunter. If you were unraveling, you'd be nervous, too, and in a way kind of eager to see how things are going to work out.

A guy I know was public-relations director for a sizable oil company. His boss was a rapidly decaying wimp. "Warren was a nervous guy with a lot of ailments, a double A–type personality," my friend reports.

> He was a scared rabbit, highly strung, terrified by upper management. He had this idea that those gods up there would one day call him in, rant and rave and fire him over some mistake, that he would stumble and end his career. His favorite saying about someone who ran into trouble was "He broke his pick."

Phallic enough for you?

> We on his staff, naturally, were the guys who would end up giving him a broken pick. Ergo we were his enemies. Of course, we had to interface with other divisions, and each time we did, to his mind, we were in a position to create problems.

The disaster hunter lurking inside the crazy boss moved the guy closer to his doom. In his defense, let it be said that he had no choice. Being sick hurts, and a guy needs his medicine.

> He took pills to calm himself, tranquilizers, I think they were Valium, and he took a lot. But they didn't keep him from getting sick. He had constant anxieties that would cause more ailments, so he would take more medicine, and the medicine would make him feel even worse. The guy was a wreck.

> He insisted on seeing everything, correcting everything, in order to avoid that horrible situation in which we would supposedly "shoot him down." I remember one lunch when we were all supposedly out to relax when someone told him Atlantic Richfield had put out a release that day on something that involved us. Warren got out his pen, took the release, and started making changes, saying, "No, no, this isn't right, you can't do it that way," and we were all saying, "Walt, Walt, you can't edit another company's release. It's out already! Calm down!"

Because he was the only one who could do anything, he was a workaholic. He worked like an insane man, very late hours. I would offer to help him, but his perception was that he was the only one would could save himself from disaster by attending to every detail.

He was inconsistent. We would write something and make it as non-controversial as possible, because he wanted it that way, bland. He'd call us in and read us out because it wasn't "snappier." So we'd think things were changing, write something snappier, and he'd get furious because it wasn't bland enough.

He had a pipe. He perceived that people who were calm smoked them. But he could never keep it. He had burns in every suit. He would set wastebaskets on fire. And he would blow up while puffing his pipe. The veins would stand out on his forehead as he screamed, "DON'T YOU UNDERSTAND?" There was no difference in his mind between a file clerk and me. We all posed a threat. I'd see him taking the time to ream out *my* secretary. He absolutely did not perceive that he could delegate.

Here, in one boss, are all five of the symptom-complexes of the crazy boss: bully, paranoid, narcissist, wimp, and disaster hunter. One day Warren's boss retired, and a woman whom Warren had always treated condescendingly got the job. She gave Warren the option of taking a smaller position or leaving the company. His nightmare of being called in and demoted had come to pass. In fact, he had made it happen. My friend concludes:

Warren was hoist on his own petard. It was a self-fulfilling prophecy. But he would have been totally worse off if he *had* gotten his boss's job. He couldn't have handled it. Maybe his crazy behavior was his own way of insuring that he wouldn't get it.

Beyond manic meddling lies the reaction on the other side of desperation, one that's even more appropriate, given the disaster hunter's situation.

## KINDA DEPRESSED?

He feels the world unraveling around him and suddenly receives a clear picture of the cause—him—and the one who's going to suffer for it—him—as well as probably the only one who can do something to atone for it—you guessed it, *him*.

Perhaps for the first time, the guy sees quite clearly through all the defenses and rationalizations he has erected to protect himself from his craziness. And the clearness of the picture is devastating.

His depression is the flip side of his go-get-'em momentum, the energy he employed to keep all the balloons in the air. It's also the closest thing to a realistic frame of mind he's enjoyed in a long time. In *Relations in Public*, Erving Goffman noted:

> We should appreciate that depression is not something that can be fully understood by looking inside the patient. It seems to me that depressed persons come to appreciate consciously how much social effort is in fact required in the normal course of keeping one's usual place in undertakings. Once an individual feels a little less outgoing than usual for him, a very large part of his social universe can easily become attenuated, simply because such a universe is partly sustained at the constantly exercised option of the actor.

As we've seen, the effort to *sustain place* in the irrational organization takes tremendous effort for employees, and even more daily exertion from the boss who is trying to keep it all in control. When the philosophical underpinnings of the job start unraveling for real, the positive, kick-ass guy may just throw up his arms and sink into despondency.

Perhaps the most pathetic specter of public depression was that of Robert McFarlane, former National Security chief, who attempted to commit suicide after he was designated one of the fall guys for the Iran-Contra scandal. "All of my life, all of my father's life, I had been consumed by the idea that devoting one's total energies to government as a way of improving the lot of my fellow man was the best thing you could do with your mind and your body and your passion," Mr. McFarlane told Maureen Dowd of *The New York Times*, in a manner Dowd described wonderfully: "his deliberate baritone even more slow and heavy than usual, his words pushed out by small, gusting sighs." Dowd continued:

> Mr. McFarlane, a 49-year-old former Marine Corps officer, was a man who seemed so intense and so tightly controlled that "you had the sense he was tied down to his desk by leather straps," a White House

colleague recalled. And yet, Mr. McFarlane lost control in the suicide attempt that left him in Bethesda Naval Hospital under psychiatric treatment for two weeks. . . . "What really drove me to despair was a sense of having failed the country," he said.

Part of McFarlane's problem was that he did not feel included in the circle of wealthy, self-made men who surrounded the inattentive president. To keep going, the crazy boss needs love from his peers. Without that love, life is not worth living. "At the White House the morning after McFarlane's attempted suicide, none of his former colleagues brought it up at the staff meeting," Dowd writes. " 'We were embarrassed by it,' a Presidential aide said. 'Washington is a town that does not know how to deal with emotion.' "

Here was a crazy boss cut off from his fellow crazy bosses, a rigid man with a huge conception of the good he could do, a need to be nothing if not great. This is lonely work—as is all crazy bossing. And loneliness is a contributing factor to more than one serious illness.

The depressed guy probably would love to be able to talk to you. He's just too darned sad. Also, frankly, kind of disappointed in advance that you didn't come up with the goods before they were ordered. "Harold isn't a good manager either at home or on the job," says a young entrepreneur of her husband:

He expects too much, and he's itching to do it all himself, and he broods, instead of talking about it with the person involved. Look at the way he acts when he tries to manage my housekeeper. He won't tell her what to do, he'll just tell *me* to tell her. And his secretary at the office. He had a problem with how she dealt with clients on the phone. She was just vacant, would forget to ask questions, never reminded patients that they had to pay when they showed up, so naturally they would walk out without paying. That really drove him absolutely crazy. So I said, "Why don't you help her, give her scripts to work from, that kind of stuff?" But that was too organized for him, too curative. He'd rather brood about it.

When a lonely, sad person and his excessively high hopes get disappointed, he may take it out on others for a good long while, but have no fear. The ultimate beneficiary of his loathing and fear will be himself.

In the July/August 1975 issue of the *Harvard Business Review*, psychologist Harry Levinson, in a discussion of executive suicide, asks, "What intense pressures for achievement or approval forced these men to comply with actions that violated their consciences?" Levinson goes on to inquire:

> What rigid self-demands made them think that death was the only way out of their dilemmas? Why do some executives attach so much importance to their roles? Why are their aspirations so high and crucial to them that if they face business reverses, their only solution is to punish themselves with long hours of fatiguing work and perhaps eventually with death?

Levinson also remarks on the "threat of failure" that leads the grandiose person to despair. Now, keep in mind that such a threat is very real today—every day, every hour of every day. In the 1980s, it was the fear of takeover and the resulting loss of power and face.

One of American business's most famous recent suicides came as a direct result of Frank Lorenzo's successful run at Continental, come to think of it.

*Time*
August 24, 1981

Continental Airlines Chairman Alvin Feldman, 53, worked for several hours with an aide Sunday, August 9 in his office at the Los Angeles International Airport. The two men were preparing a press release to be published the next day announcing that nine banks had pulled out of a plan aimed at stopping a Texas International Airlines takeover of the company. The banks had changed their minds about making a $185 million loan to a group of about 11,000 employees who wanted to buy controlling interest in their ailing company. Without the loans, the takeover seemed inevitable. After finishing work, Feldman sat alone and wrote four letters: two to his attorneys, one to his three grown children, in which he mentioned the death of their mother last year, and one to his secretary telling her what to do with the other three letters. Then Alvin Feldman shot himself.

This is certainly an extreme reaction. But the frustration of seeing one's business edifice crumble is almost impossible to describe.

I'm going to try it anyway.

When I was assistant to the president of my company several years ago, we received the news that our parent corporation, in a move to restructure itself and fend off a takeover, was going to sell off one of our most important businesses. We were left with about half our revenue stream, and our position as a diversified conglomerate involved in all corners of our industry was destroyed.

On the day the deal was announced, I, along with several others, was called into the president's office. He was ready to tell the media about this news. The story was said to be sold to the media as his own decision, one he embraced as a sage business move, terrific, in fact, for all concerned. So he not only had to announce the divestiture of his favorite child, he had to repress all his anger at the decision and feign executive pleasure.

He did a brilliant job throughout the fourteen conversations with the press. When each reporter asked, "Yeah, I understand how good it is for the parent corporation. But isn't this devastating for *you?*" Carl responded: "We developed this property for its asset value, and we're pleased to see it realized for the benefit of the company and the shareholders we serve."

Between interviews he would fall silent, rubbing his hands together gently and occasionally uttering such statements as "Good Lord." His face became increasingly pale, his eyes attained a glassy sheen, and he began to sigh and stare off into the distant landscape that lay beyond his vast plate-glass window.

From that time forth, he never really *ran* the company. Within six months, he was preparing a successor. A year after that, he had effected his own departure. Don't feel sorry for him. He's a happy man now. Rich beyond most people's capacity to understand wealth, a massive personal corporation in his own right. Our organization is building itself back, too, but it's a nervous place. Just starting to get over its lassitude, its anger, its . . . depression.

Not all depressed guys are hugely tragic, I'm happy to say. Good news comes from *Omni:* "A lot of people may be depressed and lonely because they are socially unskilled," the author writes, "and their main problem may be that they are boring."

Sadly, that is one widespread business illness for which there is no cure or solution.

## HOW MANY UNFINISHED PROJECTS ARE ON HIS DESK?

Feeding the dual tendencies toward both hysteria and depression is the disaster hunter's penchant for bad project management. The inability to see projects responsibly from start to completion is the next tip-off that impending, self-sought destruction is on the way. This form of disaster hunting is most commonly displayed by the ubiquitous procrastinator who functions even in our midst. Hey. It could be you.

A procrastinator lives life on the edge, and needs the drug of terror to get the job done not well, but at all. Here are some of his faces:

"I go to sleep knowing that it's not done, safe in the knowledge that unless it is done tomorrow morning, I will have to die," says one. "Procrastination shows confidence, even hubris. *Believing* you have the ability to get it done."

Another cliff-climber recalls: "In college, my senior year, last semester, I was taking five courses. Each had a paper due. And I left myself one day for each paper at the end of the year. Five papers in five days. Which I thought was very reasonable. What would have been bad was to have to write two papers in one day. That would have been programming failure."

And finally, one who cuts right to the bottom line: "You take all the nothingness of your existence and turn it into pressure, then pleasure. *It's about trying to stiff-arm death.*"

It takes a very strong person to maintain an aggressive procrastinatory strategy over time without melting down. My friend Rich, a financial analyst for a firm that engineered a large number of stupid acquisitions in the 1980s, explains his method.

The trick is to do as little work as possible until the last moment, and to learn how to determine what that last moment is. You need good technical skills, too, to move very quickly when you have to. Then it becomes a question of how to waste time effectively. You have to make sure you're in a profession in which they don't mind the appearance of not doing anything, where execution is all that's appreciated. People have to marvel at your ability to do things effortlessly. But it's extremely hard work. It helps to have a newspaper. Because you need to look like you're doing something, you can't just sit and stare into space in some offices.

Talking on the phone is probably the preferred time-waster for serious procrastinators. I spend a lot of time, even in the context of working, procrastinating. A business lunch talking about everything but what you're supposed to be talking about is good. Once you get to your task, it's never that bad. The operative time period to give yourself is forty-five minutes. I always say if I can sit and work for forty-five minutes, I've earned the right to get up and procrastinate again. One of the great debates is, if you're really on a roll but you're finishing too fast, do you stop—and possibly blow your momentum—rather than finish early? I think you do. The key is never to finish before deadline. Quitting while you're ahead is the point in this context. Instead of pushing on, you say to yourself, "Hey, I wrote a great sentence. Time to take a break and celebrate."

The bottom line is this: a procrastinator meets his deadlines. If he didn't, he'd have to stop procrastinating.

Most fail. And only a disaster hunter needs to push the envelope until it bursts. It's because he has something to prove to the only audience he respects: himself. That is, he's seen what he can do with the greatest of ease—and remains darned impressed with himself, too. He's contemptuous of people who need to work along more regular paths. As one do-it-later guy says, "I'm proud to be a procrastinator. It's the can-do guys who I think make it tough for the rest of us. They're grinds. Humorless. And they're always getting ahead."

Self-delusion is a critical centerpiece of the procrastinating disaster hunter's operating mentality. Aaron, a senior executive who was once in charge of training and development for his company, is now a consultant. Here's what he says:

When is the last time you heard of anyone having a long-term plan that benefited anybody? America procrastinates and feeds the world. Russia has five-year plans and is starving! In fact, the whole idea that you will carefully do a little bit every day is a very bad sign psychologically. You have to be a procrastinator or obsessed with punctuality, and there's no in between. I use procrastinating as a way of thinking obsessively about what I'm not doing. It's the best way of working.

But think of people who do a little every day. Those are sick people. It requires planning how far you're going to do it and then really getting into it and then reaching the point when you were planning to quit for that day and then just . . . stopping! Doing a little bit more tomorrow! And then stopping! And stopping! Do you realize how *sick* that is?

I think procrastinating is the healthiest people can be. It means you have a certain joie de vivre, the will to put off what is unpleasant until it must be done. What is more healthy than that? Back in the dawn of civilization, people went out and shot something when they were hungry. Now we have freezers, and it's the signpost of the downfall of civilization. People start storing stuff and then they need more stuff to store in this big freezer, and better stuff, and eventually we have gourmet stores.

Come again?

Now there's a man who knows how to construct his rationales. How can he work? By feasting on the anxiety his paralysis is wreaking on his entire life system. And waiting for the big, orgasmic rush when the fear gets strong enough to motor him to greatness. "When you really can't procrastinate any more, your work is due, there's no way out of it, and you're sitting in front of that spreadsheet, a concentration high comes that I only have when I'm on deadline when everybody's screaming at me and it really has to get done, and it's really wonderful," Aaron says. "That moment when all the pressure is on you and you have an hour to go and . . . it's like dream time. It's better than drugs. It's pressure. And adrenaline. And fear and ego. It's the greatest high. It's fabulous. You only get that payoff when you procrastinate right. I know when I'm into that. When the phone rings and I don't want it to, I know I'm in the curl."

But while the disaster hunter is searching for his fix of fear, he's got a problem. He's insane now: hyper, moody, maybe even popping pills or snorting some of that ole brain Drano, just to keep the anxiety at bay. He's in no position to judge how close he's getting to the brink from which no procrastinator ever returned except to clean out his office.

A guy I'll call Sandy is the CFO at a lending institution in the Midwest. He does a lot of reports, and finds himself often on deadline the night before the morning of a great terrible meeting where men in gray suits will decide the fates of many other people. One night he was the last left in his huge office tower. "It was the ultimate frisson of fear," he recalls.

I thought I would freeze to death. It was in the middle of the winter in our sales office in Detroit, and I'm on the forty-third floor and the heat was turned off two hours ago and the last other person left forty-five minutes ago, and I'm stuck on this one number for what seems like hours. And I'm sitting there. And then suddenly all the lights in the hallways were turned off, I guess on a timer. I was scared to death. This was Detroit, which is not like getting stuck in Cancun, and I had two choices, that's it. One was to flee for my life and lose my job. The other was to get the report in by six A.M., when the chairman got in. I sat there frozen, paralyzed with spiritual procrastination. My body was there, but my mind didn't get to work until they flipped the "off" switch and elevated me into new levels of fear I had never known before. After that, it took me half an hour. Then I had to call the security police to get me out. As I left, I felt like I was getting out of jail.

Sandy made it. But not for long. He's out of that company now and a lot happier, although not appreciably better at deadlines. As a senior manager of his department, he's simply making himself hysterical at a higher level—and hunting for his next, bigger, disaster.

Ultimately, the piper gets his and one of the big projects fails—and fails dramatically. You don't want to be around to catch any shrapnel when that happens. My friend Wally is a former big wheel at a TV/radio/programming company in New York. "As a boss, I was known for dragging everyone to the edge with me," he says. "I was much loved for it, ha-ha. If it were not for the fact that I managed to pull off good work, they would have had me shot. But for me there has always been a relationship between fear and performance." Wally continues:

But there is a time when it can shut you down. One or two times, as the deadlines approached and the fear enlarged, I was literally locked down tight, and I was close to needing a respirator. The issue is don't let it get to that point, which I did. When I was pulling off the Benzinger/Putch merger, I had been on it for five months, and suddenly it all came down to one Sunday afternoon. And I was supposed to put together the entire contract and letters of agreement and who the fuck knows whatall.

For months I had counted on putting together this masterful package of paper, and suddenly here I had to do it on deadline. The incredible horror of having to do it in the corporation's formal style, too, which was Byzantine. And I think it was the one time in my life . . . that I collapsed, that I didn't come through. I think I disappointed everyone, and it was because my fear became so great. It's a horrifying thing. Your brain won't unlock, even though you know it's important that it does. It was a nightmare.

The general counsel called and literally . . . talked me through the entire deal a piece at a time. And while I attended the meeting and everything, he's the one who got to make the main pitch to senior management.

Six months later, Wally became a consultant. A few months ago, he in fact became a consultant for this very same institution he left in distress back in the early 1980s. Did they decide he was sane again? Or are the expectations for sanity in consultants different from those necessary for senior staff?

## WHAT'S HIS ADDICTION?

AP-NY-10-30-87
White House Admonished Deaver?

WASHINGTON (AP)—A woman who worked for lobbyist Michael K. Deaver says a White House counsel complained that Deaver's contacts with Reagan administration officials were inappropriate.... Pamela G. Bailey testified at Deaver's perjury trial Thursday that Fred Fielding, the White House counsel in 1985, telephoned Deaver's lobbying firm after he became aware of Deaver's contacts on behalf of private clients.... Deaver, the former deputy White House chief of staff, is accused of lying to a grand jury and a congressional committee about his lobbying activities after he left the administration.

Deaver's former secretary, Janet Harvey, meanwhile, supported the defense contention that his memory was impaired by alcoholism. Ms. Harvey testified Thursday that the news about Deaver's drinking problem "somehow gave an explanation for Mr. Deaver and the way he was, the moodiness or depression, not remembering things."

Drunks are common in business. Studies estimate that slightly fewer than one in ten American business types have a "problem," and that where performance issues exist in the workplace, alcohol is involved up to 70 percent of the time.

Like Mr. Deaver, disaster-hunting drunks are often protected by a lot of people who should know better. It's understandable. Drunks can do excellent work, and make terrific friends. Until they don't.

Relatively recently, drunkenness has come to be seen as an illness, not a vice. This is good news for the drunk, but it's bad news, too. It means the punishment he's seeking will be long in coming.

That doesn't mean it will never arrive.

Eventually, most organizations try to do something about the drunk and his more radical counterpart, the drug addict. They seldom care about the wide variety of other addictions, the most destructive of which is the addiction to work. Alcoholism remains the favorite disease to treat, possibly because it tends to be the most flagrant, having, until recently, been considered an acceptable mode of behavior:

> O'Malley was one of these big beefy characters who hit the pub every day at 12:30 and did not resurface until about 3:30 P.M. Then, with his face Santa Claus red and his eyes all bleary, he got through the rest of the day very well until quitting time, when he repaired to the same pub again.

The guy in question is an editor at a big New York publishing house. The report comes from Tess, a woman who used to work for him.

> One afternoon he calls me into his office to discuss copy for a book jacket. Before I even sit down, he says, "This is the worst fucking piece of shit I've ever seen. I don't know how you could turn this in. This is not worth the price of the paper it's printed on!"
>
> So I finally managed to squeeze in, "But Mike, Mike, that isn't my copy!" So he slams his fist down on the desk and roars, "Don't give me any of your fucking excuses!" I still have to laugh when I think of that.

The drunk continues to thrive partly because many executives, themselves not averse to recreational libation, would like to retain the right to drink when it seems to be required, and even when it's not.

Charlie was a director in the Employee Relations Department of a Bell Operating Company. "This guy who was my boss, Otto, he managed three people, including me, and he was an alcoholic, and we all reacted to that differently," he remembers.

> I worked overtime to compensate for him; my friend quit and basically as much as possible gave up working; the third walked around in a rage all the time and tried to stab Otto in the back, to sabotage him and our whole department. He was as off the wall as the boss, which I suppose was the only sane reaction.

It was murder. Everyone in the company knew about this man's problem. They all liked him—so did I—and they wanted to cover for him long enough for him to retire early with his benefits. I would turn in work to him days early, and he would not respond. Suddenly, I would get a call from the secretary of the chief executive asking where the hell it was. I would have to scurry around, deliver them a copy, then of course when revisions were necessary do it at night or over the weekends.

He would call meetings at 4:00 P.M. and tell us he needed something on his desk the next morning, so we would have to work late. Then of course he would not get around to looking at it until 2 P.M. the next day.

He helped me in my career, paid me well, and made sure I was promoted, so in some ways I felt beholden to him. But it was one of the most miserable periods in my life.

Lots of people who serve the drunk, in fact, are helping him to get by and stay loaded. A study conducted for the New York State School of Industrial and Labor Relations at Cornell University in 1972 found:

First, deviant drinking was supported and protected by a group of significant role definers. A protective clique enveloped the executive in an intricate network of protection which effectively isolated him from the rest of the organization. Simultaneously, the clique members satisfied personal ambitions for power and material gain such that the relationship between them and the alcoholic executive evolved into symbiosis. Clique members . . . effectively controlled the president through a clearly understood, yet covert, threat of exposure, for the president's exposure would obviously mean personal humiliation, loss of status in the organization, and loss of protection for continuing deviant behavior. Thus the executive usually acceded to their wishes rather than risk exposure.[2]

A woman who works for a mean drunk suggests another reason why nothing is done about the incompetent stewpot in the corner office:

The interesting thing is that often he's terrible to the people below, but the people above don't mind it because everyone below is kept in

[2] Harrison M. Trice & Paul M. Roman, *Spirits and Demons at Work: Alcohol and Other Drugs on the Job*, ILR Paperback No. 11, Ithaca, NY: Cornell University, January 1972.

check by this lunatic. In family therapy, they have this belief that one person is the *sufferer* for the whole family, and the family doesn't really want them to get better because then *they* don't have to get better. There's an attitude in management that they don't want him to be a better manager, because as long as he's a lunatic, they can be nice and not deal with anything. People at the lower rungs go above and complain, but it doesn't do any good.

So the drunk sops off the company and the company helps the drunk and everybody's happy, sort of, except the drunk's direct reportees. It's a sodden symbiosis that keeps the disaster hunter in office and abnegates the disaster hunters up above from any responsibility. Good thing, too, because they're every bit as ineffectual as he is—without even drinking.

A guy I'll call Frank is the controller of one of the largest liquor importers and retailers in the United States. The company he describes is highly political, a place where promotion is more dependent on politics than on merit, possibly due to the fact that the firm is privately held by a family that runs it like their personal toy. "It's their candy store, and they can do what they want," says Frank. Nobody's going to argue with him.

I reported to a guy named Guido for more than a year. He was Brazilian, from one of the best families over there. He was wonderful, brilliant.

Many drunks are, by the way.

He was about five feet four inches, fat and very Latin, not at all the physical type of most of our company's executives. But he was very bright, with a tremendous financial mind. He joined the company in Toronto, and they moved him to New York. For reasons that were unclear to me, he left his family in Toronto. He was all alone in New York.

Isolation . . .

He was very lonely, very separate from his peers and not socially accepted. Despite that, Joe, the vice president he reported to, became very paranoid about Guido, decided that Guido was a real threat to him. Joe was from a lower-class Bronx-Irish background. He was not very smart, easily threatened, and his nails were chewed to the middle of the quick from sheer anxiety. As irrational as it was, he decided that Guido was a threat to him, and proceeded to make his life miserable.

Guido started drinking heavily. As his drinking became worse, Joe started avoiding him completely. Months went by, literally, when the two would not see each other at all. Joe wouldn't enter Guido's office, or hold a conversation with him. His only communication with Guido was through memos that would criticize his performance.

A bully paranoid and a depressed drunk make quite a pair.

It got so bad that ten whole months went by without either going into the other's office. As Guido's lieutenant, I was called in by Joe all the time and given all kinds of assignments. I'd say, "Look, it's kind of tough for me to get all this done . . . given the situation," and he'd say, "I don't care who does the work, as long as it gets done. If you have a problem, you should voice it."

I knew what he was trying to do. He wanted me to be the one who turned Guido in. He didn't want to do it. I don't really understand why. Maybe he just hated to bring bad news to the president, whose wife was a chronic alcoholic who just couldn't stop drinking no matter how hard she tried.

The situation got worse, of course. Finally, around the holiday season last year, they became kind of dramatic. Around Thanksgiving, Guido called in sick for one entire week. I called him at home, and I knew he was on a monster binge. I was genuinely concerned about him. I invited him to our Thanksgiving dinner. He said no. By Christmas, things were terrible. On Christmas Eve day, I kind of panicked. I'd tried to reach Guido on the phone all day. I kept thinking about what he had told me: that three days before he had applied for and obtained a gun permit. When I asked him why, he lowered his voice mysteriously and muttered, "You can't be too careful."

I got real paranoid that if he killed himself, there would be an investigation and phone records would show how often I had been in touch with him. Did this mean I had a responsibility to speak out? Did I have the right? I was freaking out. I called Joe and told him about the gun. Joe's first reaction was pretty characteristic. "Does he know where I live?" he asked. "Where my kids go to school?" He immediately called his wife and got his kids home.

I was supposed to go to my brother's house for Christmas dinner, but I was too upset. I called the police and told them the situation with

Guido, and they broke into his house. They called me back in about fifteen minutes and told me they had found my boss wrapped in a sleeping bag with the TV on, pathetic, sound asleep. They said he had "imbibed too much Christmas cheer."

The next week he finally appeared at work, but I have no idea how he even made it to the station. By 8:45 he was snoring at his desk, too drunk to sit up. I put him on a train, sent him home, and went in and told Joe, "We have to do something." So Joe finally went in to the president and told him, and the president called Guido in and fired him on the spot.

A sad ending? Not at all. That very day, Guido left the firm, stopped drinking almost immediately, and is currently running a successful private accounting practice. The sick symbiosis was broken.

The odd thing is, Frank never really felt the professional pressure resulting from reporting to two horrible bosses *because he maintained a thoroughly professional function, moment to moment.* "It wasn't hard to stay ahead of Joe," he says, "because he's not very competent and almost any kind of day-to-day performance is okay with him. I kind of resented the workload, I guess, but Guido left me pretty much alone. So it was just tough in human terms."

Helping to cover for the drunk, while it may be the short-term humane course of action, won't automatically redound to your benefit after he's gone. You're associated with his loopy administration. Charlie, the Bell Operating Company guy, is a case in point:

My drunk boss made it to retirement, thanks to my help, and then they immediately went out and hired an outsider to take over the department. I absolutely hit the roof with the boss's boss. It was the only time people ever heard me shout. After all I'd been through . . .

Yes, while the crazy bosses who permit the drunk to stay in place demand loyalty for themselves, they generally give none, believing that the joy of working for their tremendous company is privilege enough by half. So give your all for your drunken boss if you must, but don't expect anything in return except the warm feeling of knowing that you're helping the disabled.

It might make sense here to say a brief word about professional counseling. It's great for employees, sort of, sometimes. But professionals agree that your basic Employee Assistance Program (EAP) does not reach into the executive ranks. "A person at that level generally won't go," says one EAP administrator. "They're afraid for their careers, afraid it will be used against them."

And when you think about it, they don't really have to, do they? They don't have a drinking problem. *You* do.

Besides, EAP professionals tend to lump all substance abuse under one category and go for the talking cure. This approach is fine when we're talking about downers and speed. But Gorman, an attorney, has a Valium boss. "I can always tell when Eric's on it," he says. "He used to take real powerful downers, which he says he's liked since college, but now he's settled on Valium because he can get it legally. He's CFO."

Eric has a tendency to be pretty pompous and to weigh his words with tremendous care, as if every statement he utters, you know, is like of tremendous importance and wisdom. So when he's straight, he's kind of ruffled, and a little on edge, maybe, but kind of more human. But when he pops a couple milligrams of Valium, he, like, smooths out, and gets very haughty, and appears to weigh his words with extra-special care, and looks totally unflappable—which is great at meetings with adversaries, you'd better believe it—and his eyes kind of get pinpoint sharp in his totally relaxed face. And on the whole, he appears to be 110 percent the player he is when he's on his own. Which is fine, until you try to have a human conversation with the guy. Then you realize that he's miles and miles away.

Cocaine, of course, is the most terrible drug of all, particularly because there are very, very few addicts who can manage a business career. But cocaine, even after all the publicity and hype, is still quite popular. The cokehead's physiological systems are far closer to hysteria than they are to the attractive somnolence of your average drunk around 4:30 P.M. While the drunk may be cranky some of the time (particularly in the critical valley of fatigue directly after a three-beverage luncheon), the cokehead is downright mean when the buzz is beginning to fade. And while the drunk's behavior sways to and fro like a giant palm frond, the coke monster skitters from mania to murderous depression like an oscilloscope on a power surge.

All in all, I'd rather work for a drunk any day, and I believe most contemporary employees who know both feel the same. My friend

Linda is a manager at a production studio that specializes in commercials and music videos. "I was at the staff party one year and I'm a little loaded, you know, like everybody, and I happen to go to the ladies' room," she says.

> And I go in there, and I find about fifteen people actually down on their knees on the floor of the ladies' room passing around a tiny vial of cocaine, both women and men, everyone in this little space snorting and honking, and as I come in every single pair of eyes looks up at me, and I see this greedy twinkle in them, like "Get out of here, we barely have enough for *us*." And I see that one of those people is my boss. And several others are guys I'm competing with for an upcoming promotion. So I left and had to go to a completely different floor to go to the bathroom.

All addictive substances provide a *forum for belonging* to people who would normally be alienated and isolated. Cocaine is the most dangerous, creating a malevolent fraternity of nose bandits. Stay away from the cocaine-snuffling disaster hunter, however, not because he is any better or worse than his many doom-seeking counterparts, but because his doom will come sooner, rather than later. If you are around, you'd better believe it will include you. While most establishments will tolerate most forms of substance abuse, it is an odd workplace indeed that will support someone whose vice has received such terrible press. To be against cocaine is now one of the safest ways to be a solid citizen. Many's the three-martini alkie with a potbelly the size of a medicine ball who feels sanctimonious when facing the poor droid with the deviated septum.

Both are doomed, though, the minute they *become dysfunctional*. As always, function is the one and only issue that counts.

Sometimes, however, people can be *too functional*, and that, too, is an often unrecognized form of intentional self-destruction.

## WHAT'S HIS ADDICTION? PART TWO: WORK

More hazardous to your professional and mental health (which is more important again?) is the boss whose addiction is to work. There are few treatments for workaholism because society doesn't yet see a need for one. Workaholics make money, and money in itself is one definition of sanity not only in business, but in far more rational sectors of our society.

Only in rare, healthy corporations does the workaholic stick out from the pack, and cry for attention and assistance. The rest of the time he merely grows in strength and popularity with his bosses until he implodes or gets a better job somewhere else. Yet he, like all addicted disaster hunters, carries the seeds of his own destruction. Unfortunately, he carries the seeds of *your* destruction, too.

Left unchecked, the workaholic will suck the life out of his subordinates, wrecking their marriages and friendships, inflicting ulcerous pressure. No workplace disease is so contagious. And it kills the carrier last, feasting first on those infected from above.

Take a long look at the workaholic. Sure, he appears competent to a fault. But look deeper.

Notice the life devoid of the pleasure of human love and companionship, the vacuity of his relationships.

Observe the killer anxiety that can only be expunged, momentarily, by work, his obsessive need to define himself in terms of how well he performs against other people's expectations.

The only way to deal with a workaholic boss and stand a chance of keeping your job until he destroys himself is to deliver 100 percent during working hours, and draw the line the rest of the time. Doing so can be complicated and dangerous. But, if you value your life outside the office, it must be done.

A woman I will call Leslie is the senior executive at a large and very prestigious market-research firm. A miserable woman with no life to speak of, she is a thoroughly successful mixture of craziness, blending workaholic dementia with a bullying disregard for others and a righteous paranoia regarding people she cannot totally control.

Worse, Leslie has elevated this psychological stance into a management philosophy by which every one of her workers must suffer. Comments on her style are offered by Paul, a consultant whose wife works inside this crazy boss's domain and survives there only because she has drawn that mythic line in the sand. "Leslie *is* a bully," Paul says. "But that's not the overriding essence of her management. She is one of these people who thrives on chaos and who believes sincerely that unless the place is in total chaos, something is wrong. So if everything is running smoothly, she *creates* chaos. She believes she can't get the best from her staff unless she keeps them totally off-balance":

My wife, Annette, is Leslie's research director, and I had worked with the woman before. They had called me to do a study on demographical buying patterns among middle-income professionals. I made arrangements to get out in the field, and picked a typical community to look at. I turned in my work in the middle of March, and my immediate manager there said it was okay, and turned it in to Leslie. And Leslie sat on it until the end of July—two-and-a-half months—and then called me in and asked for quite a lot of changes. I made them and turned them in in the middle of August. In October, she asked for more changes, which I did. The study was now twice the length and complexity of the original plan. Once again, my immediate boss—a nice guy, kind of passive—said it was okay, it just needed a little editing. It basically told them everything they needed to know, believe me.

At the end of November, Leslie rejected the document entirely. Seven months of work down the drain. They paid my expenses and a small portion of my original fee, that's all. I've been in this business a long time, and I know the difference between good, bad, and indifferent treatment, and this was insulting. Throughout all of this, her manner was crisp and businesslike, but the basic treatment was totally unprofessional.

And that's the way she treats my wife, Annette, who works there every day, unlike me. Last month she called my wife into her office and told her that the marketing manager, who is a very crucial person, had gone in and threatened to quit because he couldn't get along with Annette. My wife was stunned—she thought she and the marketing man had a harmonious relationship. Leslie added that she had put this damaging information in Annette's personnel file, which goes up to corporate headquarters, noting that Annette is a poor supervisor and her staff can't stand her.

Now, my wife came home crying, and *she couldn't* understand it at all. And when she got a chance, she took the guy aside and asked him about it: and it turns out that it was *all a lie*. The marketing manager had received an offer from another firm, and he should have gone to Annette first, but instead he went to Leslie, and *Annette's name never was mentioned*. I believe the guy. He had no reason to lie. Annette has reason to believe that she has affection and loyalty from her staff. Once they worked all night to get a project done on time and under budget. They've won all kinds of awards and there's a good feeling there.

Leslie can't stand to be anywhere but at the office. She will routinely call for a full-dress editorial meeting at six-thirty on a Friday afternoon—because she can't abide to be home with her own two children. My wife's staff gets a big kick out of our little boy, making a big fuss about him when he shows up at the office and all. And Leslie can't stand that my wife wants to get home to be with her child. When Annette takes time off for a school conference or something, Leslie has hysterics, screaming that Annette has no right to take that kind of time off for personal reasons. And at times she'll say things like, "Oh God, my kids'll be home for the whole weekend instead of with their father!" She's divorced, did I mention? So she avoids her own kids and can't stand the fact that Annette wants to be with hers.

Finally, Annette just told her: "Look, Leslie, I'll be here in emergencies when you need me. But I will be leaving the office by 7 P.M. every night as a matter of course. When I start missing deadlines and budget requirements, you let me know. Until then, I plan to see my kid in the evening."

There wasn't anything that Leslie could do. But she gets her revenge by, for instance, giving me a hard time on a research project, or a thousand other little ways. She'll come into Annette's office and look at her desk calendar and say, "You can't go out to lunch." Or, if she didn't catch up to her until the afternoon, "How could you possibly go out to lunch with all this stuff on your agenda?"

The woman's a nut case. But . . . we need the money.

Not all restrictions on the disaster hunter need be outlined in such a bold stroke. My pal David, former community-outreach manager here at my august corporate home, remembers the day that he almost had to say no to our boss at the time, Chet, a grim workaholic with no life of his own and no discernible desire for one. "I had already set up a fifteenth-anniversary second-honeymoon trip with my wife," David says.

I was going to leave on Saturday morning, and he was toying with the idea of asking me to go to L.A. Thursday night for a Friday morning meeting, take the red-eye back, and meet my wife in the Bahamas on the second day of the trip. And the purpose of the meeting was unclear. That I had to be there was totally unclear. To represent the corporate persona at a city council meeting for no discernible reason? I said, "Normally, Chet, I would do something like this without any objection, but in this case I have some personal plans that would be severely impacted by that trip, and if I'm the only person that can do this, perhaps I can work it out, but if there's anyone else, I'd really appreciate it."

I was saved in this respect because it was not a formal request yet, so I didn't have to slam him down. There's usually a dialogue leading to a request, and before it got to me, I lodged my objection and nipped it in the bud.

You don't want to disappoint the workaholic too often, however. His expectations are high, and his RPMs are set on 78. One hard-driving Workie I know made a small career out of complaining about his secretary who was "too slow," "not motivated," and "weak." Finally, the woman quit on him. Here's his analysis of the situation, and you can see how much he learned.

When she left, Roxanne wrote an angry letter to Personnel, saying I was a workaholic, that the post was unreasonable, and intimating that my expectations were unreasonable. What she would do is go to the other editor and cry, and the other editor would go to me with tears in her eyes. And I'd say, "Look, no work is getting done, and I don't have any sympathy. I don't want to have to take somebody and give them a detailed list of what to do hour by hour, I want them to have some kind of handle, not to need that kind of organization." When you gave it to her anyway, she resented it.

The terrible news for employees is that the workaholic views his disease as an asset, and there is ample propaganda from the business media and consulting industries to keep his delusion toasty and warm.

*U.S. News and World Report*
July 21, 1980

Compulsive workers aren't necessarily unhappy, obsessed people, according to a new research study . . .

This was a report on the work of a leading apologist for workaholism, Dr. Marilyn Machlowitz, who received her doctorate in psychology on the subject from Yale University. In general, Machlowitz told American management what it wanted to hear: that workaholics were high-energy achievers who may need some management from employees and spouses, but who were essentially healthy, perhaps healthier than their more laconic and balanced counterparts.

Machlowitz was relentlessly jolly about the ailment. "I started a

half-day camp for 2-year-olds the summer I was 4," she revealed. "I
charged 10 cents a day. I enlisted my mother as head counsellor—
mostly because I wanted to serve juice and wasn't allowed to use a
can opener yet. When I got my first real job—as a summer camp
counsellor—I came home so thrilled that I told my father, 'Dad, you
can retire.' . . . In my grade-school days, I came home for lunch. If
something had been mentioned in class in the morning, I'd look it up
in the Encyclopaedia Britannica and come back that afternoon with
the answer. So I didn't have to be urged to finish my homework."

In a word: yech.

In general, analysts like Machlowitz contend that the workaholic
is a sane individual aware of his peculiar needs, that he can therefore
be managed. And to a certain extent, this is true. But not the workaholic in the last stages of disaster hunting. He can no more be
managed than a force of nature, for his anxiety, and the need to keep
it in check with work work work, cannot be managed or contained.

Once it's reached this stage, the workaholic's addiction to adrenaline is too deep to be mended. So deep, in fact, that the entire
person is involved, and all his life, including his interpersonal relationships, are yanked into the work arena and poisoned. Because his
work, literally, is the only thing that arouses him, it's only natural
that he will find an object for this stirred-up desire in the small
workplace universe that he calls home. "I've known my boss Ron for
about ten years, but I only worked for him the last two," says Lara,
administrative assistant to the senior counsel of her corporation.

He was a new associate when I started with the company. His first
year, Ron won the Superassociate Award for billing the most hours.
He ran through three secretaries that year.

One of the secretaries, the one who worked for him the longest time,
was my best friend. She worked for him for four years, during which
he fell for her. He was married, with three children. It was not recip-
rocated, however. The pressure of his overtures caused her to leave
him and go to work for another partner. Ron had a series of people
work for him for two years, then I began to work for him.

Ron would get to the office at seven, if he had gone home at all, and
he would leave at ten at night. This was his routine day after day. He
lived under incredible pressure, and it affected his work. Like if he was
out during the middle of the day at a luncheon, he would call in for
his messages, and if you'd start to read them, he'd interrupt to say he

just wanted the important ones. Then, when he got back in the office, he would rant and rave, "Why didn't you give me that message!?"

He humiliated me in front of others. He would call me stupid. I'm not stupid. I learned I had to shout back at him to preserve my sanity and self-respect. Occasionally, I would quit, after which he would always be incredibly contrite.

I came to know him very well. He went after my best friend Anne again, and this time they started dating. By this time he was a senior partner, and she was working at the firm.

His kids were totally messed up. He hardly ever saw them, but when he did, he was always correcting them. He told me once how he reduced his fourteen-year-old-son to tears by berating him so much. He was sorry about it, but he kept on doing it.

Finally, after he had dated Anne for eight months, he moved out of his home and separated from his wife. But she had a private detective follow him, found out about the relationship, and threatened to spill the beans to the company. That did it. He returned to his wife, and dumped my friend, who proceeded to try to kill herself by taking sixteen Seconals. She survived, thank God, after being in a coma for two days. But he would not visit her in the hospital. It happened on the weekend, and the following Monday when I got in, I could see he was going to adopt his bad-little-boy act. "You probably won't want to work for me now, huh?" he said. His attitude was that it wasn't his fault, that Anne must not have had a good self-image. That he would accept no blame. I stuck it out with him for two more months, and then I quit. My husband was glad I did. He could never understand why I put up with the guy. I'm not so sure now myself.

I guess when times were good and we had a case on, it was kind of a high. Once you leave, you have to learn to live without that, and get more from your family and friends.

That's hard for sick people to do. Working like a maniac, getting a bolt of high testosterone, is so much easier, and recognized as Good by the gods of business.

But don't be fooled. The addict doesn't cleave to his drug because it's Good. He does it because he has to.

When I was a young corporate man, I knew a guy I'll call Bruce. He was vice president of Something Important that kept him on the road about a hundred days a year. He had a picture of his wife and two lovely daughters on his desk, which he would regard lovingly whenever he was in town, often exclaiming how hard it was to miss his family day after day.

"Why does Bruce work so hard?" people would ask as he returned with his overnight bag from another exhausting trip to the boonies. No one really knew. We all worked hard, you know, but Bruce . . . he was a machine.

One Friday night at six-thirty, I was headed out the door and passed by Bruce's office. "Hey!" he called out from within. "Hold on a sec!"

He bounded into the corridor and slammed me on the shoulder. "Just the guy I wanna see!" he boomed. "How's about a couple of drinks and a movie or something? Just to blow off some sweat at the end of the week?"

"I got to get home, Bruce," I said. "Maybe some other time."

"Sure, sure," he said. "A short-timer, I get it. Guess I'll go home, too, in a little while."

I left him sitting at his desk reading an industry magazine, feet up, as the gathering night settled outside his window. And I got the picture very clearly. The guy didn't want to go home.

The same is true of another workaholic I know right now. One day recently, a project we were mutually involved in was completed on time and under budget on a Thursday afternoon. "Shit," said the executive in question. "Now we won't have to work on Saturday." Instead, the guy had to stick around the house, play with his wife and kids, and do yard work. I guess *that*'s the kind of work a grandiose dude could find truly daunting.

## GENDER MANAGEMENT PROBLEMS, TOO!

Adding to the list of executable offenses, the disaster hunter will probably have serious problems with "the opposite sex," whichever that may be. In general, he or she is guilty of that high sin of the late twentieth century: genderfication; that is, the need to make gender an issue, either by discriminating for or against someone based on it, or by screwing somebody because of it—in both well-worn senses of the verb.

Bad gender management goes both ways. But while depredations are daily visited upon men by inept token women placed into positions of trust and power due solely to their gender, this is still more the exception than the rule in the vast scheme of things. The workplace is still by far a man's world, and the gross distortions of character evinced by the crazy boss are visited on women far more often than on men, as contemporary men visit their rotten attitudes on women from the entry point onward. The difference today is, the sexist is just one more crazy boss doomed to the fire.

While many men seem to be toeing the line, the following statements typify the kind of disgusting things we say to each other when women aren't listening. Here's Max, director of planning for a data-processing firm:

> Women are the toughest group to hire. My experience is that because they've been socialized, they tend to look to a male as an authority figure and want constant approval from them. When I'm hiring a woman, I'm well aware of the fact that this will be somebody I'll have to deal with more than others because she'll need more approval. Women need it more than men, take my word for it. And they're horribly ambitious, too. If men were as overtly ambitious, there'd be knife fights in the halls. That's the way men are taught—to rip out each other's throats head-on. Women are backbiting.

Here's Steve, a TV producer in one of the top ten markets:

> I love women in the workplace, but don't ask me to talk honestly to them. I can't tell a woman that her work stinks, for instance. I have to go into tortured explanation as to why someone other than myself might not like it, and after twenty minutes I completely fold, and say something wormy like, "Okay, why don't we just fix it up a little bit and we'll run with it."

And while women must be included in all compulsory, strictly business events, the contemporary crazy boss still has the ability to assert sexual power by excluding them from semisocial gatherings. This is often done by judicious selection of a locale where only boys are allowed to hang their jocks. An attorney I knew tells this sad tale with proper outrage:

> A woman lawyer I know had worked on this case for months, and really felt like part of the team. There were about six lawyers on the squad, and she was the only female. But when the case was won, we had our celebration lunch at a private university club where women

aren't allowed. The woman was really upset and protested to the senior partner. The guy told her he was sorry, but that was where the client wanted to go. And they went.

While men have been forced to give up blatant displays of "on top" thinking, they still have every opportunity to exercise their members when the time comes to impose the bottom line. An entrepreneur who recently sought financing for her satellite entertainment firm comments on the process of meeting with investment bankers:

There are always a lot of reasons not to do a deal, and in our case, there is the additional issue of the femininity of the management. It's an added wrinkle that's not doing us any good. In the early stages, it does, maybe, but when it gets down to brass tacks, it's bra time at the OK Corral.

But even within the confines of the crazy corporation, male power against women may be pursued with a lot less impunity. A woman I'll call Barb is advertising sales manager for a large general-interest magazine. Her boss, John, a hail-fellow-well-met type, runs the entire sales and marketing end of the operation. He plays the role of the entrenched male dinosaur in her scenario:

A year and a half ago, I put myself on a diet program and lost about thirty pounds, and felt great. The important part of the situation is that John did not know me when I was at a heavier weight. I came to work for him after I had lost the weight. So his knowledge of my different weight status was only by hearsay. He had scheduled a meeting with a marketing consultant, and the morning of that meeting he had, sort of impromptu, invited me to join the meeting. I wasn't surprised to be asked into the meeting, because it has to do with my area. I'm out there on the firing line, and he is not necessarily out there every day interacting with clients and agencies.

This consultant is a woman John has worked with previously and I had never met before, and we had a very extensive and thorough meeting about what was needed, so she could get our ideas and come back and propose what kind of support material she was suggesting. At about noontime, John suggested that we should all go to lunch and resume in the afternoon. So the three of us went to lunch.

And, you know, I pretty much eat balanced, normal meals. I think I ordered broiled chicken, salad and vegetable, and Perrier. John, who is a marathoner and very thin, makes a statement that he can eat anything he wants, and orders bacon cheeseburger, fries, and beer. And then Julie, the consultant, orders a salad (no egg, no cheese, extra green peppers, all substitutions), a little bit dramatic about the severity of her order. She wanted them to bring her vinegar, mustard, and lemon juice on the side. So at this point, John is laughing. "Boy!" he says. "Talk about rigid diets!" So Julie says, "I've gained seven pounds, and no matter what I do, I can't seem to lose it." So John, out of the clear blue, looks at her and says, "Well, you want to learn about diets, talk to Barb here! I remember when she was a *two hundred-fifty-pound sausage!*"

Now, I might have been 145 pounds (now I'm 105), but I was never approaching 300 pounds. I was so stunned I could have fallen off the chair, and seconds later, my shock turned to sheer anger. The lunch came, and I said nothing. We ate. The consultant became aware of the situation and changed the subject to art. I looked at John and at her, and I kept my mouth shut.

We finished our lunch, finished our meeting, and I was boiling and left the office for the day. I went from anger into hurt, into tears. It was a personal assault to me. It was such a rude comment for any individual to make to another person. It was an insult. I don't think there's anything funny about that. This is a professional relationship, boss to employee, with a stranger.

The next morning, I was in my office, and he walked past, and I said, "Do you have a minute," and he comes in, and I just calmly said, "John, I just have to have a few moments with you to discuss the situation over lunch, because it caused me some real anger and a great deal of disappointment."

I said, "I had never met this consultant person before, that she was doing her own diet had nothing to do with me. I was absolutely appalled by your behavior. We can agree to disagree professionally, but personal insults or attacks I cannot or will not tolerate." He was shifting from foot to foot and was embarrassed and tried to turn it into a joke, and he says, "God, Barb, you're so damned sensitive," and I said, "John, it has nothing to do with sensitivity, it was rude and uncalled for." At which point, he opted to leave. He literally *backed* out the doorway.

Being cheek to jowl with able, attractive, independent women may be enough to drive the marginal boss right over the edge into actionable behavior. My friend Suzanne is a salesperson at a retail clothing store in St. Louis. "Matt is the owner of the clothing store," she says. "At this time, he would take me out to lunch often to talk business, and we would drink."

The meals would go on for hours—I think he was lonely and wanted someone to sit with. I would eat, and he would drink his lunch and get pretty high. There were a few times when he got kind of drunk and kissed me. I would say, "Cut it out, Matt," and that was that. I didn't take it seriously.

The situation came to a head one day last summer. Matt said, "Why don't you come out to my house and have a swim." I said, "No, it's okay, I have a lot of work to do," and he said, "No, take the rest of the day off." Which put me in a weird position—my boss telling me to take time off and relax? And I was refusing? After all, he wasn't saying, "Come have sex" or anything, but I still felt weird. I tried to get out of it, but he insisted. So I said, "I want to go home and get my bathing suit," just stalling for time. My husband, Charles, happened to be home for some reason, and I said, "I'm going for a swim at Matt's." And Charles looked at me, and looked at Matt, and said, "Yeah? I'd like to come, too." I felt relieved, to say the least. We went out there and just went swimming and then we came home.

At last, in a terminal lather of frustrated desire, Matt called Suzanne into his office the next morning, and stared at her from across his desk, doodling compulsively on the back of a purchase order.

He said, "You really looked great in your bathing suit." I said, "Come on, Matt, I'm busy." And he said, "My plan was to make love with you all afternoon." And I just cracked up. I said, "Matt, I'm married and not interested. It's not going to happen, so stop it." Next day he was having trouble putting some furniture together, so I was helping him. We were working on this étagère, sitting on the floor, and all of a sudden he lunged at me through the shelving. I didn't even know what he was doing. I thought he was having a heart attack. I said, "What are you doing?" and he said, "I was going to kiss you. I can't take it anymore!" I was really grossed out. It wasn't even complimentary after a while. It was kind of scary. And I eventually quit.

The opportunities for disaster are tremendous for crazy bosses already aroused by the proximity of big money, big offices, and personal power. And you don't have to be a sexist to be just plain horny.

As the crazy boss matures and eventually overripens, he will most probably move beyond simple bullying or paranoia, narcissism or bureaucraziness, creeping inexorably closer to his own particular, self-chosen disaster. Look for this last and most serious aspect of the crazy boss.

What are its attributes? Who is the disaster hunter? By the drama of his actions you shall know him.

He is hysterical, as befits the changing nature of his business.

He is depressed, because he occasionally sees the world as it is, with no wishes and delusions projected on it.

He is addicted to alcohol, to drugs, to work, to power over other people, power that he can express in anger, in manipulation, in sex.

He will lie when he has to, because his is the ultimate truth.

He has no insight into his problems. In fact, they're not his problems, as far as he's concerned.

Until he finds the disaster he seeks, they're *yours*.


## ACTION POINTS: THE DISASTER HUNTER

We're gonna be mean here. The disaster hunter is the crazy boss on his last legs. He's in the grip of his madness and cannot shake loose. He's hurting. He's spinning out of control. He just needs one more push.

You provide that push in exactly the right way, and you could end up rid of the crazy boss. Or at least *this* crazy boss. That's saying a lot.

Let's see how you could possibly make that happen.

- *Establish an escape route:* If you've been pursuing some of the strategies laid out in prior chapters, you know that the establishment of friendships and alliances is key to managing and surviving your crazy boss. If your tenure is too closely aligned with his, you'll go down with him. If, on the other hand, you've gained the respect and, more important, the patronage of clients up and down the company's management structure, you may be relatively safe. In his late days, you'll want to be quite clear with your pals and potential new bosses about your desire to survive. At this point, his dysfunction will be common knowledge, and it should be possible for you to approach friendly senior types with offerings of admiration and fealty. It's most effective, I believe, to work on the manager a level immediately above that of the crazy disaster hunter. Don't be oily about it. But here is a guy who's probably as fed up with his reportee as you are with your boss, which is no coincidence, because they're the same bad actor. This campaign should begin, if possible, a year before the disaster hunter reaches the critical phase. You can see it coming. So can your boss's boss. Start by making small talk. The men's room is a good place to start. After that, make sure to disingenuously ask his advice on business matters when you can. Run ideas, memos, and interesting news stories by him on occasion. Get comfortable with the guy. Hey—I don't have to tell you how to make friends with people, do I?

- *Be the organizational alternative:* Throughout your workplace, make sure it's well understood that you continue to pursue your function and occupy your place whether your disaster hunter is in the saddle or not. You're headed for an uncertain time, that's for sure. You can make things easier for yourself by establishing and maintaining solid business relations with people and projects that aren't about to change precipitously and throw you into an uproar. Don't let his meltdown drip all over you; do your best to stay one step ahead of his disaster by obviously remaining bright and effective: cc: as many people as you can on work that has widespread interest. Don't be ostentatious. But tough it out. Look on the bright side. You won't have him to be kicked around by for much longer.
- *Be calm in the face of hysteria:* As he fritzes out, your crazy boss will begin flailing about like a madman, punishing evildoers, medicating himself with long luncheons and surreptitious Valiums, festering behind his closed door like a hermit, insulting people who should be stroked, stroking people who should be insulted, doing everything he can to take you along on his ride into oblivion. Your only weapon during this phase is your composure. Presumably, people are still looking to you for continued usefulness. They'll be turning to you more and more as he turns increasingly difficult to deal with. See yourself as an island of cool sanity in an ocean of despair and irrationality. This will make you feel better than if you allow yourself to be swept along in the powerful tides of emotion that attend the death of the king.

- *Disassociate yourself:* He'll also be generating a lot of stupid projects, trying to create the illusion that he's there for some larger business purpose. Anything associated with his reign will be dogmeat in the months to come. The more you're identified with his agenda, the more doubtful your future becomes. Also, you're wasting time pursuing things that aren't important to the company. If they were important, would they be contemplating the demise of their author? Go to as many meetings as you can so that people can see you're busy and providing service. Get in early and roam the hallways with the other guys, drinking coffee and laughing at idiotic jokes and apocryphal stories. *Meld yourself into the culture.* Make sure people see you as an individual in your own right. You are, you know.

- *Do what's necessary—but never enable:* Perform your usual good job while he still seems viable. But the moment it's clear he's losing the game, do the minimum. Disaster-hunter files are full of stories about guys whose staff made their continued excesses possible. The longer you do all this work for him, the longer his bosses will think he's doing his work. It's not easy to let things slide into catastrophe. It goes against every impulse you have as a quality employee. But you're going to have to. You have your work. He has his. Go to the limit of your abilities to do your own stuff as well as you can, under the circumstances. Do not disappoint your own customers. But stop short of covering his ass when he's doing nothing. And when the fur begins to hit the fan, *make no excuses for him.* When asked, "What the fuck is going on here?" by a bigger boss, take your tongue in both hands and lay it out clearly, without obvious pleasure, even displaying a small measure of loyalty to the disaster hunter who is the cause of it all. But make no mistake about your position. Remember: you *want* the facts to come out. The only thing you should be caught enabling is the honest disclosure of your soon-to-be-former boss's craziness.

- *Keep on the periphery of the pathology:* If you're not a dummy, you can stop reading this bullet right here. If you are a potential dummy (and which of us is not?), perhaps you'd better read on. While the disaster hunter is stalking his doom, he'll be looking for company. If he's a drunk, he may want you to suck up a variety of clear fluids with him at inappropriate times. Don't. If he's sexually out of control, he may want you to join him on his midnight (or noontime) rambles or, worse, if you're a member of the opposite gender, he or she may want to conquer *you*. Do I have to suggest how stupid that would be? If he's a paranoid, he may want to spend hours behind closed doors with you, plotting insurrections and coups. Find other things to do. Perhaps most dangerous, if he's a socially stunted workaholic, he may demand that you destroy your life, as he has destroyed his, by working idiotic hours for uncertain purposes. That's the hardest to fight, but you must. Your goal is to try not to go crazy along with him. You can't do that if you're sharing his vices and excesses with him in a pathetic attempt to remain loyal. Perhaps most challenging to resist is the fact that, when he offers to share his profligacy, it may appear that he's offering friendship. He's not. His chuminess has nothing to do with you. He's looking for a partner to accompany him to perdition. That's a role you may politely decline.

- *Draw the line:* Obviously, there will come a time—whether you're resisting his bogus, drunken amity or demanding some free time away from the office—that you're going to have to come face to face with his outright displeasure. Keep in mind that you have the right, as an employee, to define the limits of your job. Yes, under the boot of a crazy boss, those limits will be stretched to the utmost. But there is a line no employer can cross over. Every company has its own definition of that—but each does have one. Make sure that you've gone the limit by any sane definition. Then act. Don't shout. Don't weep. Just face the face guy down with all the resolve and determination you have. Do not be insolent. A simple "I can't come in this Sunday, Larry. I have to be in church" is better than "I'm sick of you leeching off my free time like a vampire!" But get the message across. You'll be taking a risk, it's true. But few companies give a boss the right to fire a hardworking person for wanting to have a normal life. There are laws against that, laws that are being prosecuted with increasing frequency in these crazy times.
- *Do not assuage the loneliness:* This is difficult. A disaster hunter on the road to his destruction is a sorry thing to watch. And from your vantage point, you're going to see some things that will generate pity, remorse, and even a sort of bogus nostalgia about the "good old days" that never really existed. As we saw previously, all employees seek to love and admire the boss they work for—that's why the obverse, disappointed love turned into hatred

is so widespread in the unhappy corporation. Your inherent humanity will meld with your innate horror at seeing your authority figure unmasked, stripped of honor, and, finally, defenestrated. Throttle those higher impulses. They are the worst form of sentimentality. If you must, stick yourself occasionally with the needle of recollection. Remember the time he made you cancel your vacation to attend that stupid productivity seminar? The time he denied you your raise because the industry was "in the tank," then treated himself to that new BMW on the company? The time he took your work, slapped his name on it, and sold it as his own without a word about you to the folks who later praised it? When he reaches out for common human warmth and compassion, offer only what you must in order to terminate the exchange as easily and quietly as possible. Conserve your humanity for your friends and family. They need and deserve it more, and have done more to earn it.

- *Do not love, do not regret, and don't look back:* There is life after a crazy boss. Perhaps it involves still another, I don't know. There are certainly a lot of them around. All emotional, ethical, familial, or human issues aside, you're working for several very clear and wholly American things: life, liberty, and the pursuit of money. All reports to the contrary, money does, if wisely accumulated and spent, bring happiness. Give your love and loyalty to those who help you achieve those goals. Summon only your enmity and intelligent defiance for those who stand in your way. Good luck.

# EPILOGUE

We too have weapons.
Kafka

**M**ore than any other factor, the "tyranny of the present" is expressed by the constant need for—and the willingness to accept—short-term solutions and people prepared to carry them out, no matter how loony they may be. No set of personal strategies can alter the fact that the sorry state of the American workplace arises from economic factors that no one person, no one organization, can change. And while individuals everywhere can fight the good fight, nothing can be done, even by an entire organization, to cure the insane business environment that is churning out crazy bosses faster than they can be destroyed.

In the end, many employees solve their personal problem by running away from it, and sometimes this is the best solution, if they have another job. If they do not, and simply bolt, the action can lead to an extended period of self-examination, always a bad idea for those past the age of twenty-four.

Is jumping ship a real solution? Not at all. To leave precious years of your career smoking behind you? A spot on your résumé you can no longer point to without bursting into the kind of vitriol that scares headhunters and job interviewers silly? Besides, wherever you end up, will not a steaming, crazy boss be waiting for you?

Who's to say he won't?

The only true solution is to take matters into your own hands and *manage.* No, you may not solve things. Yes, you may be thrown out on your ear. But at least you'll be alive! Taking risks!

In short, you'll be in business.

The greatest power you have is your sanity. Not only madness confers strength. Rational thought and action, pursued with boldness and, when necessary, ruthlessness, is a mighty hammer.

# SELECTED BIBLIOGRAPHY

Bartlett, Donald, and James B. Steele. *Empire: The Life, Legend, and Madness of Howard Hughes.* New York: W. W. Norton, 1981.

Bartolomé, Fernando, and Paul A. Lee Evans. "Must Success Cost so Much?" *Harvard Business Review,* March-April 1980.

Becker, Howard S. *The Other Side: Perspectives on Deviance.* New York: The Free Press, 1964.

Berne, Eric. *The Structure and Dynamics of Organizations and Groups.* New York: Grove Press, 1963.

Crosby, Philip B. *Quality is Free: The Art of Making Quality Certain.* New York: McGraw-Hill Book Company, 1979.

Crosby, Philip B. *Quality Without Tears.* New York: McGraw-Hill Book Company, 1984.

Dahm, Charles W., in collaboration with Robert Ghelardi. *Power and Authority in the Catholic Church.* Notre Dame, London: University of Notre Dame Press, 1981.

Deal, Terrence E., and Allan A. Kennedy. *Corporate Cultures: The Rites and Rituals of Corporate Life.* Reading, MA: Addison-Wesley Publishing Company, 1982.

Drucker, Peter F. *The Concept of the Corporation* (2nd ed. Rev.), New York: Harper & Row, 1983.

The Editors of *Fortune. 100 Stories of Business Success: Case Histories of American Enterprise.* New York: Simon and Schuster, 1954.

English, O. Spurgeon, and Gerald H. J. Pearson. *Common Neuroses of Children and Adults.* Boston: Little, Brown, 1937.

Freud, Sigmund. *Group Psychology and the Analysis of the Ego.* New York: Liveright Publishing Corporation, 1949.

Fromm, Erich. *The Art of Loving.* New York and Evanston: Harper Colophon Books, 1962.

Ghodse, A. Hamid. "Drug Dependence and Intoxication." *Handbook of Psychiatry 2: Mental Disorders and Somatic Illness,* ed. M. H. Lader. Cambridge, London, New York, New Rochelle, Melbourne, Sydney: Cambridge University Press, 1983.

Goffman, Erving: *The Presentation of the Self in Everyday Life.* Garden City, NY: Doubleday Anchor Books, 1959.

Goffman, Erving. *Relations in Public: Microstudies of the Public Order.* New York: Basic Books, 1971.

Goffman, Erving. *Stigma: Notes on the Management of Spoiled Identity.* Englewood Cliffs, NJ: Prentice-Hall, Inc., 1963.

Grunewald, Donald, and Henry Bass, eds. *Public Policy and the Modern Corporation.* New York: Appleton-Century-Crofts, 1966.

*Harvard Business Review. On Management.* New York, Evanston, San Francisco, London: Harper & Row, 1975.

Horney, Karen, M.D. *The Neurotic Personality of Our Time.* New York: W. W. Norton & Company, 1937.

Kanter, Rosabeth Moss. *Men and Women of the Corporation.* New York: Basic Books, 1977.

Kanter, Rosabeth Moss, and Barry Stein, eds. *Life in Organizations.* New York: Basic Books, 1979.

Katz, Daniel, and Robert L. Kahn. *The Social Psychology of Organizations.* New York, London, Sidney: John Wiley & Sons, 1966.

Kernberg, Otto F. "Regression in Organizational Leadership." *The Irrational Executive: Pyschoanalytic Explorations in Management,* ed. Manfred F. R. Kets deVries. New York: International Universities Press, 1984.

Levinson, Harry. "On Executive Suicide." *Harvard Business Review,* July-August 1975.

Levinson, Harry. "When executives burn out." *The McKinsey Quarterly,* Spring 1982.

Maccoby, Michael. "The Corporate Climber Has to Find His Heart." *The Irrational Executive: Psychoanalytic Explorations in Management,* ed. Manfred F. R. Kets deVries. New York: International Universities Press, 1984.

Maccoby, Michael. *The Gamesman.* New York: Simon and Schuster, 1976.

Machlowitz, Marilyn. *Workaholics.* Reading, MA: Addison-Wesley Publishing Company, 1980.

Mills, C. Wright. *The Power Elite.* New York: Oxford University Press, 1956.

Moore, Burness E., M.D., and Bernard D. Fine, M.D., eds. *A Glossary of Psychoanalytic Terms and Concepts.* New York: The American Psychoanalytic Association, 1968.

Naisbitt, John. *Megatrends.* New York: Warner Books, 1982.

Peters, Tom, and Nancy Austin. *A Passion for Excellence: The Leadership Difference.* New York: Random House, 1985.

Peters, Thomas J., and Robert H. Waterman Jr. *In Search of Excellence: Lessons from America's Best Run Companies.* New York: Warner Books, 1982.

Rodgers, Buck, with Robert L. Shook, *The IBM Way: Insights into the World's Most Successful Marketing Organization.* New York: Harper & Row, 1986.

Sampson, Anthony. *The Sovereign State of ITT.* New York: Stein and Day, 1976.

Schrank, Robert. *Ten Thousand Working Days.* Cambridge, MA: MIT Press, 1978.

Shapiro, David. *Autonomy and Rigid Character.* New York: Basic Books, 1981.

Shapiro, David. *Neurotic Styles.* New York: Basic Books, Inc., 1965.

Shook, Robert L. *Ten Greatest Sales-persons: What They Say About Selling.* New York: Harper & Row, 1978.

Tobias, Andrew. *Fire and Ice, The Story of Charles Revson—the Man Who Built the Revlon Empire.* New York: William Morrow and Company, 1976.

Trice, Harrison M., and Paul M. Roman. *Spirits and Demons at Work: Alcohol and Other Drugs on the Job.* Ithaca, NY: New York State School of Industrial and Labor Relations, Cornell University, 1972.

Vare, Robert. *Buckeye: A Study of Coach Woody Hayes and the Ohio State Football Machine.* New York: Harper's Magazine Press, 1974.

Victor, Maurice. "Mental Disorders Due to Alcoholism." *Handbook of Psychiatry 2: Mental Disorders and Somatic Illness,* ed. M. H. Lader. Cambridge: Cambridge University Press, 1983.

Wall, Jim. *Bosses.* Lexington, MA: Lexington Books (D. C. Heath and Company), 1986.

Zaleznik, Abraham. "Charismatic and Consensus Leaders: A Psychological Comparison." *The Irrational Executive: Psychoanalytic Explorations in Management,* ed. Manfred F. R. Kets deVries. New York: International Universities Press, 1984.

Zaleznik, Abraham, Manfred F. R. Kets deVries, and John Howard. "Stress Reactions in Organizations: Syndromes, Causes and Consequences. *Behavioral Science,* Vol. 22, 1977.

Zaleznik, Abraham. "Why Authority Fails." *Executive,* Vol. 6, No. 3 (Summer 1980), reprinted by the Division of Research, Graduate School of Business Administration, Harvard University.

# PERMISSIONS